FAMILY THERAPY WITH HISPANICS

Toward Appreciating Diversity

Maria T. Flores
Marriage and Family Institute of San Antonio

Gabrielle Carey
Marriage and Family Institute of San Antonio

Allyn and Bacon

Boston   London   Toronto   Sydney   Tokyo   Singapore

Series Editor, Social Work and Family Therapy: Judy Fifer
Editor-in-Chief, Social Sciences: Karen Hanson
Editorial Assistant: Julianna M. Cancio
Marketing Manager: Jackie Aaron
Production Editor: Christopher H. Rawlings
Electronic Composition: Omegatype Typography, Inc.
Editorial-Production Service: Omegatype Typography, Inc.
Composition and Prepress Buyer: Linda Cox
Manufacturing Buyer: Julie McNeill
Cover Administrator: Jennifer Hart

Copyright © 2000 by Allyn & Bacon
A Pearson Education Company
160 Gould Street
Needham Heights, MA 02494

Internet: www.abacon.com

Library of Congress Cataloging-in-Publication Data

    Family therapy with Hispanics : toward appreciating diversity / Maria T. Flores, Gabrielle Carey, eds.
       p.   cm.
    Includes bibliographical references (p.   ) and index.
    ISBN 0-205-28532-5 (alk. paper)
    1. Hispanic American families—Psychology.   2. Hispanic American families—Social conditions.   3. Family psychotherapy—United States.   4. Hispanic Americans—Cultural assimilation.   5. Hispanic Americans—Ethnic identity.   I. Flores, Maria T.   II. Carey, Gabrielle.
    E184.S75F35   2000
    616.89'156'08968073—dc21   98-49518
                                                          CIP

Printed in the United States of America
10 9 8 7 6 5 4 3 2 1   04 03 02 01 00 99

CONTENTS

PREFACE

The purpose of this book is to assist therapists in their understanding of cultural issues that impact clinical treatment of Hispanic Americans. This text is about working therapeutically with people from a diverse culture. It is a book about similarities and differences, but its emphasis is on the diversity of the people that make up the fabric of what is commonly referred to as Latino culture. We use the words "Hispanic" and "Latino" interchangeably to refer to people and their descendants from countries where Spanish or Portuguese is the dominant language. We also use both terms to be respectful and inclusive of the entire population. Similarly, we use the terms "Anglo American" or "non-Hispanic White" to refer to English-speaking people. "African American," "Asian American," and "Native American" are also terms we have used although we would prefer not to group diverse peoples and cultures under such general labels. We have chosen to use culture instead of color because of the variety of hues and races within distinct countries. Culture honors personal stories in a unique way that no other concept captures. The chapters contain theory, clinical cases, and strategies for therapy. Our goal is to enrich the vision of diversity embraced by the word Hispanic. The book will be useful to psychotherapists, other professionals, and students engaged in treating Hispanic families.

We asked each of our authors, most of whom are Hispanic or bicultural, to include personal information to enhance their narratives, hoping to capture their creativity, opinions, and expertise. We invite you to attune your ear to each voice, as each has its own tenor, its own timbre, its own musical chorus. With diversity comes a complex pattern of voices; for this reason, we have asked the authors each to use the first person at times. We ask you to train your ear to the varied styles and diversity of the authors. Each brings unique experiences and a wealth of information to the subject at hand, namely, diversity in the treatment of Hispanic families. The process of appreciating diversity requires tuning one's ear to hear not only the similarities that so often resound in clustering Latino cultures, but also the unique qualities of the "us" in the "other." Recognizing differences that count and developing that essential curiosity about the experience of another is at the heart of each author's therapeutic approach.

OVERVIEW OF THE CHAPTERS

The chapters are organized into four sections: Part I contains three chapters focused on people; Part II is focused on the therapist; Part III contains six chapters about clinical issues, emphasizing healing relationships; and Part IV summarizes the acculturational processes and the current demographics of Hispanic people in the United States. We invite our readers to appreciate the rich diversity of the Hispanic cultures existing in the United States today: Hispanics from twenty-one nations reside in the United States. The three largest populations include Latinos from Mexico (59 percent), Puerto Rico (14 percent), and Cuba (5 percent). This book will focus primarily on these groups.

Part I: Focus on the People

Chapter 1, entitled *"La Familia Latina,"* written by Maria T. Flores, focuses on clinical issues useful in understanding and treating Hispanic families. Although there are similarities among most families in the United States, Hispanic families need to be understood in a cultural context. The multiplicitous distinctions among country of origin, geographical region of the United States, gender, acculturation, and socioeconomic class lend to the vast diversity seen within Latino cultures. The author discusses the reflexive process of identity formation within bicultural and familial contexts. She echoes her clients' voices as she asks, "Who am I?" "Who are we?" The chapter explores the narrative diversity inherent in language. Case studies are used to illustrate common themes and pitfalls in working with Latino families.

Chapter 2, "*El Latino:* Transgressing the Macho," written by Gonzalo Bacigalupe, dons a distinctly postmodern lens and invites us to observe the diversity of Hispanic men. When we socially construct cultural stories, labels, definitions, and stereotypes, we can make some grave mistakes and generalizations. In becoming "culturally resonant," therapists can appreciate contemporary Latino males and transcend the myths concerning their "macho mystique." Political discussions and case studies will illuminate the clinical implications. Bacigalupe's emphasis is on a therapist's ability to have confidence in people's strengths and resources and their capacity to change. He reviews literature and research to underline his perspective.

Chapter 3, "*La Mujer Latina:* From Margin to Center," written by Yvette G. Flores-Ortiz, describes the location of and the changing role of Hispanic women in the family and in society. The traditional role for Hispanic women, as characterized by *marianismo,* was to run the household, raise the children, and take care of others. The struggles of Latinas who wish to keep cultural traditions alive while seeking to integrate career and educational goals are explored. Latinas fight oppression in the United States on a variety of levels, within the family, and on a larger societal scale. Myths and stereotypes are exposed as the diversity of women's lives are understood. Case studies and personal experiences display the diversity of Latinas and portray the implications for therapy. Family therapy is highly effective, even with Latinas who seek therapy for themselves, as the family relationships are always present in the room and interwoven in the therapeutic dialogue.

Part II: Focus on the Therapist

Chapter 4, "Culture Clash or Not?" coauthored by Gabrielle Carey and Laura Manuppelli, describes interviews with therapists of different ethnic and cultural backgrounds, which yield some interesting opinions and answers to this question. The factors of importance in working with Hispanic families are debated and described. The authors argue for the necessity of examining one's own cultural presuppositions and prejudices. The need for cultural training and experience treating Latino families is growing.

Chapter 5, "Supervision and Consultation with Latino Therapists," written by Gonzalo Bacigalupe, focuses on the roles of supervisor and supervisee considered in terms of gender and cultural influences. The author outlines some basic themes that emerge when dealing with collaborative and postcolonial perspectives in supervision and consultation. Cultural sensitivity on behalf of supervisees and the ability to supervise with a culturally resonant lens are the important factors in cross-cultural supervision. Collaborative approaches open new ways of exploring any culture.

Chapter 6, "Group Psychotherapy: Adolescent Latinos," written by Cynthia de las Fuentes, explores the effectiveness of group therapy with Hispanics. Groups play an important role with adolescents who need to understand who they are and where they are going. Adolescents need support, and if the family system is not helping them, groups can help them to adjust and become what they are capable of becoming. Groups are particularly useful in preventing future problems. Examples, rationales, and techniques are presented. A group case study illustrates adolescents struggling to learn and grow from each other.

Part III: Clinical Issues: Healing Relations

Chapter 7, "The Hispanic Couple in Therapy," written by Thelma H. Duffey, views the nature of intimacy as the quality of the relationship. The author explores the search for intimacy and satisfaction among Hispanics in the United States. A case study that involves a professional couple illustrates the benefits of marital therapy for negotiating conflicts that arise within a multicultural couple context. Using a theoretical model, in this case, an Adlerian model, as a base for cultural assessment can be a very useful mode of working with couples and their cultural differences. New opportunities for women and minorities along with the changing U.S. economy present unique problems for Hispanic couples and therapists who work with them.

Chapter 8, "Life-Cycle Development, Divorce, and the Hispanic Family," written by Randall R. Lyle and Flor Faure, presents a new life-cycle development model and illustrates the way in which it can inform the therapeutic process. The structure and definition of the Hispanic family is changing dramatically. This model offers a more fluid and accepting conceptualization of family development. Intimacy through communion as well as identity through separation provides a backdrop for working with Hispanic families throughout their developmental milestones and crises. A case study involving divorce is used to portray the way the model can enhance the therapeutic process.

Chapter 9, "Therapeutic Sensitivity to the Latino Spiritual Soul," written by Rosendo Urrabazo, describes how religious influences are intimately entwined in the Latino cultures. The importance of religious influences to the Latino family is examined. The author explores the immigrants' plight in searching to belong in a foreign country and how belief in God and church offers a beneficial resource. He explores ways spirituality enters the therapeutic conversation and how a therapist's perspective can help affirm healthy responses for Latinos.

Chapter 10, "Healthcare Today: Treating Hispanic Families and Children with Chronic Illnesses," coauthored by Heather J. Ambrose, Maria T. Flores, and Gabrielle Carey, is grounded in the first author's research with Hispanic families who had recently had a child diagnosed with juvenile *Diabetes mellitus*. The chapter contains several examples of clinical work with chronically ill children. Although the diseases are very different, there are many similar factors in the family's therapeutic processes. It is cost-effective to provide family therapy and to work collaboratively with others in the healthcare field.

Chapter 11, "Injustice in Latino Families: Considerations for Family Therapists," written by Yvette G. Flores-Ortiz, sketches for us a view of how violence and culture can take on distinct twists and how culture can be lost in violence, drugs, and alcohol. She offers a model to predict familial violence and ways to work with abuse in families.

Chapter 12, "A Multisystemic Look at Mexican American Gangs: Adolescents at Risk," written by Lucille Marmolejo Romeo, looks at the widespread phenomenon of Mexican American gangs in the United States. Who is a member? The author argues that a broad, multisystemic view of our society is conducive to understanding the Mexican American gang member. She helps us see how identity crises in youth create a desire to join a gang in which they find a voice. The author employs a variety of lenses to explore the history and the attraction of gangs and ways in which therapists and other mental health professionals can collaborate with law enforcement and community groups to combat the problem.

Part IV: Hispanic Families in Acculturation

Chapter 13, "Acculturation and Family Therapy with Hispanics," written by Cynthia Diez de Leon, explores how the forces of acculturation produce great changes over time and for each new generation of Hispanics born in the United States. The differences in first-, second-, and third-generation Hispanic families are outlined, and the implications for therapy are presented. How acculturation is manifested in behavioral, emotional, and cognitive levels of functioning is addressed.

Chapter 14, "Demographics: Hispanic Populations in the United States," written by Maria T. Flores, provides current statistics and forecasts about Hispanics in the United States. The need for culturally resonant therapy is growing. In order to gain a basic understanding of Hispanic families and their cultural realities, the author suggests therapists explore their clients' country of origin, present location, social contexts, and economic needs.

In summary, this book provides a broad clinical perspective that will help therapists working with Hispanic Americans in the United States. Our focus on clinical studies was deliberate to help therapists struggling to find treatment approaches helpful to working directly with Latinos. The voices of Hispanic therapists working with Hispanic clients and families are an important beginning to helping other therapists from different cultures understand cultural concepts and issues. Research in this area is limited, and clinical work with Latinos is even less accessible and needed. We hope that this book is the first of many books that will focus on the treatment of Latino Americans in family therapy. This text can provide a guide to professors searching for a textbook to help students grapple with the tough issues of working with another culture. Clinicians who want to expand their repertoire of skills and general knowledge of Latinos in the United States will also find the book useful. We are aware that this work is somewhat limited in depth and breath because of the lack of intense research or training being done in this area. However, our contributors present many key ideas and original concepts to help guide us on our journey toward cultural resonance.

ACKNOWLEDGMENTS

We appreciate the valuable contributions of our reviewers: Kaye W. Nelson, Texas A&M University, Corpus Christi, and Josè B. Torres, University of Wisconsin, Milwaukee.

CONTRIBUTORS

Heather J. Ambrose, Ph.D., is a therapist at the University of Texas at San Antonio Counseling Services, San Antonio, Texas.

Gonzalo Bacigalupe, Ed.D., is an assistant professor at the University of Massachusetts in Boston and associate consultant with Latin American Consultancy Services.

Gabrielle Carey, M.A., is in private practice at the Marriage and Family Institute of San Antonio and a Ph.D. candidate at St. Mary's University, San Antonio, Texas.

Cynthia de las Fuentes, Ph.D., is an assistant professor of psychology in the department of psychology at Our Lady of the Lake University in San Antonio, Texas and has a private practice in Austin, Texas.

Cynthia Diez de Leon, Ph.D., is in private practice in San Antonio, Texas, and is an adjunct instructor in the graduate psychology program of Our Lady of the Lake University.

Thelma H. Duffey, Ph.D., is an assistant professor in marriage and family therapy in the department of educational administration and psychological services at Southwest Texas State University in San Marcos, Texas.

Flor Faure, Ph.D., is a clinical therapist at the Center for Health Care Services in San Antonio, Texas.

Maria T. Flores, Ph.D., is in private practice at the Marriage and Family Institute of San Antonio, Texas.

Yvette G. Flores-Ortiz, Ph.D., is a clinical psychologist and associate professor in Chicana/o studies at the University of California, Davis. She has a private practice in family and individual justice-based therapy in Berkeley, California.

Randall R. Lyle, Ph.D., is an assistant professor at St. Mary's University, San Antonio, Texas.

Laura Manuppelli, M.A., is in private practice at the Marriage and Family Institute of San Antonio, Texas, and a Ph.D. candidate at St. Mary's University, San Antonio, Texas.

Lucille Marmolejo Romeo, Psy.D., is a clinical psychologist in private practice in El Paso, Texas.

Rosendo Urrabazo, Ph.D., is doing consultation and research in Rome, Italy.

PART I

FOCUS ON THE PEOPLE

1

LA FAMILIA LATINA

MARIA T. FLORES

*It is through music that you may touch my soul and I
yours. It is there where our eyes meet that we can laugh
and cry together. It is through the profound love you have
to give and take "con tu corazon" [with your heart] that
life makes any sense at all. Life's designs, its delicate and
tender interchanges, and its intricate patterns are then
revealed and you understand what it is to be. It is faith in
God and Mary that opens and lights the way on your
journey. And it is in the intimacy of family, the whole
family, where you learn who you are.*
—MY MOTHER, MARIA TAMEZ FLORES

My parents were immigrants from Mexico who came to the United
States because of the revolutionary war. Their dream was to return to
Mexico once they retired. They loved Mexico and being Mexican. I
grew up thinking I was *pura Mexicana* (pure Mexican). I knew, with-
out contradiction, that my ancestry was easily traced: on my mother's
side to Spain—with just a dash of Italian blood; on my father's side to
Mexico—with a mixture of Spanish and Indian blood. My Native
American Indian ancestors were probably the Kickapoos, a North

American Indian tribe, although there might have been an additional tribe. *Pura Mexicana* means a heritage of Spanish Mediterranean ethnicity combined with indigenous American Indian ancestry. In Mexico, there are other Native Indian–European mixtures that often remain unclaimed or simply ignored. And, of course, there are the totally indigenous Indian people of Mexico. In later years, my Dad claimed he was *Tejano* (Texan) first and foremost. This process of changing identity depending on where one locates oneself is a natural process for many Latinos and Latinas.

This chapter focuses on clinical issues that are useful when attempting to understand and treat families as they change through time and circumstances. I will demonstrate how family therapists can view critical concepts and formulate clinical interventions that are informed by a cultural context. Therapeutic work, enhanced with cultural understanding, gives a therapist a fundamental grasp into a person's behavior, belief system, and emotional mode of being.

CULTURAL CONTEXTS

Cultural understanding is an essential backdrop for therapy designed to utilize family resources and stories as concepts of empowerment. Cultural information enhances options and broadens perspectives for therapists dealing with Latino families. I will deal with a number of issues that have a direct impact on cultural negotiation, specifically, identity, personalism and socioeconomic class, the extended family, language, prejudice and discrimination, common clinical errors, and the bicultural narrative. Each of these sections will include case studies and intervention guidelines.

Understanding diversity and uniqueness within and between the Latino populations is a basic guiding principle for therapists dealing with Latinos. My work with Latino families is based on three basic assumptions about diversity in Latino families: (1) diversity in family interaction needs to be understood in a cultural context; (2) diversity within and between Latino groups once clearly addressed, often breaks with ethnocentric or stereotypical views and their absurd implications; and (3) diversity, on the personal, familial, and cultural levels, expands and changes with the narratives of meaning. Researchers have come to recognize the extreme diversity present in Mexican American families (Rueschenberg & Buriel, 1995). Therapists can help families and individuals draw from their personal and collective resources to deal successfully with stressful situations. These suggestions are based on my experiences as a family therapist working with Latino families, literature reviews, and research studies.

The Reflexivity of Identity and Culture

"Quien soy yo?" ("Who am I?"), we ask, when seeking an identity. What are my talents and gifts? What will I become? What is my potential? Where do I belong? Where can I find meaning and love? These are universal questions and the "stuff" of reflective individuals, questions that are often attended to by a therapist. These questions can be intensified in Latino families because ethnic identity is continually changing. *"Quien soy yo?"* is impacted strongly by parents, religion, family of origin, migration, settlement, and social class on one hand, and by the media, television, radio, school environment, and geographical settings on the other hand. Of course, individual education, spirituality, intelligence, personality, and interactions with others also help create our identity stories.

Negotiating Cultural Identity

A therapist will wonder together with clients who are negotiating their cultural identities by defining personal stories or new "narratives." Questions such as, "Who are we as a family?" will emerge. Culture is not a specific list of traits or characteristics. Culture is a set of values, beliefs, and thoughts embodied in a musical score of language, customs, products, art, and music that creates interactions among a group that by its very nature changes in time. Culture can be as simple as a song or as complex as a symphony. The melody is the thread that holds the cultural composition together, yet its expression varies with tempo, key, harmony, crescendos, and other dynamics. Culture can take any format: classical, jazz, rock, alternative, hymns, country, or opera within Hispanic groups.

Case Study 1: "Quien Somos Nosotros?"

Pablo and Maria came from El Salvador. Both parents spoke of trying to teach their son, Roberto, the American ways. They said that they tried to teach their son the right values, but their fear was that he did not accept them and did not care. He had been suspended from school for fighting with another student—yet again.

Pablo worked as a laborer mending street holes for the city. He was proud of his work, but his son seemed ashamed of him. Roberto was born in Indiana and grew up in a middle-class school environment. His experience of reality was so distinct from his family's that he felt great alienation from his family and from himself. Roberto did not speak Spanish with his parents, which upset them, although both parents admitted encouraging their son to learn English so that he could succeed.

An important intervention in therapy was to help this family create space and respect for distinct cultures and the personal choices each member adopted. Roberto claimed no cultural identity other than as a United States citizen. He is looking for acceptance in this culture only. In order to help the family reconnect, we looked for an open space where a new sense of culture could emerge. For Roberto reconnecting with culture meant reconnecting with his family roots, which is often the case in families that migrate and have two cultures to negotiate.

Maria and Pablo shared the unique choices involved in choosing to emigrate from El Salvador and start a new life. As Pablo recounted tales about the war and their family back home, he caught Roberto's interest. He spoke of how they immigrated to this country to give Roberto and the other children a safe place to live. Roberto spoke of his struggles in trying to fit in. Together, Roberto and his parents created a common bond that all could embrace. This bond, formed by sharing understanding of each other's culture and in cocreating something new, became the driving force for reconnecting. When therapy was completed, Robert's grades improved, his relationship with his schoolmates took a turn for the better, and he felt reconnected to his parents and siblings. Processing immigration experiences with the family can be an essential part of helping families adapt to U.S. culture and help with needed generational changes and reorganization (Falicov, 1998; Minuchin, 1980). Roberto began to identify himself in terms of two distinct cultures. The family interactions were strong enough to accept their son's radical new identity. His parents were sustained by another world Roberto knew little about but became eager to know.

Negotiating Socioeconomic Class

Personalism is an intricate concept often missed or misunderstood by non-Hispanics. I deal with it here because it can make a critical difference in therapy and can affect whether a person succeeds. Personalism is a concept that developed in Latin America in response to a sociocultural caste system. Historically, social mobility was limited. Personalism, or a sense of uniqueness and personal goodness, was at the core of interactions between people in the community (Ho, 1987). Personalism is, essentially, a group norm that emphasizes that relationship formation must be established before a task can be accomplished (Flores, 1994; Levine & Padilla, 1980). Personalism is an inner quality of respect (*respeto*) and dignity (*dignidad*).

In many Hispanic families and communities, tasks are assigned because of the relationships that have been established based on this inner respect. This part of the class structure made it clear who could be trusted with loved ones and who could be given responsibility. The goodness of the person determines the nature of the task he or she is given.

In contrast, many "Anglo" societies assign goodness or value to a person based on his or her actions. The term Anglo is often used by Latino people to signify English-speaking people or those descended from Northern Europeans. The perception to Latinos is that relationships are often established because a task has been accomplished. The Protestant work ethic is partially responsible for this phenomenon in the United States. The accomplishment of a task, not the person's goodness, is what is most valued. The distinction between a person's value and the worth of his or her task is not an either/or concept, for they exist together. However, our perception is that one concept leads and the other follows.

The Latino concept is that when a person or the community accepts me as a trustworthy person, then I have permission to accomplish something. In the Anglo community, it means that when I accomplish something, then I can be in relationship and be given

respect. It is, therefore, important to help the Latino or Latina understand that relationships are not a prerequisite for accomplishment in
the United States.

A therapist can help the Latino client understand that, in the dominant United States culture, usually the task or an accomplishment
comes before a relationship is given an opportunity to form. The application of this concept is often a real eye opener for Hispanics. The
difference across cultures is clear, although there are no absolutes
when it comes to diversity in any cultural group. The fact that Latinos
are more likely to put relationship before task than Anglos does not
mean that all Latinos do this. Nor does it mean that all Anglos put
task before relationships. I find this relational view especially helpful
when working with immigrants or the first generation of United
States–born Latinos and Latinas who are directly affected by the cultural mores of their Latin country within their family of origin. This
also can become a messy issue in all sorts of relationship endeavors.

Case Study 2: The Concept of Social Class

Juan and Linda were from Mexico. Their parents had come to Texas
during the Mexican revolution of 1910. The Lopez family had lost
large amounts of land and money. Yet, Juan was enterprising and
began a small lumber company. He regained the status his parents
had lost, and now has one of the largest Latino-owned companies in
the nation. Juan married Linda after he was well established. He,
Linda, and the children traveled back and forth to Mexico routinely to
visit relatives and friends.

Linda was also from an upper-class family from Mexico. Her family members were fluent in both Spanish and English. Juan was proud
of what he had done and often referred to himself as "a real Mexican."
He spoke of the poor Mexicans as "*los Indios.*" It was to his utmost
surprise when his eldest son and daughter confronted him with this
"class issue." Latinos, who have grown up with a class system among
themselves, are aware of social boundaries that should not be crossed.
This class concept is not easily translated to their children who are
born into a pluralist society, part of a minority group that is steadily
eking its way into the middle classes.

Juan and Linda faced the fact that their children saw themselves as
Mexican American and, even worse, "Tex-Mex." This horrified both
parents, but they reluctantly began to accept their children's new def-

inition of themselves. Giving up their class system was something that they could not do, but they were open to the fact that it was different for their children. When their son announced that he and the son of one of Juan's salespersons, a Latino schoolmate, were going into business together, another new reality was defined for this family.

Each member of the Lopez family had a clear self-identity and could redefine the reality in how they existed with each other. The family's belief and meaning systems that created the cognitive and behavioral dilemma could be resolved. The socioeconomic status of the parents added to the children's ability to decide for themselves what was right (Bohon, Singer & Santos, 1993). However, their economic status did not completely protect their children from prejudice or their minority status. This led to the need to unite with other Hispanics.

Most Latinos and Latinas are not as fortunate as the Lopez family for they are poor. Many come to the United States to better themselves economically. Central Americans and Cuban immigrants come to this country in order to escape political oppression and yet many remain in poverty. Latinos and Latinas are hard workers willing to take on the most menial jobs to support their families. Although Hispanic men have the highest labor-force participation than any other male ethnic group in the United States (U.S. Bureau of the Census, 1996), Latinos remain the poorest group.

Interestingly, political surveys of Hispanics in the 1990s show that although Hispanic Americans are increasingly middle class (Castro, 1993), the overall economic statistic indicates a much lower income level. This statistical skew occurs because of especially high immigration from Mexico, and increased immigration from some Central and South American countries. These immigrants are typically of very low income. There is an obvious need to distinguish between immigrants and United States–born Hispanics. Due to acculturation and economics, the two groups have different perspectives and very different needs, although sometimes they may be from the same family.

Poor immigrants experience psychological distress including cultural shock, marginal and social alienation, posttraumatic stress, psychosomatic symptoms such as palpitations, dizziness, and insomnia, as well as anxiety and depression created by uprooted values and exposure to life in the United States (Falicov, 1996). American-born Hispanics experience a variety of psychological states that will vary according to such factors as their income, degree of discrimination experienced, stress levels at work and at home, and their degree of bicultural ability. Low-income and unicultural Hispanics may suffer in ways similar to their immigrant counterparts.

However, poor immigrants are in a transitional situation and are often off-balance and need to regain the ability to cope and use and establish resources. Therapy for low-income but nonimmigrant Hispanics may be geared to help in meeting basic needs and developing the capacity to cope. Poverty-stricken areas have great needs and insufficient resources. Some *barrios* (neighborhoods), border towns, and inner cities have situations so desperate that social services is the first call of action before therapy can be attempted. Middle-class Hispanics, however, adjust to normal stress in a fashion similar to middle-class Anglo Americans (Flores & Sprenkle, 1989).

Common Therapeutic Errors Due to Cultural Perceptions

A common therapeutic error is putting a Hispanic or Latino family or person in a position of having to choose between Anglo versus Latino cultures. This creates an "us and them" mentality. Working with the family to continually reevaluate their many options in particular situations usually helps the family develop skills to find different and better choices. Many Latinos have learned to move easily from one language to another or one culture to another while respecting both. But others find themselves "stuck" if faced with a decision set that might result in a possible split from culture or forces an either/or decision between their Latino heritage and their new identity as a citizen or resident of the United States. Therapists can help clients move beyond the idea of Latino culture as static or fixed. Their new bicultural identity can be seen as a process of becoming or a process of recreating—weaving in the old with the new. It is possible to use a postmodern social constructionist approach to reconstruct decisions and maintain core Latino values.

For example, a traditional Latino view is that proper young women stay in the family home until they marry. It would be unwise for a therapist to assume that leaving home is "better" than staying at home with the family. The belief that one should move away from home at 18 years of age is merely a myth, a cultural norm that may or may not apply to Latinos or others. However, the prospect of moving back in with the family may be met with resistance by a young Latina woman returning from studying at a university, away from home, or out of state. The young woman and her family may find themselves in conflict especially if the young woman looks like she is taking on the "rough individualism of the United State's ways." The therapist can reframe "living at home," as one way of "choosing to remain connected in a Latino way." It then becomes a distinct choice rather than a requirement. And if she chooses to leave home rather than stay, she remains true to the essence of her Latino heritage by maintaining strong familial connections. This process of focusing on what is important to the family culture establishes within the family a means of negotiating differences while remaining true to their distinct interpretations and meaning systems.

Another common error, known as an alpha error, occurs when a therapist assumes incorrectly that culture is central to the presenting problem (Hardy & Laszloffy, 1994). This might mean a therapist asks about culture when the client has made no reference to culture as part of the problem or blames culture as the reason for the client's problem. A young Latino having difficulty with Anglo, Asian, or Black peers might have a personality problem in relating to others. Thus, to attribute his inappropriate relational skills to his culture can mask the real problem. The most obvious blunders in bringing up culture occur when a family is dealing with the death of a child, a financial problem, a divorce, a natural disaster, or any variety of crises. To bring up culture at these crisis points is to miss the point of cultural awareness. The message is *not* to avoid the subject of culture or ethnicity, but not to automatically interpret every Latino's presenting problem as culturally related.

The most common alpha errors I find happen under certain circumstances to therapists. The first case occurs when a therapist cannot help the client distinguish between a situation when a person from another cultural group is just being rude, indifferent, or self-centered and when that person's behavior is due to cultural prejudice. A second example occurs when a therapist does not know how to help the client process whether a situation is prejudiced. This might be a therapist who is reluctant to ask questions about prejudice, fearing he or she may appear prejudiced. The therapist may avoid gathering clear information from the client. In this case, the client is uncertain about a situation, yet jumps to the conclusion that the situation was a result of prejudice. Usually, this is a client who was not affirmed when prejudice was in play and has learned to distrust situations using the ethnic card to escape responsibility. In this regard, therapists themselves must not jump to a prejudiced conclusion without helping the client evaluate the pros and cons of the particular situation. A third situation occurs when a well-meaning therapist holds an internal residual echo, a dominant Anglo cultural voice that maintains Hispanic culture itself is what is holding the client back from success and life.

On the other extreme are the beta errors. These occur when culture is central to the presenting problem but is ignored or dismissed as unrelated by the therapist (Hardy & Laszloffy, 1994). This type of error can pack a fatal blow to self-esteem and create confusion in personal judgment. If a person is ignored and purposefully not praised for a job well done, he or she develops doubts. This is especially painful when he or she sees others less competent advancing while he or she is not encouraged or given merit for work.

A therapist needs to help a person identify these issues. Once a person can identify these obstacles, the therapist can help the person cope, adjust, or protest. If a group excludes a person based on culture, it is very important for the therapist to affirm this reality in order to help the client successfully overcome such an obstacle. Drawing on family support can help sustain the type of environment needed to get through such an ordeal. This process helps the person not feel "crazy" or become so defensive that other opportunities are passed up.

Case Study 3: Cultural Discrimination

A young engineering student who came to see me began to cry over her instructor's constant putdowns of her projects. The young Hispanic women had one of the highest SAT scores entering school and was on scholarship. She had always been an honor student. At first, she thought her professor was joking, then she was insulted by his comments. When the professor gave credit to others with less well-designed projects, she became despondent and confused. This was her first disillusionment with authority figures. She thought that all professors were fair and that the quality of her work would speak for itself. She retreated into silence, which I find to be a common Hispanic response to confusion. Alarmed, her parents brought her to therapy.

I affirmed her perceptions of what was happening, and that was an important step. Soliciting her family members for support was also critical to helping her. Her mother, father, and older brother explained how they had dealt with prejudiced teachers. She eventually strategized on how to avoid this teacher. Other professors in her academic department used more objective criteria than her cultural identity to judge her work, so she did not have to transfer schools. This young woman could have been simply diagnosed as depressed and given medication without addressing the culture component. This typical form of treatment does not have long-lasting effects, as it fails to explore the cultural factors that are highly influential in Latinos' lives.

The Extended Family

In therapy, Latino families often express their greatest fear about the future as the fear of losing connection with each other. The breakdown in the extended family is seen as the loss of a means of support and nurturing for its children's children. The extended family is probably the most valuable, cherished, and sacred characteristic that Mexican American and other Latinos hold. This value appears to transcend national boundaries, forming a global community, and underlining a fundamental similarity in Latino people.

The extended family has roles, rules, and players that differ with each family. This information can be critical for a therapist when dealing with a changing family. Most extended family members are closely related by blood, such as grandparents and parents, uncles and aunts, siblings and cousins. But there are also some adopted "family members" who are intimately close to the family.

Primos are cousins. Yet, some first cousins are so close they call themselves *primos-hermanos or primos-hermanas* (cousins-brothers or cousins-sisters). This speaks of relationships formed by growing up together almost like brothers and sisters. Weekly visits occur as parents gather and share child care for their young. Weekly and extended visits for a Sunday meal at the grandparents' home are common. And, of course, all holidays and Church celebrations are times to gather the family.

Tias (aunts) and *Tios* (uncles) are based on generational boundaries. For example, if the relationships are close, the children of first and second cousins would call each other cousins, and their parents *Tio* and *Tia*. And, in turn, these children are considered nephews and nieces. There are *Padrinos* and *Madrinas* (Godparents) that may be considered extended family members. There are *compadres* and *co-madres* (more than friends) that have achieved a "relatives" status and are often called *Tio* and *Tia* by the children. These are some of the common relationships, but there are no hard-and-fast rules, so other combinations may exist.

A therapist has to ask about the extended family to see who is important and how they are connected to the presenting problem. *Who* is important is probably different from each child's or adult's perspective. It is common that the mother's family is more prominent, or close. However, I have seen families in which it is the father's family that takes the lead, and occasionally I have seen a family in which a balance between two families is achieved. Each family is unique and there is also a unique extended family culture. The extended family works for the young because it has a variety of adults in the network to help them. Studies have shown that a greater number of healthy social connections is a key element in resistance to disease, healing, and a long life (Ornish, 1998).

How can extended families survive? This is a critical issue that Hispanic Americans are facing and can be facilitated by the therapist. The extended family offers an emotional and physical support system for a group of relatives. Extended families carry a universal truth about culture. Every culture has something very important to share with the universe and this is intuitive to the groups (Hall, 1959/1981). The concept of this universal truth reminds me of the Kokopelli Legend made famous by the illustrations of Robert Montoya (Hill, 1995).

The Kokopelli is a mythical character dating back to ancient times often depicted as the flute player that brought wisdom and joy. The Kokopelli is a mythical magician, teacher, storyteller, healer, trickster, and one who brings good fortune and fertility to all living things. As legend has it, the flute player travels up from Mexico visiting the four corners of Earth, as symbolized by visiting many Southwestern Indian communities spreading music and happiness (Kidder & Guernsey, 1919). The flute song carries aesthetic, spiritual, and psychological impulses that form a bridge to ancient times while appreciating their modern manifestation. If this music is lost, will the culture follow?

The fear perhaps is that if the extended family dissolves, then the culture will also dissolve and this valuable song will be lost. Can Latinos maintain extended families in the United States? The high mobility, the individualism, and materialism of the United States culture threatens the extended family. If the extended family survives, how will it last? What new arrangements and negotiations will take place? Responses to these questions open up dialogues of empowerment. Each family has its own strengths and means of being in connection.

When change is in process, whether through crisis or through natural development, extended families will change, using the families' natural strengths and resources, which will ease the transition and help maintain connections. Family is, itself, a wellspring of strengths and resources. Clients often tell me that without the support and love of the family, life would not be as worthwhile. Jorge and Diana share how the happiness of seeing their *Abuelita* (grandmother) playing quietly with their child is one of the fundamental joys in life. Or teenager Julio told me how he keeps out of street gangs because he has his brothers, sisters, and cousins to hang with.

There are both positive and negative factors to having extended families. Most extended families are composed of families living in close proximity to each other as in the same neighborhood, town, or city. Contact is frequent among grown children, their families, and grandparents. Adults are seen as responsible for the children in the family. They are a resource in time of need. Elders are given authority and respect; they have a real say in the attitudes, values, and decisions the family makes. Extended families can be a place where people feel support, love, and care, and it can be a place where each member can find refuge and help during times of conflict. However, along with these close connections come some problems and hierarchies. Change comes slower in extended families since tradition may play a big part in the family organization.

At times, it may be difficult for younger members because so many people know what is good for them. Some privacy is sacrificed when most people know what is happening to a person in the family. However, nuclear families hold confidentiality and have a protective system that must be studied to be understood. Families may ask for help depending on who they believe can help, and other members respectfully remain silent. The important thing is that the child, adolescent, or adult knows that he or she has access to seek help from the person they choose. This is the ideal, but it is not always followed.

There are, of course, functional and less functional extended families. Less functional families do not handle stress well and can become severely dysfunctional so as to not support their members and even hurt them emotionally, physically, and psychologically. Although a functional family may handle crisis and struggle with a major change, such as its grown children moving out of state with their new families, it somehow manages to support and help its members. The opposite may be true for dysfunctional families. If a family is dysfunctional, then the natural breakdown accelerated by our mobile society may be welcomed by the younger generations in these families. The members want the freedom to escape or create their own family miles away from the dysfunctional system of their past. The cacophony of pain and unresolved issues often seems too hard to face. Leaving bad situations and people that hurt them can be a journey to new life. This breakdown may also create alienated persons with nowhere to call home. In these cases, mental problems, drugs, alcohol, gang or criminal activity increase with the breakdown of the family. The dysfunctional cycles continue or get worse. These families often stay together as they remain paralyzed and consumed with their problems. Therapeutic intervention for these families is desperately needed and yet these families and their members may not seek help except in crisis.

NARRATIVE DIVERSITY

Language is considered to be one of the best carriers of culture by social scientists (Cuellar, Harris, & Jasso, 1980; Montiel,1978), philosophers (Crossley, 1996; Mead, 1967; Merleau-Ponty, 1992; Ricouer 1991; Schutz, 1972; Vygotsky, 1986; Wittgenstein, 1953), and therapists (Anderson, 1997; Freedman & Combs, 1996; Watzlawick, Beavin, & Jackson, 1967; White & Epston, 1990). Language is the carrier of meaning systems, and language organizes how a person perceives and thinks about our world (White & Epston, 1990). How these cultural values match or mesh between Latino groups has not been examined extensively. However, preliminary exploration as in Marin, Vanoss-Marin, Sabogal, Otero-Sabogal, and Perez-Stable (1986) found that with the exception of Cubans, who share Anglo values of complete independence, there is more similarity than difference among Hispanic groups in the United States.

Language

Another feature that unites diverse Hispanic groups is the Spanish language. Language is an element that bonds the Hispanic community. Spanish is the most common of the Romance languages in the world today (*Microsoft Encarta Encyclopedia*, 1996). Although English is the first language in the United States, Spanish is prevalent as well. It is kept alive in the United States for a variety of reasons, such as our proximity to Mexico and Latin America, a strong Spanish-speaking immigrant population, and the ease of travel. Spanish media, local and international Spanish television, and cyberspace connections create a strong cultural and linguistic community whose emotional bonds transcend geographical and political boundaries (Sotomayor, 1991). In Roy's (1998) survey, 55% of Latinos in the United States preferred both Spanish and English to using only one language.

There are, however, Hispanics who do not speak Spanish well. Some understand it and don't speak it, and others simply do not understand it or speak it. In these cases, Latinos depend on the unspoken and implicit language as manifest in Hispanic families and the community, church, spiritual ideas, and neighborhoods to help carry on the Latino culture. This can also be named the unconscious, silent language of behavior, emotions, spirit, and psyche developed by culture (Hall, 1959/1982).

Case Study 4: Spanish Interpretations

Anna's family came from Cuba and Rolando's family from Columbia. They came to a Mexican American family therapist because they wanted someone who spoke Spanish. I was the only person with a Hispanic surname on their referral list of providers. They said they were struggling over communication issues especially over Anna's wanting to work outside the home. Anna was planning to return to her career as a legal assistant, and Rolando wanted her home with the children. He felt that now that his law practice was doing well, she did not need to work.

The three of us had Spanish as an anchor to help facilitate the career and gender issues. Yet the Spanish language varies in style among different families, communities, and countries, which can compound the difficulties in understanding between a man and woman. For this couple, to see a therapist who did not understand

Spanish would have delayed dealing with the intricacies in meaning of each one's perspective. Translating from Spanish to English can completely change the meaning of what one is attempting to communicate. I often hear couples and families turn to each other and say things like, "See, I knew choosing a Latina would make a difference for us. She understands our culture." Other families ask for a Spanish-speaking therapist and tell me, "I speak English well, but we needed the cultural part. We already saw a non-Hispanic psychotherapist. So I used this excuse of language to get a Hispanic therapist." Of course, some clients simply need the Spanish-language therapist. Probably one of the most interesting and frequent comments that I hear is, "We Latinos can access our emotions and affections so easily, and we are good at reading others' emotions. Our passions overflow. I picked a Latina therapist because I didn't want to scare off or be misinterpreted by an Anglo therapist." Emotions are a type of language. They tell the story of our fears and affections, and are expressed differently in different cultural groups.

Therapy for Anna and Rolando could have been conducted in English, since both were fluent. In fact, both languages were used during the session. Language is the essential tool of a therapist, so matching the clients' language is crucial to the process (Anderson, 1997; O'Hanlon & Werner-Davis, 1989; Walzlawick, Beavin, & Jackson, 1967). The dropout rate among Hispanics receiving mental health services is well documented (Acosta & Evans, 1982; Ho, 1987; Padilla & Lindholm, 1984; Sotomayor, 1991) and may be due to language and cultural clashes between therapists and clients. Latinos need to be encouraged to enter the counseling profession, and training therapists to work with the Latino population is essential if we want to provide service to this group. However, I have found that having a Spanish-speaking therapist is not as critical when doing individual therapy with a bilingual person, as it is for a couple or a family problem. If a Spanish-speaking or a culturally trained therapist is not available for a couple or family preferring to speak Spanish, therapy may take longer.

I often work with couples from different Hispanic groups who claim that their cultural differences are a fundamental problem in their relationship. Not only do these couples have to integrate the voice of the dominant culture, but they have to negotiate their respective cultural voices. Studies by Keefe and Padilla (1980) indicate that although externally a family may be very actively participating in United States society and using English as its primary professional language, internal family systems remain relatively unchanged. Family-of-origin patterns will reflect the language and country of origin. One's family of origin is a purveyor of culture, but each family develops unique patterns of interaction that influence the interpretation of that culture. It is important to help couples distinguish family-of-origin issues from cultural ones.

I often find that the cultural issue is brought up as a negotiating tool. One partner attempts to get the other partner to understand that to give up a particular idea would be to give up their culture. This negotiation attempt is often effective when the other partner understands the value of holding on to cultural values. A deep respect for new ways of interacting can be engendered as a family creates its own version of its new culture together.

Discrimination and Rage

Hispanic skin color ranges from a light tan to a dark brown. We usually have brown eyes, with dark brown hair or black "Indian straight hair." Many Hispanics with darker brown skin experience discrimination. Those with Latino accents or surnames also continue to experience discrimination in the United States. Some Latinos fall into the "invisible minority" category (Montalvo, 1991). This term, coined by political scientists of the 1950s, refers to Hispanics who blend into the White "melting pot" of Americans with varying ethnicities. Hispanics in this category are still well aware of discrimination as they watch the Black-White racial issues unfold in the United States, and see a similar racial divide applied to themselves in their workplaces and educational institutions. For the "invisible" Latinos and Latinas, discrimination is more subtle, but the impact is painful, nevertheless. Almost everyone has a story of discrimination as an individual or a family. Yet there are some Latinos that seem to go personally unscathed by prejudice.

Anglo American culture seems to many Latinos to be obsessed with the preference of light skin over darker skin. This color theme is imposed on minority groups by a dominant Euro American discourse.

Although it is difficult to trace the beginnings of color discrimination, its roots were well established when the Aryan nation concept ravaged Europe in the nineteenth and twentieth centuries, pitting Nazis against Jews, and resulting in the extermination of millions of people. Some other examples closer to home are the annihilation of the American Indians in the United States and the tradition of slavery pitting White slaveowners against Black African slaves in the southern states. More recent examples include the imprisonment of Japanese Americans during World War II and the racial riots of the 1960s. Even today, White supremacist groups enact hatred against their fellow Americans of color. Tragically, this awareness of color inferiority is now integrated into the Latino's own discourse as they compare themselves to Anglo Americans. Though Latinos have struggled with oppressive color distinctions since the Spanish conquests over the Native Americans, I find that Latinos in the United States are much more color conscious than Latinos in their native land. As one Latino man told me, "Back home, we were white and brown, and no one said anything or made such a distinction because we are all Latinos and this is what was important."

Racism, ethnocentrism, socioeconomic barriers, and other oppressive structures from the Anglo society that do not allow room for Latino cultures, create bonds between Hispanic groups that might not otherwise be acknowledged. One noticeable feature about ethnic groups is that they feel comfortable with each other and need togetherness to support ideas and philosophies. This is evidenced with Latinos by their tendency to cluster in particular states and areas.

Prejudice causes serious problems for a family. Therapists need to know that clients will introduce topics of discrimination or cultural clashes when it is pertinent to the presenting problem. The condition of trust must exist for this type of sharing to take place. Therapists look for elementary clues such as clients feeling alienated, isolated, or rejected in the context of society, school, and career. They may need to reaffirm these issues when they are shared, to help clients overcome them, cope with them, or remove themselves from the context.

If an adult is experiencing discrimination, they usually suspect it; children have to learn about prejudice from others. If Latinos get paid less for a job than Anglo counterparts, they eventually find out. If a Latino is passed over in a career opportunity and a less qualified

Anglo is hired, this reality is usually discovered. If a Latina is given the unwanted jobs in the office whereas the Anglo staff member gets the more visible, perky jobs; she quietly and painfully has to deal with this reality.

Case Study 5: Prejudice in the Workplace

Sergio, a 45-year-old Mexican American, came into therapy because of panic attacks. He had quit his job because he was often afraid. Sergio had worked for the government on the civilian side all his life. He was an air-conditioning specialist and worked on very large systems. He was aware of discrimination at the plant, but because of his expertise, he enjoyed respect from his fellow workers. He told me that once he worked on a team, the men would include him in the next project. Sergio was a troubleshooter. Give Sergio an air-conditioning unit's brand name and model and he automatically had the design in his head. Once a problem was identified, he usually knew what part of a system would probably break down and under what circumstances.

When the Air Force downsized, he was transferred to a smaller unit where his expertise was not as valued. Smaller systems were usually replaced rather than fixed, but there were still big systems to work on. "My new boss is prejudiced," Sergio told me. "At first, I thought he was just a bad fellow, but I quickly learned otherwise. He singled-out me and the Polish immigrant for toilet duty." All the men had E8 status and should have been rotating this cleaning job. This was around the time Sergio had his first panic attack.

Sergio took action and wrote a memo to his boss' superiors and within a week the problem was rectified. Toilet duty was now rotated among all E8s. Things went well for about a month and then his boss asked him if he would take on a part of an E2 employee's job for one week. Sergio wanted to show his good will, so he agreed. A week turned into two weeks, then a month, and then three months at which time Sergio's panic attacks got worse. What disturbed Sergio the most was that he had to clean a patio where people smoked. Because of the design of the patio, he could not just sweep it; he had to pick up the butts one by one that had fallen into the cracks. He felt demeaned and the smell got to him. Sergio became so distraught that he left his job. He said, "The boss was harassing me, that boss wanted to humiliate me. He tricked me, by relying on my good will."

Once Sergio left, the ratings on the plant dropped. His ex-boss called Sergio several times, asking him to return. The damage, however, was done. Sergio continued for six months with panic attacks. Sergio knew he had been discriminated against. He had to deal with the sadness of prejudice before he could return to another job.

His wife was supportive and was relieved when Sergio broke his silence. Their youngest son did not understand what everyone was arguing about. Their daughter thought this discrimination was something of the past. Their eldest son wanted his father to sue. He argued loudly with his father, "What do you mean we Mexicans don't sue. We are Americanos."

Facilitating a Bicultural Narrative

The "Bicultural Model" (Ramirez, 1983) supports diversity within each culture. One of the most consistent findings in acculturation research and theory is that Hispanics who are bilingual and/or bicultural have stronger ties with their culture and have a stronger sense of family identity (Elizondo, 1992; Montiel, 1978; Ortiz & Arce, 1984; Ramirez, 1983). These strong ties are associated with better academic achievement (Kimbell, 1968) and identity formation. Bicultural individuals and families are more competent and less anxious than Hispanics who attempt to give up their culture (Laframbose, Coleman, & Gerton, 1993).

In contrast, a longitudinal study by Ramirez (1983) shows how adolescents who become overly acculturated to the Anglo culture at the expense of their Hispanic identity experience negative consequences. For example, they have poor psychological adjustment to education and their environment, and have a higher probability of antisocial behavior. This attempt to disown a Hispanic identity results in more psychological problems and drug use (Ramirez, 1971).

If a family makes no attempt to teach its children its customs, values, and language because of its own need to fit into U.S. culture, then an exaggerated intergenerational gap may develop in the family. This can put a young person at risk. A study of 55 Cuban families with adolescent drug users and mothers with drug usage found that these mothers and adolescents were out of sync with their own culture and had an exaggerated generational gap as compared to nondrug-using families (Ramirez, 1971; Szapocznik & Kurtines, 1980). This was illustrated earlier in Robert's family.

This finding seems to cut across Hispanic groups. The less connected a person is with his or her culture, the more poorly he or she does in adapting and succeeding in the United States (Montiel, 1978). The stronger a family or person identifies with his or her culture, the more positive he or she feels about it and the better he or she does in life and with his or her own family. The school systems' concern for bilingual education uncovers the grim educational difficulties that Hispanics face. Hispanics have the highest dropout rates and the fewest graduates on all levels of education of any ethnic group (U.S. Bureau of the Census, 1996). It makes one appreciate why Hispanic communities fight to maintain the Spanish-language fluency and bilingual programs in school settings.

Bilingual education increases the chances for language competence and success for Latinos (Lambert, 1977). When parents and children speak different languages, it creates alienation and suffering. The knowledge of two or three languages enhances the first and will better serve our future leaders who will be working in a global community. My community as well as others have included a multilingual "magnet" high school and middle school with great success (Tofolla Elementary, San Antonio, Texas, in 1998). A graduate therapy program with multicultural and bilingual teams in this community spearheads a revolutionary effort to help families (Our Lady of the Lake University in 1998). Using Spanish in therapy is essential for some Mexican American families. Bilingual education will enhance our educational system—for all Americans—as well as provide the necessary remedial work for new immigrant children of the Americas.

Also, studies that have evaluated crisis intervention programs have discovered that children and adolescents who can learn to identify with their cultural background can enhance their self-concept, reduce role conflict, and become better adjusted emotionally (Derbyshire, 1970). Moreover, treatment approaches (whether individual, group, or family) of drug abuse and behavior problems found that Mexican American adolescents receiving any therapeutic treatment that included a component to increase cultural awareness and family values had better outcome results than treatments where the cultural component was not included (Dominguez-Ybarra & Garrison, 1977; Freudenberger, 1975).

Taking a broad ecological approach that includes cultural influences enhances therapy with people of all backgrounds, but especially those marginalized by the dominant culture. Fontes and Thomas (1993) focused on how family therapists can empower clients by making cultural issues explicit when pertinent to the presenting problem. What family values can clients claim as their own to help them through a difficult time? What culturally rich experiences can clients call on to regain self-dignity and thus become empowered to enjoy life and give to others? How can a client claim difference as a contribution to community and society? What family stories of immigration, oppression, and bravery call forth courage and pride in one's own ancestors? Therapy is a means by which a therapist taps the client's resources to help him or her adjust and supercede difficulty.

Fontes and Thomas (1993) list seven helpful interventions for establishing a cultural identity:

(1) Encouraging clients to value and be proud of their cultural background; (2) fostering self-esteem by acknowledging clients' cultural uniqueness; (3) validating clients' cultural values and experience; (4) acknowledging clients' attempts to preserve and express their cultural traditions and practices; (5) encouraging the strengths of clients' culture; (6) recognizing clients' bicultural competence; and (7) acknowledging the social forces of discrimination that may have led them to positions of reduced power in society and contributed to their presenting issues (p. 265).

These interventions give a basic framework for a commonsense approach to acknowledging one's birthright and experience. Once this basis is established, it is necessary that the Latinos and Latinas be affirmed in creating new bicultural realities in the United States. I would add nine other helpful interventions in facilitating a new "bicultural narrative" in a family therapy context:

Steps to Facilitate a Bicultural Narrative

1. Facilitate clients' attempts to craft their own definition of themselves as bilingual, bicultural persons
2. Enhance clients' ability to go back and forth between two world views with ease and enjoyment without a dualistic focus
3. Help family members understand that the new generation will redefine what it is to be Hispanic, that is, class and gender
4. Encourage clients to continue their career and educational pursuits based on their self-evaluation, while acknowledging that they may meet discouragement and discrimination

5. Explore how social class and poverty issues within the culture can lead to family and community problems
6. Validate strong emotional, cultural, linguistic family ties as healthy
7. Consider grief issues for immigrants as a natural process
8. Match language whenever possible
9. Help distinguish family-of-origin issues from cultural ones

CONCLUSION

Diversity is the discourse that is most needed when dealing with *la familia Latina*. Therapists need to acknowledge that Hispanic families are set within a diversity of cultures from distinct countries with Spanish as their uniting language.

Hispanic families come from a blend of cultures yet have a unique and clear identity. Their ability to blend, grow, and change is a dynamic reality that taps the resources of the individual and family. Therapists treating these families must have an ear for their unfolding music and verse. When discord, pain, and dysfunction disrupts family life, culturally resonant therapists will understand how to facilitate growth and orchestrate the necessary resources for healing.

REFERENCES

Acosta, F., & Evans, L. (1982). The Hispanic American patient. In F. Acosta, J. Yamamoto, & L. Evans (Eds.), *Effective psychotherapy for low-income and minority patients.* New York: Plenum Press.

Anderson, H. (1997). *Conversation, language, and possibilities.* New York: Basic Books.

Bohon, L. M., Singer, D., & Santos, S. (1993). The effects of real-world status and manipulated status on the self-esteem and social competition of Anglo Americans and Mexican Americans. *Hispanic Journal of Behavioral Science, 15*(1), 63–79.

Castro, M. (September 5, 1993). Hispanics in the '90s: Time for a new image? San Antonio: *Express-News*, Vista Section, pp. 6, 26–27.

Crossley, N. (1996). *Intersubjectivity: The fabric of social becoming.* Thousand Oaks, CA: Sage.

Cuellar, I., Harris, L. C., & Jasso, R. (1980). An acculturation scale for Mexican American normal and clinical populations. *Hispanic Journal of Behavioral Science, 2*(3), 199–217.

Derbyshire, R. L. (1970). Adaptation of adolescent Mexican Americans in United States society. In E. B. Brodsky (Ed.), *Behavior in new environments: Adaptation of migrant populations* (pp. 275–290). Beverly Hills, CA: Sage.

Dominguez-Ybarra, A., & Garrison, J. (1977). Toward adequate psychiatric classification and treatment of Mexican American patients. *Psychiatric Annals, 7*(12), 86–96.

Elizondo, V. (1992). *The future is Mestizo.* New York: A Meyer-Stone Book.

Facundo, A. (1991). Sensitive mental health services for low-income Puerto Rican families. In M. Sotomayor (Ed.), *Empowering Hispanic families: A critical issue for the '90s.* Milwaukee, WI: Family Services of America.

Falicov, C. J. (1996). Mexican families. In M. McGoldrick, J. Giordano, & J. K. Pearce (Eds.), *Ethnicity and family therapy.* New York: Guilford Press.

Falicov, C. J. (1998). *Latino families in therapy: A guide to multicultural practice.* New York: Guilford Press.

Flores, M. T. (1994). The Latino seminarian. In R. Wister (Ed.), *Psychology, counseling and the seminarian.* Indianapolis, IN: National Catholic Education Association: The Lilly Endowment.

Flores, M. T., & Sprenkle, D. (1989). Can therapists use *Faces III* with Mexican Americans? A preliminary analysis. In D. Olson, C. Russell, Q. D. Sprenkle (Eds.), *The circumplex model: Systemic assessment and treatment of families.* New York: Haworth Press.

Fontes, L., & Thomas, V. (1993). Cultural issues in family therapy. In F. Piercy & D. H. Sprenkle (Eds.), *Family therapy sourcebook* (pp. 256–282). New York: Guilford Press.

Freedman, J., & Combs, G. (1996). *Narrative therapy: The social construction of preferred realities.* New York: Norton.

Freudenberger, H. J. (1975). The dynamics of treatment of the young drug abuser in a Hispanic community. *Journal of Psychedelic Drugs, 7*(3), 273–280.

Hall, E. T. (1959/1981). *The silent language.* New York: Doubleday.

Hardy, K. V., & Laszloffy, T. A. (1994). Deconstructing Race in Family Therapy. *Journal of Feminist Family Therapy.* Binghamton, NY: Haworth.

Hill, W. (1995). *Kokopelli ceremonies.* Santa Fe, NM: Kiva Publishing.

Ho, K. M. (1987). *Family therapy with ethnic minorities.* Thousand Oaks, CA: Sage.

Keefe, S. E., & Padilla, A. M. (1987). *Chicano ethnicity.* Albuquerque: University of New Mexico Press.

Kidder, A. V., & Guernesy, S. J. (1919). Archaeological exploration in Northwestern Arizona. *Bulletin 65.* Washington, DC: Bureau of American Ethnology.

Kimbell, W. L. (1968). Parent and family influence on academic achievement among Mexican American students. (Doctoral dissertation, University of California, 1965). *Dissertation Abstracts International, 29*(6), 1995A. (University Microfilms No. 68-61, 550.)

Laframboise, T., Coleman, H. L. K., & Gerton, J. (1993). Psychological impact of biculturalism: Evidence and theory. *Psychological Bulletin, 114*(3), 395–412.

Lambert, W. E. (1977). The effects of bilingualism in the individual. In P. W. Hornby (Ed.), *Bilingualism: Psychological, social, and education implications* (pp. 15–27). San Diego, CA: Academic Press.

Levine, E., & Padilla, A. (1980). *Crossing cultures in therapy: Pleuralistic counseling for the Hispanic.* Monterrey, CA: Brooks/Cole.

Marin, G., Vanoss-Marin, B., Sabogal, F., Otero-Sabogal, R., & Perez-Stable, E. J. (1986). *Subcultural differences in values among Hispanics: The role of acculturation.* San Francisco: University of California, Hispanic Smoking Cessation Research Project.

Mead, G. H. (1967). *Mind, self, and society.* Chicago: University of Chicago Press.

Merleau-Ponty, M. (1992). *Texts and dialogues.* Princeton: Humanities Press.

Microsoft Corporation. *Microsoft Encarta Encyclopedia* [CD-ROM]. (1996). Redmond, WA: Author.

Minuchin, S. (1980). Families and family therapy. Massachusetts: Harvard University Press.

Montalvo, F. (1991). Phenotyping, acculturation, and biracial assimilation of Mexican Americans. *Empowering Hispanic families: A critical issue for the '90s.* Milwaukee, WI: Family Services America.

Montiel, M. (1978). Chicanos in the United States: An overview of socio-historical context and emerging perspectives. In M. Montiel (Ed.), *Hispanic Families* (pp. 19–40). Washington, DC: COSSMBO: National Coalition of Hispanic Mental Health and Human Services Organizations.

O'Hanlon, W. H., & Weiner-Davis, M. (1989). *In search of solutions: A new direction in psychotherapy.* New York: Norton.

Ornish, D. (1998). *Love and survival: The scientific basis for the healing power of intimacy.* New York: HarperCollins.

Ortiz, V., & Arce, C. H. (1984). Language orientation and mental health status among persons of Mexican descent. *Hispanic Journal of Behavioral Science, 6*(2), 127–143.

Padilla, A. M., & Lindholm, K. L. (1984). Hispanic behavioral science research: Recommendations for future research. *Hispanic Journal of Behavioral Science, 6,* 13–32.

Ramirez, M. (1971). The relationship of acculturation to educational achievement and psychological adjustment in Chicano children and adolescents: A review of the literature. *El Grito 4*(4), 21–28 [On-line]. Azteca: University of Kansas.

Ramirez, M. (1983). *Psychology of Americans: Mestizo perspectives on personality and mental health.* New York: Pergamon.

Rueschenberg, E. J., & Buriel, R. (1995). Mexican American family functioning and acculturation: A family systems perspective. In A. M. Padilla (Ed.), *Hispanic psychology: Critical issues in theory and research.* Thousand Oaks, CA: Sage.

Ricoeur, P. (1991). *From text to action.* London: Athlone Press.

Roy, D. (1998). Strangers in a native land: A labyrinthine maze of Latino identity. *Latino Attitude Survey* [On-line]. Azteca: University of Kansas.

Schutz, A. (1972). *The phenomenology of the social world.* London: Heinemann.

Sotomayor, M. (1991). *Hispanic families: A critical issue for the '90s.* Milwaukee, WI: Family Services of America.

Szapocznik, J., & Kurtines, W. (1980). Acculturation, bicultural adjustment among Cuban Americans. In A. Padilla (Ed.), *Acculturation: Theory, models and some new findings* (pp. 139–159). Boulder, CO: Westview Press.

U.S. Bureau of the Census. (1996). *Statistical abstract of the United States: 1996.* (116th ed.). Washington, DC: Author.

Vygotsky, L. (1986). *Thought and language.* Cambridge, MA: The MIT Press.

Watzlawick, P., Beavin, J., & Jackson, D. (1967). *The pragmatics of human communication.* New York: Norton.

White, M., & Epston, D. (1990). *Narrative means to therapeutic ends.* New York: Norton.

Wittgenstein, L. (1953). *Philosophical investigations.* Oxford: Blackwell.

2

El Latino: Transgressing the Macho

GONZALO BACIGALUPE

What's a man without a family? Nothing.
—OSCAR HIJUELOS, 1989

People's strengths play a central role for postmodern practitioners of family therapy, especially those who espouse solution-focused psychotherapy, collaborative language approaches, and feminist relational therapies. Strengths are also important in recent organizational behavior models, in participatory research, and in the popular education models of Latin America and Africa. Practitioners of all these approaches question the status quo. One major assumption is that having more confidence in the future depends on gaining a better understanding of people's strengths and their capacity to change. Postmodern professionals believe solutions are found in collaboration with others.

In contrast, the research and clinical literature emphasize a rather pessimistic perspective concerning the roles of Latino men within the family and within the therapeutic system. A review of the literature in psychology and the social sciences shows that deficit models prevail as ways to construe knowledge about Latino or Hispanic men. Latino men appear as deficient individuals who lack something, or who are embedded in contexts of oppression, in which they usually play a negative role as victim or oppressor.

What can practitioners learn from this research? How do the dominant discourses about men shape our therapeutic practices and affect our own discourses with this population? I must question myself. As a well-educated Latino man, with a reportedly successful, professional, and academic experience, and as a recent immigrant to the United States from Chile, what questions do I find relevant? Anyone who works with Latinos might ask these questions. In addition to questions that deconstruct ideas we take for granted or ideas we have construed as the *truth* regarding Latino men and their families, what else needs to be asked?

THE SOCIAL CONSTRUCTION
OF DOMINANT DISCOURSE

Taking an affirmative postmodern perspective (Rosenau, 1991), and, more specifically, a social constructionist perspective of family therapy (Anderson, 1997; Friedman, 1995), I struggle with the constructed *reality* of multiple oppressive discourses that inscribe Latino men. Considering that "what we focus on becomes our reality" (Hammond, 1996, p. 20), there is a wealth of ideas and questions yet to be raised. We can question the status quo and create new perspectives that appreciate the heterogeneous quality of the subject at stake. This chapter is what Bakhtin (1981) calls heteroglossic text, a critical, although incomplete reading of the socially diverse and competing discourses in this author's experiences and in the literature on Latinos.

The construction of the social discourse about Latino men and Latino families is a joint activity carried out by hundreds of men and women writing about Latino men and by those whose lives are inscribed by these texts. Although a joint activity, the construction of these texts has not been dialogical. The authors have not entered a communal discourse. The men and Latino families have not participated equally in defining the social identities represented in the literature. Written texts contain many voices, although not all are public or present.

In listening to those who have been silenced in texts that speak of them, I join a postcolonial perspective that emphasizes the heterogeneous nature of any text or social organization. We explore the assumptions of those who investigate, treat, evaluate programs, educate, and produce knowledge regarding Latino men. We hope to deconstruct the notion of "Latino inscribed in a model of deficit," while bringing to light the multiple, complex, and slippery theme of Latino men in families and family therapy.

El Latino

The Latin American men I describe in this chapter are from South and Central America, and some of the Caribbean countries. Although I have decided to focus on those men whose Hispanic heritage is hegemonic, I consider men from Latin America who speak Portuguese, French, Dutch, or other European languages Latinos. Those who speak Native American languages, indigenous to Latin America, are also considered Latinos. The observations developed in this chapter refer to all those who came from Latin America, or who have links to ancestors from Latin America.

I am a biased observer, a writer who emphasizes the exploration of multiple discourses and the effects of these discourses on people's lives (Bacigalupe, 1995). This article was inspired by questions about Latino men and their role in a book on the diversity of Hispanic families. The literature in family therapy has paid little attention to the subject of Latino men in families. Reviewing the major journals of family therapy is disappointing if one wants information on this theme. The topic of Latino men in families and family therapy is virtually invisible. This chapter addresses some of the ways to frame the therapeutic process when working with Latino men. I hope to offer an alternative, to take some distance from approaches that define *for* Latinos "what needs to be done."

Labels and Definitions

As we question the effects of creating discourses regarding Latino men in families, and in family therapy, it will be useful to agree on some working definitions. Family is a construct designed to help us understand how people live within a web of intimacy. It is a story about how individuals survive and thrive in that web where struggles of gender and power are central. Family therapy is defined as an approach that emphasizes a relational understanding of clients and characteristic ways of carrying out therapeutic conversations with individuals or groups of people.

Some of the questions family therapists might ask are: (1) Can therapists describe and define the intersection between Latino and man without resorting to stereotypical and all encompassing descriptions? (2) How do we challenge internalized conceptions about the role, position, and power? (3) Are we reconstructing a definition of men that reproduces heterosexist, patriarchal biases (Jardine & Smith, 1987), addressing masculinity in universal terms while neglecting racial and cultural variations? or (4) How do we integrate an affirmative and dialectical practice in the treatment of Latino men?

So, what is *Latino*? Like many terms that describe groups of people, *Latino* or *Hispanic* includes men from cultures and societies that share characteristics, but show a tremendous amount of internal variability. *Latino, Hispanic, Americano* and other more localized terms like *Chicano* and *New Rican* are just a few of the terms suggested to label the group. Latin Americans in the United States are a heterogeneous set of groups and communities. Although we have some common internalizations about being disadvantaged minorities in the United States, not even our language is shared by all. *Hispanic* and *Latino* are language labels that evoke struggles and create specific realities for each participant in a therapeutic conversation. The labels not only pose rhetorical problems to researchers and clinical practitioners, they are the source of psychosocial and existential conflicts for Latinos.

The constitution of self is a social event and the reality of our Latino identity is constituted in imaginary and always evolving *novelas* (Bacigalupe, 1997). Clinicians, researchers, and administrators need to recognize the diversity of Latinos and of Latino men and their contexts. Latino men live in very different contexts and even one individual in a family may experience contexts that the others in the family do not experience. Some groups of Latinos do not interact with each other due to language, ethnic, or racial barriers, but most are disconnected by economic differentials that result in residential segregation. Race, social class, and the history of immigration are key factors that differentiate the experiences of Latinos in the United States.

What are the themes and images that create the reality of and about Latino men? What is the image of Latino men in the United States? I find these questions relevant since the therapeutic encounter occurs in the context of wider social relationships, and family therapy may recreate the same social relationships that exist "outside" the clinical context. What does recent research discuss concerning Latino men, their families, and family therapy? These questions are framed differently, depending on who is the researcher, writer, or clinician attempting to define these categories. Ideally, I conceive a situation in which these researchers, writers, and clinicians take hold of their assumptions and enter into a dialogue regarding the impact of the construction of *Latino* and *La Familia* within the therapeutic conversation.

Statistics: The View from the Top

One traditional but useful tool to describe Latino men and Latino families is the epidemiological study. These sometimes painstaking studies are based on data from a census or large survey and then generalized to the whole population. The results can then be revised to fit Latino populations and supposedly show reliability and validity, statistically. Quantitative studies based on large samples derive "sound and objective" conclusions by quoting statistics about the "reality" of Latino men in the United States (Bacigalupe, 1998; Dimedo, 1980). From this perspective, the relevance of the subject is defined by comparison and contrast. Latino men are defined as similar to other people under the umbrella of *Americanos,* but they are also differentiated as part of a different group: the other—the one that needs categorization. These generalizations fail to acknowledge the diversity of this other.

However, this form of research may introduce us to the U.S. Bureau of the Census (1996) statistics reporting that 10.2% of the population in this country is Hispanic. That is, about fifteen million Americans are "officially" of Hispanic origin. This research attempts to predict future patterns, like the one suggesting that by the year 2050, 22.5% of the United States population will be constituted by Hispanics. If one were to take these studies seriously, a sound conclusion is that the relevance of knowledge associated with Latinos in the United States should have increased proportionally. If more than a fifth of the population is Hispanic, social policies would have to reconsider any long-standing decision based on this dramatic population change. For example, changes in immigration, education, and tax laws, plus business and international treaties, have a direct impact on the way Latino families acculturate, enculturate, and/or transculturize in the United States.

Reportedly objective and seemingly neutral statistical research can support radical changes in the way Latino men position themselves in their families. A more critical analysis demonstrates how a superficial consideration of these statistics can have deleterious consequences and further the unjust conditions in which the majority of Latinos are placed. From a clinical perspective, statistics about income, employment, and housing can inform clinicians not only about the "issues" that may be affecting Latino men, the socioeconomic conditions will enter the therapeutic relationship in complex but comprehensive ways. For instance, there is a strong relationship between the social location of clients and income level with the relationship they may have with the larger system. This relationship will affect a central aspect of the therapeutic relationship: the confidentiality of the therapeutic relationship and the privacy of family life. The larger the capacity to control economic resources, the largest the capacity to stay disconnected from social control agents that may attempt to inflict change in the family. Thus, intimacy and secrecy of the family will be ensured by income level.

GENDERED ISSUES

We Spanish-speaking people live in a language-gendered world. We are unavoidably immersed in the world of gender characterized by oppositional terms for male and female: *el/ella, eso/esa, el/la.* Gender classifications apply not only to people and animals, but inanimate objects and abstract concepts too. The ocean and the sky are masculine, *el mar y el cielo,* the earth and writing are feminine, *la tierra y la escritura.* Using gendered descriptors for all that surrounds us does not necessarily make these objects and abstractions acquire what one might consider male or female characteristics. Yet, the roles of *El Latino* and *La Latina* are clearly defined and differentiated by gender.

Given that our languaging of reality is oppositionally defined by gender, the nonheterosexual world is noticeable only by its absence in the daily naming of what surrounds people. Not having a "third gender" (Morales, 1996) makes the dichotomy one that may preclude the realities of Latino gays in families and couples. Being a man in the Latino world assumes being a heterosexual male; being manly is not associated with the "nonworld" of gayness. This is so pervasive that the "strong Latino emphasis on a masculine-feminine gender dichotomy predisposes many Latino gay men to use heterosexual relationships as templates for their own relationships" (Morales, 1996, p. 292). Despite the stigma, Stavans (1996) writes, "homosexuals have been a ubiquitous presence in the Hispanic world . . . they are the other side of Hispanic sexuality, a shadow one refuses to acknowledge—a 'they' that is really an 'us'" (p. 155).

Most Latinas who live or have lived with a Latino experience him as participating in structures of domination at home. In most cases, this experience of domination reflects the Latino's reaction to the lack of access to a higher status in a social milieu.

> *The public/private distinction is relevant only for the white middle and upper classes since historically the American state has intervened constantly in the private lives and domestic arrangements of the working class. White feminists' concerns about the unhealthy consequences of standards for feminine beauty, their focus on the unequal division of household labor, and their attention to childhood identity formation stem from a political consciousness that seeks to project private sphere issues into the public arena. Feminists of color focus instead on public issues such as affirmative action, racism, school desegregation, prison reform, and voter registration—issues that cultivate an awareness of the distinction between public policy and private choice. (Hurtado, 1994, p. 145)*

A majority of Latino males live within the constraints of poverty, unemployment, and blatant racism. Latino men, however, independent of their social class upbringing or actual status, are challenged in the United States by the increased demands for gender equality and feel their status is threatened by these changes (Davenport & Yurich, 1991). They feel that their sense of masculinity and their role as provider are in danger. Latinos resent the change and react in a number of ways. Some are privileged enough, like some middle-class and upper-middle-class men, not to *feel* the need to change. Others have partners who continue to pretend that the social context has not changed. Some Latinos threaten their female partners. Usually, the recent immigrant continues to interact with others as if he were still back home. If that role is threatened, he may resort to aggression, threats, or other forms of overt control and power.

Gender Roles

A married couple, both graduate students, and their teenage daughter sought family therapy for assistance in parenting. This case demonstrates how those who are recent immigrants have difficulty changing their relationship in response to their the new context:

Case Study 1: Parenting While Acculturating

Ricardo and Marta were arguing about how to discipline their teenage daughter who refused to do chores until "everybody at home did their part." Their daughter was raised with a firm sense of fairness and democratic values. Her experiences visiting her classmates' homes in which fathers had a more active role at home made her more aware of the inequalities at home. However, the father could not see the value of her statement since "everybody at home is doing what we have always done." In therapy, we listed each family member's chores, clarified responsibilities, and defined some new arrangements.

The following week, Ricardo expressed pride in how everybody did his or her share. But, on further inquiry, Marta admitted she was covering for him. Ricardo could not let go of rules that prevailed in his home country, where men would not do chores at home or would not admit they did. Socially, Ricardo was not adapting to contexts that were different from his country of origin. In the eyes of the members of the extended families, changing his behaviors or beliefs about gender roles would jeopardize Ricardo's dominant role. Marta's mother-in-law accused her of lacking the strength to adapt to the new American ways. In her opinion, Marta was not a good wife and mother if Ricardo helped out with "women's activities." It was a sign that her daughter-in-law was too demanding and not supporting her husband.

Gender arrangements that resemble the traditional roles in Latin America are difficult to change, even if men believe their socioeconomic position to be underprivileged. It is not women working out of the home that makes the difference; most Latin American women have always worked outside their homes, in addition to maintaining the full array of household chores and management. The difference is in the perception of who should be in charge and who is construed as more important in the marital relationship. Even if the extended family is not nearby, the family's traditional values exert a powerful influence. This is particularly true for those who emigrated without their extended families; the power of the extended family reaches beyond their physical presence. Memories and family myths, combined with limited contact, act as a continuous reference to how lives should be lived and thus how gender arrangements should work out.

Paradoxically, Latina women have been socialized to feel that they are spiritually superior to their men and thus able to endure the pains of their less enlightened partners. Espin (1985) has suggested that Latinas have been socialized to believe that men are both indispensable and undependable. This is part of the *marianista* code (Garcia-Preto, 1996; Montecino, 1991; Stevens, 1972). Considering the metaphor of who takes responsibility in a relationship (Bepko & Krestan, 1985), men are abusive and seemingly in control of the relationship, but the definition of the relationship relies on the women who, as a Latina therapist reported, "let the guy misbehave since he is unable to handle the complexities of life." Reported beliefs may be concordant with patriarchal ideas, but wives may challenge that dominance on a behavioral level. What appears to happen compared to what actually happens can bewilder researchers (Baca Zinn, 1979) and therapists alike.

MACHISMO: CHALLENGING STEREOTYPES

The term *machismo* is often employed to explain the violence that Latino men exert over women, although the dynamics of gender violence are found throughout the world. Denis, Brandt, Fand, and Quiroz (1993) suggested that *machismo* is the underlying element in the violence exerted against women. *Machismo* is an ideology that affects everybody—an expression of power that provides benefits for one group over others. She compares it with racism and classism because it sustains inequality—the power of men over women. According to Quiroz, the physical violence inside the home is an expression of a greater social violence against women and minorities in society.

Men, Women, and Power

When men are oppressed by power relations at work and in the community, they, in turn, come home and oppress their wives. This *machismo* ideology immobilizes women who complain. They feel ridiculed for their attempts to fight back. *Machismo* is characterized by expressions like: "Women like to be beaten." "She must have done something to deserve a beating." "The man who loves you is the one who hits you." *Machismo* ideology spreads the belief that men are violent because they are "crazy, alcoholic, uneducated, poor, or from underdeveloped countries." These expressions narrow the scope of the problem so it is perceived as an issue that affects only some individuals and not óthers, and makes unequal gender arrangements invisible. When used to explain power dynamics, the original meaning of *machismo* is distorted.

Traditionally, *machismo* was utilized as a label to name the efforts that men make at being in charge of the well being of family. In a recent research study about masculinity and *machismo* in the Latino culture, Mirande (1997) found a complexity of patterns. "Latino men are internally diverse, so that intra-ethnic differences are perhaps as great or greater than interethnic differences" (p. 114). Utilizing a conventional, unidimensional conception of Latino men obscures their differences. And yet, "The assumption that acculturation and greater exposure to the dominant culture leads to rejection of traditional conceptions of gender and the male role was not supported by the findings. The findings suggest that there is a distinct Latino cultural ethic, surrounding masculinity and fatherhood that is radically different from dominant American conceptions (pp. 114–115).

Diversity versus Generalization

Clearly, some generalizations may apply, but one must also examine diversity among individuals. Mirande's study (1997) backs up findings by others. Baca Zinn (1995) and Zavella (1991) recognize that gender is a basic organizing principle of society and "no assumption about Latino families is more deeply ingrained than that of male dominance." However, studies "found that Mexican American families exhibited many different patterns of marital decision making" (Baca Zinn, 1995, p. 182).

In family therapy (e.g., McGoldrick, Giordano, & Pearce, 1996; McGoldrick, Pearce, & Giordano, 1982), as well as in traditional anthropological studies, men have been described within the constraints of ethnic and cross-cultural perspectives. Cross-cultural approaches generalize after careful disclaimers at the beginning of the texts, in which Latinos are initially defined as heterogeneous, but end by focusing on similarities.

Roschelle (1997) reviewed the traditional studies on Latino families based on the culture of poverty paradigm. The studies contain assumptions about Latino men that are biased, predicated on a white, middle-class, normative model.

Underlying this approach is an assumption of the superiority of white, middle-class culture and the devaluation of all other family forms (Staples & Mirande, 1980). Studies focus on male dominance and female passivity as the key to explaining Latino family disorganization. Chicano families are presented as radically different from the dominant (presumably egalitarian) Anglo American family. The primary focus of this perspective is on the debilitating effects of *machismo* (the spiritual, physical, and sexual domination of men over women). Social and economic inequality experienced by Chicanos is blamed solely on the patriarchal structure of the Chicano family (Mirande, 1985). In fact, it is argued that *machismo* produces maladaptive pathological responses in Chicano family members (Mirande, 1997, pp. 8–9). Mirande (1997) posed the need to search for a variety of masculinities and thus ways of being male among men.

Macho o Machismo?

Morales (1996) noted a distinct difference between *machismo* and *macho,*

> *Machismo* refers to a man's responsibility to provide for, protect, and defend his family. His loyalty and sense of responsibility to family, friends, and community make him a good man. The Anglo-American definition of *macho* that describes sexist, male-chauvinist behavior is radically different from the original Latino meaning of *machismo,* which conveyed the notion of "an honorable and responsible man." (1996, p. 274)

In my experience, when I ask graduate students, clients, clinicians, and peers, "What do you associate with being Latino?" The words *macho* and *machismo* emerge as negative descriptors. The therapist, De La Cancela (1986, 1990) questioned the concept of *machismo* as the central descriptor of Latino male behavior and identity. *Machismo* and ideas about masculinity among Latino men serve to perpetuate negative conceptions and myths of Latinos and legitimizes economic and political subordination.

An associated myth is the assumption that Latino men are more violent and aggressive than the dominant race. I found Martin Espada's writing inspirational. He writes,

> *Latino males in this country are in fact no worse in that regard than their Anglo counterparts. Arguably, European-American males have set the world standard for violence in the twentieth century, from the Holocaust to Hiroshima to Vietnam. Yet, any assertiveness on the part of Latino males, especially any form of resistance to Anglo authority, is labeled macho and instantly discredited. (1996, p. 88)*

Despite the biases demonstrated in social science research, which seems stuck in the intrinsic association between Latino man and *machismo*, there are men who fight the *machismo* set of values. Shorris (1992) writes, "The venerable rules of machismo require that a man have some effect in the world. . . . For the lack of it men behave as if they were mad" (p. 438). In defining us by *machismo, El Latino* becomes another very general category that says less about the particulars of that individual.

TRANSGRESSING THE MACHO

> *To be critical of one's culture is not to betray that culture.*
> *We tend to be very righteous in our criticism and indict-*
> *ment of the dominant culture and we so often suffer from*
> *the delusion that, since Chicanos are so maligned from the*
> *outside, there is little room to criticize those aspects from*
> *within our oppressed culture which oppress us.*
> —*MORAGA, 1986, p. 180*

A systemic view emphasizes contexts. The problems that Latino men present in family therapy occur in context. Context includes the nuclear family, the extended family and intergenerational stories, the neighborhood, the agencies that provide services, the work environment, and any other significant participant in the lives of these men. It also includes the belief system of each of the cultures the men have been immersed in, past and present. Finally, it encompasses some of the effects that the broader context has on the males at the intersection of racial, gender, and economic systems. Latino men and women do not exist in isolation. We Latinos coexist, affecting others and being affected by those in the world around us. The issues described in the previous pages reflect the evolving, changing, and complex contexts in which Latino men are immersed and have a direct impact in the ways therapists engage with them.

Immigration and the Impact of Economic Changes

The immigration process is a central marker in the family lives of Latinos. If Latinos have lived through generations in the United States, stories of their ancestors' immigration forge a distinctive identity for the family. Authors can rescue some of these significant stories. Our identity as Latinos is shaped by our memories of growing up and our making sense of the social conditions and struggles of our parents. Therapists who access these tales will find a wealth of diversity among their Latino clients. They will introduce a different nuance into the therapeutic conversation.

My observations refer to Latinos who come from or have links to the Latin American continent. There are those men who may not only sustain themselves and their families, but their extended family in Latin America. There are Latinos who speak little or no Spanish and/or have never visited (nor will they) their parents or grandparents in their home countries. One aspect that seems to unite them is how their psychosocial identity has been shaped by the experience of immigration and a new label that encompasses not only their country of origin, but a whole continent. This awareness is not experienced in the daily lives of Latinos in Latin America who experience themselves as belonging to one country rather than a continent. Many second- and third-generation Latino men and their families thrive in a capitalist environment and participate in the structures of power. Yet, others continue to suffer from the inherent social inequality fostered by advanced capitalism. If our families were here when the United States government expanded to the South and West, our experiences will take a particular form that will differ from the experiences of those Latinos who have recently immigrated and find themselves integrated or marginalized into a vast, undifferentiated, conglomerate of "people of color."

Structural economic shifts, the growth of service jobs, and the elimination of manufacturing positions affect Latinos and people of color in disproportionate and acute ways compared to white workers. These changes reorganize or reinforce the cultural changes associated with immigration and the way traditional gender arrangements are challenged. Thus, economic changes will have a great impact on men and their families after they adjust to some of the challenges faced in the process of immigrating to the United States. What Baca Zinn (1989) describes as the "opportunity structures decline" will foster a traumatic transformation in families and in the roles men play in families. This structural shift will separate working-class or poor males from those who constitute the middle class and move to the suburbs or better-off neighborhoods. This structure will also create further schisms that may have been challenged during the time of immigration due to exile, the search for educational opportunities, and/or better economic opportunities.

The socioeconomic schism that existed in Latin America will be reproduced in the United States. Men from distinct social classes will not get together and may not even see each other. Considering the upward mobility myth of United States society, Latinos will not have access to the networking opportunities created by the few who are successful. Those men who are successful will be disconnected from the plight or experience of those who are less able to make it in the system with the exception of those who make their work or political commitment the betterment of Latino communities independent of social upbringing.

Roschelle (1997) cautions us about the pervasive myths of the reportedly impressive support Latinos provide for each other, "the informal social support network typically found in minority communities are not as pervasive as they were in the past" (p. xi). The myth of network support or the *compadrazco* system is much more a goal to achieve through clinical interventions, as it may have little connection with the reality of isolated individuals and families boxed within the constraints of economic hardship, urban decay, hostility, and the uncertainty of immigration status in the United States. This lack of connection, or participation in support networks, undermines ingrained ideas about solidarity held by men in Latin American culture. Feeling a continuous pressure to perform, earn, and make it in America alienates Latino men from friends and family. Substance abuse, violence, gang-related activities, and other destructive lifestyles might actually be attempts to reconnect.

The perspectives of therapist and client regarding a problem are influenced by their reference points concerning economic hardship. Any clinical, educational, and preventive program should take into account the effects of social class and lack of access to economic resources in designing services. Despite conditions of poverty, it is not unusual to find clients who lack an understanding of these issues. This is especially true for more recent immigrants or migrant farm workers, whose "pattern of identifying serious problems may reflect respondents' use of Mexican poverty conditions as a referent point. Life difficulties in the United States may be assessed as not serious when viewed in relation to experiences in Mexico" (Zambrana, 1995, pp. 96–97). This may partially explain why therapists see so few recent immigrants in their offices and agencies.

The following is an example of how economic inequality hinders Latino men's full participation in counseling opportunities. In Massachusetts as well as other states in the United States, men who are found guilty of abusing their partners are mandated to attend a domestic violence program that focuses on issues of accountability and responsibility. The men demonstrate they are accountable by regular attendance to a batterers' group and payment of the fee. Making men accountable for the violence and for being safe to others is a laudable goal. For Latinos, however, the group fee may be an added burden to a community that has little access to resources. An implicit cultural assumption of capitalism is that income is directly associated with moral worth and accountability. Yet this dominant discourse directly contradicts some core values of many Latino men.

Dignidad

Dignidad (dignity), a core value, is a social agreement that may have a stronger relationship with accountability than the capacity and willingness to pay a fee. For many Latino men, the internal qualities of the person demonstrate one's worth, not one's behaviors. Financial constraints may prevent Latinos from demonstrating accountability but will not detract from their internal dignity. However, society's reaction may serve to discriminate against Latino males, silencing the difficulties they have in obtaining and maintaining jobs. This example illustrates the need to look beyond our own taken-for-granted cultural discourses to understand people of other cultures.

Another constraint in demonstrating accountability can result from the distance between Latino communities and the services needed. Many Latinos have to travel greater distances to attend the sessions than others. Placing programs directly in Latino neighborhoods will help alleviate this problem. And, as I suggested for one batterers' program that was trying to expand its services to the Latino community, demanding a monetary fee could be replaced by other forms of accountability, such as community service. This solution has a double effect: It increases the batterer's accountability, and the payment of the "debt" aids the Latino community. Ideally, the organization or program transforms its clients into active founders of the Latino services.

CONSTRUCTING COLLABORATIVE *CONVERSEMOS*

A systemic approach can be defined by its relational emphasis that can be translated into considering reality as socially constructed (Gergen, 1994). Accounts of the world, from this perspective, are embedded in social practices and thus "a critical question to be put to various accounts of the world is what kinds of practices they support. Do they enable us to live in ways we hold valuable or do they threaten these social patterns?" (p. 130). The aim of social constructionist researchers is *destabilization* by focusing with "acute sensitivity to the perspectives of other peoples and times" (Gergen, 1994, p. 137). But, the work of social science as briefly related before tells us little about the specifics of how to carry on therapeutic conversations that will move men forward toward a more just relationship in their families and with themselves. What follows is an account of therapeutic practices within the greater domain of systems work, an approach that attempts to destabilize taken-for-granted ideas held by clinicians and their clients.

The Culturally Resonant Therapist

There are excellent examples in the family therapy literature about how to introduce cultural competency in family therapy work. Dyche and Zayas (1995) and Falicov (1995) provide outstanding guidelines in this regard. Practicing family therapy within the Latino community is not ensured by "right matches" between the therapist's and client's cultures. A Dominican therapist working with a family from El Salvador would be working cross-culturally. Within this difference exists both the potential for an enriching therapeutic process and the danger for potential misunderstandings and alienation. Believing only in similarity may obscure the differences, thus obscuring the complexity and multiplicity of worlds that exist among Latinos. Curiosity in the process of knowing the client will be balanced by exploring commonalties. These commonalties should also be acknowledged. For instance, the immigration process can be viewed as one experience rather than multiple ones, allowing for the sharing of the same media outlets, choices of code words, and so on. If the therapist draws from an ethnic perspective, some shared normative cultural values emerge (Morales, 1996). However, a position I find that fits better with a collaborative stance is to understand Latino men from a minority perspective that "uses a conflict analysis rather than culture as a focus" (Ginorio, Guitierrez, Cauce, & Acosta, 1995, p. 242).

Accepting Initial Ambiguity, Listening, Advising, and Reflecting

Instead of developing culturally specific therapies, therapists have addressed the issues of members of marginal groups by reframing them as individual problems arising from the psychology of an oppressed person (Hurtado, 1994, p. 145). Ethnic and racial political leaders fight vehemently against the use of therapeutic treatments that depoliticize and individualize their concerns. On the other hand, individuals like to be recognized. In this chapter, names and other identifying variables have been changed. When I tell my clients about including their histories in one of my writings, they show interest and feel proud of their inclusion. However, when I tell them I change their names and keep our conversations confidential, some reject this anonymity. They want to stand for their story and feel awkward about concealing their real names.

Reconnecting: Case Study 2

Juan was referred to psychotherapy while attending an in-patient alcohol treatment program, in which he was the only Latino patient in the facility. He found access to one bilingual case worker who referred him to me, as the only male bilingual therapist in the community mental health clinic. I worked with Juan for a year and a half on a biweekly basis. Juan, who was 46 years old, had abused substances for more than two decades. The case worker described him as "always angry and paranoid" toward his peers in the recovery treatment center. Juan's perspective was that many of the patients in the treatment unit belonged somewhere else, "*estan todos locos ahi*" (they are all crazy there). Juan came from a rural area of Puerto Rico to the United States after being abandoned by his wife because "he was a drunk" with little hope for recovery. He lived with friends in the streets or in homeless shelters, and he did not think about connecting with his family.

During most of our therapy sessions, Juan maintained a reserved tone and did not disclose his inner thoughts. When speaking about his daily routine in the residential facility, Juan seemed "factual" and perceptive about the actions of others. As we developed a relationship, he more readily shared his thoughts about his interactions with peers. He was able to observe himself and became more accountable for the problems arising in his relationships with others. Still, he remained physically marginal with his peers, characterizing them as less human and lacking basic social skills.

In counseling, I helped him develop skills to stay in a skills training course that would help him find work and, later, keep a regular job. In the process, he began recognizing the need to reconnect with his family and relatives back in Puerto Rico. Any question that directed his thoughts to his own impact on others was met with a mix of indifference, anger, and silence. I provided advice on "experiments" he could carry with his peers that may have allowed him to reflect on his own ways of constructing his social reality at the time. By resolving some of the interactional problems, he began to think *about* reconnecting with his family and establishing links between his actions and of those who "abandoned" him.

Personal Confidences

Certain conversational practices are contradictory to Latino values. Contrary to popular brief and solution-focused therapies (Berg & Miller, 1992; Cade & O'Hanlon, 1993; de Shazer, 1991; O'Hanlon &

Weiner-Davis, 1989; White & Epston, 1990), it may not be necessary to set clearly defined goals at the outset of therapy. A therapist who can accept a lack of initial historical information and an ambiguous initial goal will be more successful at joining and engaging Latino men in family therapy. In general, within the Latino culture, therapists and researchers may find it difficult to gather information, because some groups believe certain data about "family matters" are "not to be shared with strangers" (Zambrana, 1995, p. 97).

In my own experience with clients, and in the experience of those therapists I consult or supervise, Latino men often appear to dominate family conversations, limiting the topics discussed. They are reluctant to disclose personal information, share "deep feelings," or submit "to a situation in which they perceive themselves as helpless and weak" (Torres, 1998, p. 21). In the Puerto Rican culture, several assumptions concerning psychotherapy "are inconsistent with Puerto Rican values, particularly among those who are bicultural or of low acculturation levels. Among these is the view that it is appropriate and beneficial to discuss personally sensitive issues, and the belief that achieving an intellectual understanding of a problem is likely to reveal a course of action that can rectify it" (Torres, 1998, p. 21). Men may dominate the conversation by speaking for other members of the family, by explaining it all, by staying silent, or by being *amurrados* (a complex mix of anger, indifference, silence, and a controlling gaze).

Personal Style
Speaking with men in family therapy may not be easy due to a "familiocentric" style of speech (Castaneda, 1996) that can be defined as the "impulse to speak with fervor, loudly, state things clearly and without hesitation, expecting a vigorous exchange of ideas that has no winners or losers but solutions to problems communally obtained" (p. 38). This style is rejected or misunderstood in the United States and seen as motivated by negative intentions.

In teaching, Castaneda and his colleagues have found this ferocious style circumvents issues and intimidates students. Students may accuse professors of not being nurturing. This same style silences children and women who witness the man of the house speaking forcefully and surely about almost everything. If he is not knowledgeable about the topic, he will correct others about a detail he may know something about. Frequently, he will interrupt others to establish a conversation on the side, behaving as if he was unaware of the conversation with the other members. On a positive vein, passionate speech is useful during political campaigns, festivals, and other ritualistic occasions. "Yet the underlying cultural code for this way of speaking manifests itself in daily conversations with enough frequency that Anglo-Americans often believe Latinos are aggressive, arrogant, or blustering speakers" (Castaneda, 1996, p. 44).

Familiocentric speech is opposite to the "nurturing" style that may prevail among Whites. Castaneda believes that the latter style is more presumptuous and arrogant because it assumes that we can know the psychology of the other and thus protects the interlocutor from what may be seen as too intrusive. "The Anglo-American speaking style is arrogant, by psychoanalyzing the listener, and it is aggressively intrusive, by attempting to manipulate the listener." From his perspective, the Latino style assumes the listener is positioned on equal footing, "able to hear anything and able to respond freely" (Castaneda, 1996, p. 45). Finally, another characteristic that is common to conversations among family members is that of addressing a larger issue (philosophical, political, community related, etc.) that is not just located in the specifics of a family problem. These conversations may seem "strange" to therapists who may perceive this as a form of indirectness or plain avoidance of the internal family problems.

Engaging in conversation may be more effective if it is based initially on giving "expert advice" at the request of the men and not necessarily exploring the inner interpersonal aspects of the conflict. The therapeutic work is further enhanced if the therapist is willing to offer direct advice and engage actively with the larger system at the beginning of the therapeutic work. It is useful to help clients develop strategic alliances with others rather than fostering the finding of a mentor, a task that can be too difficult because successful Latinos may be overwhelmed by requests for mentoring and support. In sum, a conversational and collaborative approach is reachable if men are given advice within the context of choices and as a commentary rather than direct directive. Being direct may not necessarily mean being directive.

Predicting, understanding, emancipating, and deconstructing (Hindmarsh, 1993) are intertwined practices in family therapy with

Latino men. These practices have differential effects in the kind of services provided. Including rather than excluding questions can move the therapeutic conversation beyond a relativistic apolitical stance that does not acknowledge the social construction and the "real" effects of what therapists and clients construct. That is, having the world be socially constructed is not to say that that category has no significance in our world (Crenshaw, 1994). Like the *mestiza* consciousness (Anzaldua, 1990), this kind of therapy simultaneously rejects and embraces—so as not to exclude—what it rejects: "It is a mestiza consciousness that can perceive multiple realities at once" (Hurtado, 1994, p. 148).

Reflecting in Public and about the Public

Anderson's (1997) notion of reflecting in public is useful. I encourage a reflexive process in sessions that foster the sharing of different voices within the client, the therapist, and the family members (Hoffman, 1993), but particularly in terms of how others in the community and in the family may be perceiving and creating opinions about the client. There are few opportunities for Latino men to obtain constructive criticism in the social arena, that is, without having to defend themselves. There are few opportunities to listen to what others are thinking or their assumptions. Therapy becomes a way of reflecting about those voices that have a concrete impact on the lives of these men. Later on, the reflective process turns to how they are shaping their relationships with those they love, and finally with their own selves.

This reflexive process is rewarding and painful because it may lead men to recognize patterns of racism, classism, sexism, and discrimination, patterns in which they actively participate as victims, survivors, and perpetrators. Thus, they are subjected and powerless as well as responsible and accountable. This polyphonic (Bakhtin, 1981) perspective allows for the sincere exploration of strong biases and difficult themes and at the same time keeps all the statements provisional and ready for further review. This provisional approach deviates from the usual structural attempt at changing what men say in families and instead invites them to consider these ideas and then to acknowledge or construe those ideas in different contexts and realities.

Learning about these men and thus about myself occurs within that sort of dialogue in which tentativeness coexists with a forceful exchange of ideas. It is a dialogue in which acceptance of different voices is balanced with the best of political exchanges in which each participant is absolutely convinced of the truthfulness of his or her political perspective. Client and therapist enter into therapeutic conversations bringing into the session the identities assumed in their daily lives, and within the context of social and economic realities, they influence each other as participants of these contexts, and although they may not expect it, they will affect each other.

Ghostly Guidance: Case Study 3

Carlos was an unemployed twenty-year-old Puerto Rican man who had lived in a small city in Western Massachusetts for the last three years. He complained of insomnia and was afraid of becoming aggressive toward his wife or other adults. He slept with a knife under his pillow because he believed that someone could break into his house at any moment during the night—a real possibility in housing projects. Yet, most of the time, he talked about his abusive father whom he left three years ago in Puerto Rico.

Carlos repeatedly discussed his efforts in "rescuing" each of his siblings from the abuse of his father. Although he was the emergent "leader" in his extended family, he was virtually powerless in his daily life. After three to four months of discussing his story, he began to pay attention to his own needs, as well as that of his family. He realized how restrained he was becoming in his role.

During one session, I asked him to write to some of the people who had been important to him while he was growing up. It was a difficult task because he could not focus on getting in touch with his relatives until he told me the story of his sister. She had been murdered by her husband the year before. At that moment, it was important for me to point out the connection between the unacknowledged grief and sadness, and the connotation of a "manly" behavior in the Latino culture. Despite this conversation in which he understood that the roles given to men in his particular culture were keeping him from exploring important emotions, he was caught up in the idea of taking revenge instead of experiencing his inner pain. Later on, he was able to report, in a more specific way, what was happening at home. I asked him, "If a healthy ghost entered your house for a day or two, what would it report to us in a session?" "If I were invisible and I were visiting your home, what would I see?" "If you were to join me and share your thoughts at that moment, what would strike you?" These questions facilitated a conversation between his wife and himself and his brothers concerning stereotypical Latino roles. The questions were not threatening to his sense of manhood, although they accounted for his feelings. In addition, they were mediated by a fictionalized or "unreal" companion. The conversation integrated the spiritual aspects of Carlos and his family's beliefs. The ghost was transformed into a spiritual guide that he could "control" and attune to his family and individual needs each time he needed to reflect on his problems.

In therapy, the telling of stories about ourselves is not trivial because stories constitute and actively shape our lives by specifying our psychological identities and location in the larger social context (Bacigalupe, 1990; Roberts, 1994). What I have learned in accounts provided in supervision, clinical meetings, professional videotapes, and in discussions with peers is that the way the stories about Latino men are told and the way therapists listen to them—the context of the telling—can affect the quality of the therapeutic relationship and its effectiveness.

Weaving Conversations with Men into Family Therapy

In my experience, there is at the core of the clinical work a high level of reflexivity in the process of redefining what is considered as the problem and/or the solution. In this framework, the therapist may need to deal with higher degrees of ambiguity as the relationship develops since there is no particular pattern to follow and no "fill in the blanks interview." Many would agree with the assertion that developing a collaborative relationship is a difficult task, thus many authors bypass this crucial aspect by assuming that the only possible relationship with Latino families implies reproducing a hierarchical therapeutic system as in the structural family therapy approach or modified psychoanalytic approaches. Our challenge is to develop a more democratic relationship to sustain a truly therapeutic opportunity for Latino men. Finding rigid hierarchical decision-making processes in Latino families does not call for a method characterized by the same features; the process should parallel the desired outcome.

Many practitioners assume that Latino families do not like to be in a reflexive therapeutic context and need to be directed, making the therapist an expert on what well-adapted families should look like. Others have proposed that exploring intergenerational legacies is a useful paradigm to help families connect with their larger heritage and address their need to feel connected and supported. In both cases, the notion that "familism" is common in every family is at stake, as well as the idea that Latinos "are more action-oriented." With these notions, therapists will find that control and manipulation can become the center of the process. In these approaches, the expert technical psychotherapist defines the problems to be resolved by the family or explains how to resolve them.

In contrast, although I find these approaches problematic, elements of them could be useful in some circumstances, since families and clients may need different kinds of relationships that may take diverse timelines and forms. Moreover, as I have written elsewhere, some families will require the therapist to actively engage with the larger system and become an advocate and cultural mediator. Those who can obtain clear results will win the trust of the family and deepen the therapeutic work. As therapists we have the opportunity to introduce the novelty of reflexivity in conversations in the therapeutic arena. In other cases, safety will develop as the therapist witnesses how the story unfolds without expecting immediate changes.

I find it useful to define clear and collaborative relationships with those who referred the family, since they will probably become important players, if they are not already important in the lives of the families. This is particularly relevant in cases in which protective services, the courts, or the schools are involved since decisions made by these entities affect the maintenance of the family. Weaving connections among all potential participants seems like an effective collaborative position for the therapist and those involved in addressing identity markers like racial and ethnic background, religion and popular religiosity, immigration stories, assimilation and integration, alien status, background of clients and therapists, income history, social class and cultural status, history of political struggle and level of alienation, language and bicultural status, health, gender, her/story and history in the context of the family and in the world at large.

In the clinical context, although I am curious about these identity markers, I make no assumptions about the specific connection between identity markers and the experience of Latinos or the way they present their problems. I believe that identity markers can potentially affect clients, but each client will be affected differently. Thus, I am curious, approach it from a nonexpert position, and ask questions about stories I do not know instead of filling in the blank questions with my expected answers.

As in critical historical accounts, I prefer a collaborative and reflexive approach in order to prevent "silencing the past" (Trouillot, 1995). Since stories by Latino men in families are packed with secrets, shame, silences, and oppression, it would be antithetical and unethical to suggest a therapy that only enforces the therapist's discourse. A critically reflexive and reflective listener describes what I believe are the significant characteristics of an effective and ethical therapist working with Latino families.

An effective therapist puts emphasis in social and dialogical participatory processes, and in the recognition of how power struggles are contested in each interaction, even the ones defined as therapeutic. Another important aspect of the therapeutic process compels us to reauthor our clients' lives by working directly with their sense of agency so that they can shape their lives and build a supportive community anew. This cannot be done only "in the minds" of clients. Clients and their families need to develop coalitions to challenge institutional practices aimed at people's disempowerment. A coalition could start by asking clients to participate in as many institutional spaces as possible in the agencies, as well as in the process of creating policies. Finally, the therapist recognizes the multiplicity and alternative meanings that can be relevant in the lives of clients influenced by those who live with the client, the client's communities, as well as those who attempt to listen to their stories.

CONCLUSION

If, in writing this chapter, I have generated more questions than I answered, I have achieved my purpose. In questioning the nature of difference we embrace a more humane, critical, and reflexive clinical practice with Latino men in family therapy. What I find relevant is not, "What is a Latino?" or "What is a Latino characteristic or even a Latino identity?" but rather, "What are the relationships between Latinos and others?" and "How do others construct their relationship with Latinos and their world?" Latino men become who they are in the relationships they and others believe they inhabit. Family diversity grows as part of a constellation of social, economic, migratory, and racial patterns rather than as the sole result of ethnic characteristics. An effective therapist listens to the variety and array of voices because clients are at the intersection of numerous of these "variables" as they develop their own agency.

REFERENCES

Anderson, H. (1997). *Conversation, language, and possibilities: A postmodern approach to therapy.* New York: Basic Books.

Anzaldua, G. (Ed.). (1990). *Making face, making soul—Haciendo caras: Creative and critical perspectives by feminists of color.* San Francisco: An Aunt Lute Foundation Book.

Baca Zinn, M. (1982). Chicano men and masculinity. *The Journal of Ethnic Studies, 10* (Summer), 29–44.

Baca Zinn, M. (1989). Family, race, and poverty in the eighties. *Signs: Journal of Women in Culture and Society, 14*(41), 856–875.

Baca Zinn, M. (1995). Social science theorizing for Latino families in the age of diversity. In R. E. Zambrana (Ed.), *Understanding Latino families: Scholarship, policy, and practice* (pp. 177–189). Newbury Park, CA: Sage.

Bacigalupe, G. (1990). Voices under arrest: Political violence and a Chilean family. *Family Therapy Case Studies, 5*(2), 31–38.

Bacigalupe, G. (1995). *Family violence in Chile: A qualitative study of interdisciplinary teams' perspectives.* Unpublished doctoral dissertation, University of Massachusetts, Amherst.

Bacigalupe, G. (1997, October). *El miedo no pasa rapido, se estanca: Therapists listening to the stories of trauma by Latino families.* Paper presented at the Hispanics in the U.S.A.: Cultural Locations, University of San Francisco.

Bacigalupe, G. (1998). Cross-cultural systemic therapy training and consultation: A postcolonial view. *Journal of Systemic Therapies, 17*(1), 31–44.

Bakhtin, M. (1981). *The dialogic imagination.* M. Holquist (Trans.). Austin: University of Texas Press.

Bepko, C., & Krestan, J. A. (1985). *The responsibility trap: A blueprint for treating the alcoholic family.* New York: The Free Press.

Berg, I. K., & Miller, S. (1992). *Working with the problem drinker: A solution-focused approach.* New York: Norton.

Cade, B., & O'Hanlon, W. H. (1993). *A brief guide to brief therapy.* New York: Norton.

Castaneda, O. (1996). Guatemalan macho oratory. In R. Gonzalez (Ed.), *Muy macho* (pp. 35–50). New York: Doubleday.

Crenshaw, K. W. (1994). Mapping the margins: Intersectionality, identity politics, and violence against women of color. In M. A. Fineman (Ed.), *The public nature of private violence* (pp. 93–118). New York: Routledge.

Davenport, D. S., & Yurich, J. M. (1991). Multicultural gender issues. *Journal of Counseling & Development, 70*(8), 64–71.

De La Cancela, V. (1986). A critical analysis of Puerto Rican machismo: Implications for clinical practice. *Psychotherapy, 23,* 291–296.

De La Cancela, V. (1990). Working affirmatively with Puerto Rican men: Professional and personal reflections. *Journal of Feminist Family Therapy, 2*(3/4), 195–212.

Denis, A., Brandt, P.-Y., & Quiroz, G. (1993). The function of negation in argumentation. *Journal of Pragmatics, 19*(1), 23–38.

de Shazer, S. (1982). *Patterns of brief family therapy: An ecosystemic approach.* New York: Guilford Press.

Dyche, L., & Zayas, L. H. (1995). The value of curiosity and naivete for the cross-cultural psychotherapist. *Family Process, 34*(4), 389–399.

Espada, M. (1996). The Puerto Rican dummy and the merciful son. In R. Gonzalez (Ed.), *Muy macho: Latino men confront their manhood.* New York: Doubleday.

Espin, O. (1985). Psychotherapy with Hispanic women: Some considerations. In P. Pedersen (Ed.), *Handbook of cross-cultural counseling and therapy* (pp. 165–171). Westport, CT: Greenwood Press.

Falicov, C. J. (1995). Training to think culturally: A multidimensional comparative framework. *Family Process, 34*(4), 373–388.

Friedman, S. (Ed.). (1995). *The reflecting team in action: Collaborative practice in family therapy.* New York: Guilford Press.

Garcia-Preto, N. (1996). Puerto Rican families. In F. Walsh & M. McGoldrick (Eds.), *Living beyond loss: Death in the family* (pp. 183–199). New York and London: Norton.

Gergen, K. J. (1994). *Realities and relationships: Soundings in social construction.* Cambridge, MA: Harvard University Press.

Ginorio, A. B., Guitierrez, L., Cauce, A. M., & Acosta, M. (1995). Psychological issues for Latinas. In H. Landrine (Ed.), *Bridging cultural diversity to feminist psychology: Theory, research and practice.* Washington, DC: American Psychiatric Association.

Hammond, S. A. (1996). *The thin book of appreciative inquiry.* Plano, TX: CSS Publishing.

Hindmarsh, J. H. (1993). Alternative family therapy discourses: It is time to reflect (critically). *Journal of Feminist Family Therapy, 5*(2), 5–28.

Hoffman, L. (1993). *Exchanging voices: A collaborative approach to family therapy.* London: Karnac Books.

Hurtado, A. (1994). Relating to privilege: Seduction and rejection. In A. C. Herman & A. J. Stewart (Eds.), *Theorizing feminism: Parallel trends in the humanities and social sciences* (pp. 136–154). Boulder, CO: Westview Press.

Jardine, A., & Smith, P. (Eds.). (1987). *Men in feminism.* New York: Routledge.

McGoldrick, M., Giordano, J., & Pearce, J. K. (Eds.). (1996). *Ethnicity & family therapy* (2nd ed.). New York: Guilford Press.

McGoldrick, M., Pearce, J., & Giordano, J. (Eds.). (1982). *Ethnicity and family therapy.* New York: Guilford Press.

Mirande, A. (1985). *The Chicano experience: An alternative perspective.* South Bend: University of Notre Dame Press.

Mirande, A. (1997). *Hombres y machos: Masculinity and Latino culture.* Boulder, CO: Westview Press.

Montecino, S. (1991). *Madres y huachos: Alegorias del mestizaje Chileno.* Santiago, Chile: Editorial Cuarto Propio-Cedem.

Moraga, C. (1986). From a long line of vendidas: Chicanas and feminism. In T. d. Lauretis (Ed.), *Feminist studies, critical studies* (Vol. 8, pp. 173–190). Bloomington: Indiana University Press.

Morales, E. (1996). Gender roles among Latino gay and bisexual men: Implications for family and couple relationships. In J. Laird & R. J. Green (Eds.), *Lesbians and gays in couples and families: A handbook for therapists* (pp. 272–297). San Francisco: Jossey-Bass.

O'Hanlon, W. H., & Weiner-Davis, M. (1989). *In search of solutions: A new direction in psychotherapy.* New York: Norton.

Olmedo, E. L. (1980). Quantitative methods of acculturation: An overview. In A. M. Padilla (Ed.), *Acculturation: Theories, models and some new findings.* Boulder, CO: Westview Press.

Roberts, J. (1994). *Tales and transformations: Stories in families and family therapy.* New York: Norton.

Roschelle, A. R. (1997). *No more kin: Exploring race, class, and gender in family networks.* Thousand Oaks, CA: Sage.

Rosenau, P. M. (1991). *Postmodernism and the social sciences: Insights, inroads, and intrusions.* Princeton: Princeton University Press.

Shorris, E. (1992). *Latinos: A biography of the people.* New York: Avon Books.

Staples, R., & Mirande, A. (1980). Racial and cultural variations among American families: A decennial review of the literature of minority families. *Journal of Marriage and the Family, 42*(4), 157–173.

Stavans, I. (1996). The Latin phallus. In R. Gonzalez (Ed.), *Muy macho* (pp. 143–164). New York: Doubleday.

Stevens, E. (1972). Machismo and marianismo. *Transaction-Society, 10*(6), 57–63.

Tomm, K. (1988). Interventive interviewing: Part III. Intending to ask lineal, circular, strategic or reflexive questions? *Family Process, 27,* 1–15.

Torres, J. B. (1998). Masculinity and gender roles among Puerto Rican men: Machismo on the U.S. Mainland. *American Journal of Orthopsychiatry, 68*(1), 16–26.

Trouillot, M.-R. (1995). *Silencing the past: Power and the production of history.* Boston: Beacon Press.

U.S. Bureau of the Census. (1996). *Statistical abstract of the United States: 1996* (116th ed.). Washington, DC: Author.

White, M., & Epston, D. (1990). *Narrative ends to therapeutic means.* New York: Norton.

Zambrana, R. E. (Ed.). (1995). *Understanding Latino families: Scholarship, policy, and practice.* Newbury Park, CA: Sage.

Zavella, P. (1991). Mujeres in factories: Race and class perspectives on women, work, and family. In M. D. Leonardo (Ed.), *Gender at the crossroads of knowledge: Feminist anthropology in the postmodern era* (pp. 313–336). Berkeley: University of California Press.

3

La Mujer Latina: From Margin to Center

YVETTE G. FLORES-ORTIZ

I feel that wherever I am now, with my parents or at work,
or in Mexico, I carry home inside of me.
I don't erase myself anymore.
I know who I am.
Frankly, I don't care if others want to ignore me.
The fact they need to erase me is proof
of my very powerful existence.

—ANA

Culturally competent family therapy can be delivered when practitioners understand the diversity of families and people of color in the United States. Such understanding calls for an integration of historical facts, cultural sensitivity, and a willingness to listen to people's stories without preimposing Eurocentric, male-centered notions of family health and dysfunction (Flores-Ortiz, 1997b). A popular *dicho* (saying) in Latin America expresses it best: *cada cabeza es un mundo* (each head is a world). Thus, to provide ethical, effective, and culturally congruent family therapy, the therapist must facilitate a dialogue wherein the unique experiences of families can be heard and situated within their own, not the therapist's, sociopolitical and cultural realities.

This chapter offers my reflections about the location of Latinas within the family and society. In 1970, while a first-year undergraduate, I was invited to work as a family therapist with migrant Mexican families. I was 18 years old and only knew my family's experience. I was Central American and immigrant. I knew next to nothing about Mexican migrant families. However, I was the only bilingual/bicultural student in the university's psychology department. Although many culturally competent Mexican community workers were available, the county services appeared to prefer hiring an 18-year-old inexperienced college student than a seasoned, mature individual from the same community. Thus began my learning about families, service delivery systems, the feminization of mental health services, and the marginalization of women within and outside the family. In this chapter, I offer some of what I have learned over the past three decades in hopes that through these pages we can engage in dialogue about processes of change.

LATINAS IN THE UNITED STATES OF AMERICA

Women of Hispanic origin, as defined by the U.S. Department of Labor (1997), include all women who identify themselves as Mexican, Puerto Rican, Cuban, Central American, or other Hispanic origin. The term *Hispanic* includes the racial diversity of the continent as well. Hispanic women are one of the fastest growing population groups in the United States, showing an increase of 54.1% in the decade between 1986 and 1996. (U.S. Department of Labor, 1997). The largest growth occurred among women of Mexican origin. The largest proportion of Hispanic women are Mexican origin (59.4%), followed by Puerto Rican (24.2%), and Cuban (11.4%). Women from other Latin American countries comprise 5.0% (U.S. Department of Labor, 1997) of the female Hispanic population. These gains include increased births and documented migrations.

The sociodemographic diversity among Latinas in the United States is partly determined by nation of birth or origin, age, years of residence in the United States, generational level, history of family migration, and each woman's level of education and degree of participation in the labor force. Although women of Mexican and Cuban origin have had consistent labor force participation, their employment rates are lower than White women and tend to concentrate in the service sector, particularly for Mexican women. Cuban women generally have higher educational attainment than other Hispanic females, are also typically older, and evidence lower unemployment rates (U.S. Department of Labor, 1997).

Labor force participation influences economic status. Consequently, Puerto Rican– and Mexican-origin women remain at the lowest socioeconomic strata. Marital status also influences women's economic position. The number of female-headed Hispanic households grew by 64% between 1985 and 1995. Women maintained a fourth of all Hispanic families (1,485,000 out of 6,200,000 families); the average size of these families was between three to four persons. Such families had lower median incomes than similar African American families; that is, female-headed Hispanic families had a median income of $13,474 compared to $15,004 for African Americans and $22,068 for female-headed households. Hispanic male-headed families with no wife present had a median income of $22,257. For married couples, the median income was $29,861. In sum, Hispanic families, particularly female-headed ones, continue to suffer economic disparities (U.S. Department of Labor, 1997).

However, even college-educated Latinas, who comprise less than a fraction of 1% of all Hispanics, do not fare much better economically with less than 2% college-educated Latinas earning more than $50,000 annually (U.S. Department of the Census, 1994). Thus, whether a Latina seeks family therapy may depend largely on economics. Most Latinas in the United States occupy jobs that provide minimal if any health benefits (de la Torre, 1993). Few working Latinas benefit from managed care or HMO services. Furthermore, for Latinas, as with other women, mid-twentieth-century notions of what or who constitutes family have significantly changed. A family therapist is more likely to see a Puerto Rican– or Mexican-origin female-headed family than the idealized two-parent extended family depicted by earlier social scientists. The economic and social position of a Latina must be contextualized, however, in terms of the historical factors that help shape her current status.

HISTORICAL OVERVIEW: WOMEN'S POSITION IN SOCIETY AND *LA FAMILIA*

From the time of the European conquest of the Americas and the U.S. incorporation of the Southwest and Puerto Rico to the present, Latinas' position within society and family has been constructed on the basis of the family's social standing, as determined by race, class, and gender. In turn, patterns of gender socialization have supported the social and familial construction of womanhood. Consequently, although Hispanic values of *familismo* are at the center of gender socialization for men and women, women receive a stronger dosage of those values that foreground loyalty and devotion to the institution of the family, respect for patriarchal authority, interdependence with other family members, sacrifice in the service of the family, and a blend of Native American–Hispanic–Christian beliefs that support woman's purity, abnegation, and reify the maternal role (Flores-Ortiz, 1997b).

Moreover, the degree to which women are expected to obey these religiocultural ideals often depends on the family's race, social class, and appraisal of their daughters' expected place in society. For example, women who occupy the bottom of the social strata, who realistically expect little advancement for themselves and their children, often emphasize the virtue of *aguantar* (endurance) to younger females in the family (daughters, nieces, granddaughters, goddaughters), as they promote *familismo* in order to potentiate resilience and quiet survival. Economically and socially marginalized women may socialize their daughters to be strong, to work hard, to endure. These attitudes may be seen by outsiders to this class as passivity and tolerance, when in fact they ensure the young women's social invisibility and thereby protect her from the more powerful (de la Torre & Pesquera, 1993).

Middle-class women, on the other hand, may socialize their daughters to aspire to better things, to demand respect, to expect men to treat them well, while still promoting respect for patriarchal authority. Furthermore, by example, they may teach young women how to get things indirectly, while seeming to honor the established order. In both instances, mothers and elders enforce the prevailing social construction of females as pure, virginal, and respectful (of self and others), who in adulthood will marry and enter heterosexual relationships with males deemed appropriate by the family. That socialization in turn is socially reinforced, thereby maintaining the racial/social stratification that has existed in the Americas for over 500 years (Bernal & Flores-Ortiz, 1984; Flores-Ortiz, 1997a, 1997b).

There are always women and family members, however, that also teach subversiveness and promote social justice. The degree to which Latinas develop and exhibit *un espíritu de lucha* (a fighting spirit) may well depend on the family's social position and their degree of political consciousness. This historical fact has contributed to the diversity of Latinas across the continent. Thus, how each woman lives out her history and negotiates cultural mandates should be a key part of therapeutic inquiry.

ECONOMIC, RACIAL, SOCIAL, AND RELIGIOUS DIVERSITY

Latinas throughout the continent share similarities on the basis of a collective history of colonization and miscegenation (Bernal & Flores-Ortiz, 1984). However, cultural, racial, ethnic, religious, and historical diversity are grounded on the particularities of each country's experience with European conquest and the resulting race and class stratification. Questions of Latina identity, therefore, are complex. A middle-class Nicaraguan woman's social positioning very likely will differ from that of a rural Chicana born in the Central Valley of California. Each woman's connection and sense of belonging to her place of birth will be influenced by her social location as well as her family's. Latinas' cultural and gender identity is influenced by social class, her color and body shape, her family's cultural values, and expectations for their daughter's place in the world (Flores-Ortiz, 1997b; Latina Feminist Collective, 1997). Thus, it is a challenge to write (or speak) of Latinas without essentializing.

LAS DE AQUÍ Y LAS DE ALLÁ: IMMIGRANTS AND U.S. BORN LATINAS

The experience of migration and adjustment to the United States promotes the diversity of Latinas. Critical considerations for psychotherapists include an understanding of each woman's and family's migration history, the influence of immigration on the family (Sluzki, 1979), and the subjective experience of being in the United States. What is often foregrounded in women's narratives of migration and life in the United States is the experience of otherness and marginality (Anzaldua, 1990; Latina Feminist Collective, 1997).

Irrespective of class, but somewhat dependent on racial background, immigrant Latinas may first experience overt racism in the United States. Such experiences mark the psychology of Latinas (Latina Feminist Collective, 1997; Souza, 1997; Vasquez, 1994). Varying degrees of exposure to the dominant culture and institutions within the United States may create different experiences within the same family and can bring about intergenerational conflicts (Bernal & Flores-Ortiz, 1984). A common concern for immigrant and second generation families is the apparent "acculturation" of women, who are seen as challenging or contesting traditional gender values (Flores-Ortiz, 1997b; Vasquez, 1984). For U.S. born Latinas, the psychological task often is to negotiate a site of belonging in a country that denies their patrimony, to heal the wounds of racism, sexism, and heterosexual privilege in order to develop effective coping strategies (Flores-Ortiz, 1997a, 1997b).

LATINA IDENTITIES

As the patriarchal state defines race, class, gender,
sexuality, nationality and ethnicity, it dents the fusion
we embody and the complexity of our lives is erased.
—*LATINA FEMINIST COLLECTIVE, 1997*

Ultimately U.S. and foreign born Latinas must forge an integrated identity that does not challenge or privilege race, class, gender, or sexuality but embraces and interweaves them into a psychological and lived tapestry. However, *familismo,* homophobia, and racism often create barriers to such integration. Universal assumptions of heterosexuality are common among Latinos. Thus, Latina lesbians face the added pressures and pain of simultaneously contesting heterosexism in the larger social context and within their families (Anzaldua, 1990; Trujillo, in press). A woman who defies the heterosexual script may be viewed as traitor to her culture, her family, her religion, and a violator of patriarchal rule. Families may seek the assistance of a family therapist in hopes of finding an expert who can guide the daughter back to compliance with cultural/familial/social rules. Explorations of sexuality with Latina clients, however, cannot occur without regard to the multiple identities they must negotiate on a daily basis. Furthermore, Latinas often are positioned to make a choice between and among these identities, without consideration to the impossibility of such choice and the psychological cost of trying (Fiol-Matta, 1997).

KEY ISSUES FOR FAMILY THERAPY

Culturally competent family therapists must examine the unique patterns and expectations of each Latino family and woman they see in therapy. This information needs to be placed within the larger context of immigrants and U.S. born Latinas in order to avoid overgeneralizations and prevent clinical errors. Whether responding to an extended, blended, heterosexual, or lesbian family, an individual or a network of comadres, the therapist must consider the intersection of gender, race, class, sexuality, nationality, spirituality, oppression, and resilience. The following vignettes from my own clinical work are offered as examples.

VIGNETTE: THREE GENERATIONS OF *SUFRIDAS:* WOMEN CONTESTING OPPRESSION

Case Introduction: "Nicas" in the United States

Margarita, a 38-year-old Nicaraguan nurse, was referred for family therapy by her individual therapist. Margarita had been in therapy for 5 years, attempting to recover from addiction and childhood sexual abuse. In the past year, Margarita had overdosed on morphine twice, was on disability, and likely to lose her job unless she could demonstrate her addiction was under control. Margarita was the eldest daughter and granddaughter of an immigrant family who had left Nicaragua in 1975, during the civil war. Margarita was 13 at the time of migration. She lived by herself, a few miles away from her mother Flor, grandmother Estella, and youngest brother, Rick. Rick was a chronic alcoholic who was homeless but who came to the maternal home for money and a change of clothes now and then. The second daughter, Alicia aged 35, was a heroin addict who had lost custody of her three children and lived, at the time, with a man she met at a 12-step group. Alicia occasionally came by to "borrow" money or items she could resell.

When Margarita phoned for an appointment, I invited her to bring her family to therapy. She arrived with mother and grandmother, having been unable to find her brother or sister in time for the session. Doña Estella, the grandmother, was 75 years old. She had been born into an upper-middle-class European-identified family and had been a businesswoman in Nicaragua. She had owned a pool hall in Managua. Her husband Manuel, now deceased, had been an "errand boy" for her father. When Doña Estella married Manuel against the family's wishes, the family disowned her for marrying beneath her class. She opened the business with some money her mother gave her (unbeknownst to the father) and hired her husband to work for her. Manuel, in turn, spent his married life drinking, womanizing, and molesting children. Doña Estella's eldest child, Flor, now 55, in turn married Juan, a soldier in Somoza's army, and had three children. Juan was an alcoholic who died shortly before the end of the revolution. Margarita was the eldest of Flor and Juan's children.

Narratives of Oppression

Mother and grandmother sat on the sofa together, facing me. I was struck by their resemblance; they were both frail-looking women. Grandmother was light-skinned, with soft gray eyes. Mother's brown skin reflected the indigenous roots of her father. However, the sadness in their eyes and the dignity in their demeanor brought out the family resemblance. They seemed strong proud women. Margarita sat to my side, facing them. In contrast to the elder women's apparent softness, she depicted a rough, tough stance. But in her features and coloring, Margarita, too, embodied her country's racial history.

After a few minutes of *plática*, Margarita opened in English:

M: [to therapist] I have brought these women here to tell them a few things.

F: *¿Hija, pero por qué persistes en hablar inglés cuando sabes que tu abuela no entiende?*
(Daughter, why do you insist on speaking English when you know your grandmother does not understand?)

M: I want to tell you both the reasons why I asked you to come to therapy. I am not the good girl you both think. I have problems.

E: But what problems could you have, child? You have a good job, you are educated. You are not a whore like your sister or a drunk like your brother.

M: [crying] My sister is not a whore, and my brother, sister and me are quite screwed up; I want to tell you why.

E: Hija, why talk about the past, the past is past, gone, forget about it.

T: *¿Señoras, sería posible que en veces el pasado susurra en el oído y no nos permite escuchar lo que dicen nuestros seres queridos?*
(Señoras, might it be possible that the past sometimes whispers in one's ear, making it difficult to hear what our loved ones try to say?)

[All three women looked at me, as if seeing me for the first time. Margarita continued:]

M: I am trying to tell you that all the problems in our family are related. Grandma, none of us kids want to talk to you because we feel so betrayed. Remember what happened when I was five, when the neighbor came to tell you that grandpa had touched her daughter, and you told her she was a liar? You knew, you knew he was a child molester, how could you not know? And yet, you and mom, mom you must have known it, too, you left us with him when you went on shopping trips, [screaming] you left us alone with him. Do you know what he did every time, as soon as you left? He would take me, my sister, and my brother to his bed, your bed grandma, and force my brother and sister to watch him do things to me. They were babies, mom, he was going to penetrate Alicia, she was only 3, so I told him he could do it to me instead, because she was too little, but he made them watch even though I begged him to send them out of the room. How could you grandma, how could you mom, how could you leave us with him?

[As the mother cried, grandmother responded:]

E: *Hay hija yo pensaba que esas eran mañas de hombres, yo pensaba que todos los Nicas hacían eso.*
(Oh child, I thought those things were just bad habits men had, I thought all Nicaraguan men did that.)

M: Do you see now why Juan is a drunk, and Alice and me are addicts? I am an addict grandma; I steal the morphine from my patients and shoot it up myself. I am no better than my brother and sister. I am an addict because it is the only way I can survive your silence, your blindness, and my pain.

Key Issues for the Family Therapist

My work as a family therapist is informed by the Contextual Therapy model of Ivan Boszormenyi-Nagy (1987) and the Social Justice Therapy of the Family Centre of New Zealand. These theoretical and clinical frameworks guide both my conceptualization of the problems clients present and my search for relational justice and balance within families.

In this family, Margarita embodied the multiple levels of oppression and injustice prevalent in abusive families; primary among these are the relational injustice that leads to spousal abuse, parentification, sexual exploitation of children, lasting patterns of sacrifice in the service of maintaining secrets, and creating a false sense of normalcy (Flores-Ortiz, 1993, 1994, 1997a). A multigenerational pattern of child molestation and incest was hidden beneath a cultural façade ("I thought all Nicaraguan men did that"). Such a statement exemplifies the internalized oppression and colonialism prevalent in families of color who abuse their loved ones (Almeida, Woods, Messineo, & Font, 1996). A complex interaction of historical, social, economic, racial, and gender factors are externalized as a male trait, decontextualizing the behavior from its multiple origins. In this way, men are not held accountable—"that is how they are, what they do"—leaving women feeling powerless to confront, avoid, or change what is.

With such a case, in my role as therapist, I needed to examine the full context of the family in order to understand the historical and cultural legacies Nicaragua as a country has faced. Likewise, I had to consider the possible impact that multiple decades of dictatorship, institutionalized injustice, the colonial status of the country, and its people as a function of U.S. intervention, civil war, and forced migrations had had on the nation and its citizens.

Having considered the larger context, I then examined the family's own history within that context, the intersection of class, race, and gender on the development of symptomatology and resilience in the family, as well as the family's experience with oppression in the United States. For example, I saw grandmother's rebellion against her country's social-class structure and her family's expectation to marry within her class as a legacy consideration for the rest of the family. Her marriage was not happy; in fact, her husband's behavior was a constant reminder that her parents had been "right" in disapproving of her choice of partner. She had violated societal, cultural, and familiar expectations and paid the price of her disloyalty.

However, while she acknowledged her own victimization in the marriage, grandmother did not see that her marital problems incurred many other victims as well. Her husband, possibly in response to the marginalization imposed by society and family for his social position, exacted the price of violence against his daughter, granddaughters, grandson, and the children of her affluent neighbors. Men who internalize the repudiation they experience in society may in turn aggress and abuse those they are supposed to love and protect. His behavior brought Estella a great deal of shame and pain. But women in her class were taught to swallow such violations to protect their dignity and the family's reputation. So, she marginalized him further, and kept the silence, ignoring the evidence of the abuse. She rationalized his behavior as typically male.

Moreover, Margarita's and her siblings' addiction also reflected the multiple losses of war, migration, and displacement. Postmigration, grandmother was unable to be as strong as she had been in Nicaragua. Confronted by a new set of cultural demands, she abdicated the matriarchal role to her daughter, who was not prepared for the role and was unable to provide the family stability her children needed to navigate being Latinos in this country and face the historical traumas they had suffered. The children attempted to actualize the grandmother's migration dreams, but could not manage the pain. They turned to addiction, self-destruction, and despair. Yet, the elders could not see this because, in seeing, they would have had to acknowledge the facts of their own history and pain.

Thus, the family continued in a downward spiral of silence and despair until Margarita broke the silence. Her individual therapy encouraged her to separate from her family in order to save herself. Her culture, personal ethics, loyalty, and familismo would not allow it. She brought her family to therapy as a final attempt to save her family, and thereby herself.

Contesting Oppression

The therapy focused on fostering understanding of how the multiple layers of oppression had created unjust relationships and a legacy of dysfunction that they, now, could change. Through reconstructive dialogues (Boszormenyi-Nagy, 1987; Flores-Ortiz, 1997c), the family members became accountable to one another, developed clear communication, and strategized to balance loyalties and legacies that might free Margarita and her siblings from decades of addiction and despair. Through dialogue and accountability, the women began to question the legacy of oppression, the roots of their victimization, and vowed to develop more ethical modes of relating in order to change the course of the family history for the next generation. The first steps in that direction came as Margarita, after a year of sobriety, became legal guardian of her sister's children and initiated family therapy with them.

VIGNETTE: "I DON'T BELONG ANYWHERE, I AM INVISIBLE": ON BICULTURALITY AND FINDING HOME

Case Introduction: "Soy Chicana pero con corazón Mexicano" (I am Chicana but with a Mexican heart)

Ana called requesting individual therapy for personal issues. I met her in the waiting room. She glided into my office, tall and elegant, she moved with the grace of a dancer. She sat gently, as if plié-ing into the couch. You must be a dancer, I said. "How did you know, how could you tell, no one ever sees me that way," she replied. "Because you move like a dancer, you are so graceful and elegant," I said. With eyes tearing, she whispered, "So you see me, you really see me."

I wondered how anyone could not see this beautiful, elegant woman, with jet-black hair, high cheekbones, and hair pulled back. She reminded me of a much younger Lola Beltrán. "That is my problem," she said. "No one sees me." "I am 38, unmarried, stuck in a dead-end job, working as a secretary with other women who seem to hate me, and I don't know why." "I walk down the street and no one notices me, not like in Mexico *donde los hombres te miran y te admiran*" (where men see you and admire you).

Narrative of Belonging and Marginality

Ana was born and raised by immigrant Mexican parents in the Central Valley of California, primarily an agricultural area with a large Mexican and Mexican American population. Ana described her parents as culturally and politically conservative. They were agricultural workers who wanted the best for their daughters. Therefore, they wanted her to become a secretary. Ana, however, wanted to dance. She had joined local ballet folklórico companies and was considered quite good. Her parents could not understand her passion for dance. Instead, they told her repeatedly that she could not make a living as a dancer; that she would find herself in the future without marketable skills and without a man because men did not like women who wanted more out of life than their "social place" offered.

After graduating from high school, Ana decided to go to Mexico to study dance. Her parents would not give her their blessing. They thought it was indecent for a single young woman to travel to a foreign country alone. She persisted and left for Mexico with $500 in cash to pursue her dream. A distant cousin she had never met received her there. He drove her to a pensión and never contacted her again. Despite the absence of extended family support in Mexico, Ana described her arrival there as if she had found her home. She sensed familiar smells from her childhood kitchen, when her mother would make beans and tortillas by hand, before "she discovered the 'international' food section at the local grocery store." She heard the sounds described by her father when he told the children bedtime stories. She realized he had not made up these stories; instead he had kept Mexico alive through his tales and, to her surprise, had given her the gift of memory so she could recognize her homeland.

Shortly after her arrival, Ana contacted the major ballet folklórico dance company in Mexico City. She indicated she wanted to apprentice. The director insisted that she audition. Ana danced, feeling awkward because she "had never danced for 'real Mexicans'." To her surprise, the director invited her to join the company as a principal dancer. "I couldn't believe it; I never thought I was that good." As a principal dancer, while on stage, Ana found a home. She created a home outside the theater as well by making friends, socializing, and immersing herself fully in the exciting city life. However, she found that her independence, her strong sense of self were anathema to some men. "*A pesar de que eran hombres finos*" (despite the fact that they were cultured men), "they wanted to change me into someone I wasn't. They wanted me to become a real Mexicana, that is, to leave the stage for the home and children they offered me. I insisted I wanted and could do both, that seemed to turn them off." She added, "it seemed that I couldn't be a Mexican American in the United States and a Mexicana here in Mexico. Neither place wanted me as I was, but at least in Mexico no one tried to totally erase me. I was visible!"

After dancing for ten years, her back and legs could no longer stand the rigor of folklórico, but without formal education, Ana could not remain in Mexico and make a living. She returned to the United States. Her family found her *muy cambiada* (very changed). She was now more mature and independent. Her family saw her as different, a woman nearly 30 and unmarried. Ana began to feel there was no place for her in her family, even though her sisters embraced her and her nieces welcomed *la tia de Mexico* (the Mexican auntie).

Ana found work as a secretary; in the back of her mind ever present was her father's prediction before she left. She felt disappointed in herself. However, Ana did not passively accept "her fate." One day feeling quite disgusted by "Anglo's appropriation of Mexican cuisine," she decided to attend chef school and eventually open a "real classy real-Mexican restaurant" here. Before that, however, she planned to return to Mexico to perfect her culinary skills. She plans to welcome her fortieth year onstage, at a reunion of former dancers organized by her former company. In the meantime, Ana continues to struggle to integrate her two cultures, to feel whole. She sees herself as a Chicana with a Mexican heart. She longs to feel at home in both her countries.

KEY ISSUES FOR THE FAMILY THERAPIST

While Ana sought psychotherapy for herself, her family was present in the room through the pain and anger interwoven in her narratives. Therefore, I needed to address their context, as if they were in the room. The therapy focused first on Ana's examination of how she felt her family had failed her by not acknowledging her unique gifts, by trying to hold her to religious/cultural values and ideals that did not fit her reality as a Chicana. She could not be the kind of Mexican they desired in a daughter while growing up in Central California.

Ana's family appeared to uphold frozen cultural values (Flores-Ortiz, 1997b), particularly in terms of their preference for traditional gender roles. Moreover, the family espoused the working-class view that a good job and material possessions equal success, while Ana aspired to be an artist, a dance performer. Such interests may have been seen by the family as belonging to middle-class families and inappropriate for their daughter (Bernal & Shapiro, 1996). Ironically, the parents did not see how Ana's desires to dance Ballet Folklórico was an expression of cultural pride and loyalty. Ana felt that her parents devalued her efforts to remain connected to their country and culture of origin. Her efforts to actualize the parents' "American dream" remained invisible to them.

On Biculturality and Finding Home

Since the family was not in the room to offer an alternative discourse, I invited Ana to imagine what motivated their wishes for her. In a very moving session, Ana expressed a profound understanding of her parents' fears for her, their desires to protect her from the poverty and hardship of migrant work. Given the parents' history of poverty, they could only imagine the highest position their daughter could attain was that of secretary. Ana assessed her anger at the poverty of Mexico, the economic hardship that forced her father to join the *Bracero* program and eventually settle in Central California, where, at nearly 70, he still worked the fields.

Ana gradually understood that her anger and resentment toward her parents masked the pain she felt for their oppression and the guilt she felt at her relatively comfortable lifestyle. Ultimately, Ana understood that her parents could never imagine her own oppression because all they could see was what they considered privilege: she had a job, a car, an apartment. Although she grieved the fact that her parents did not support her in the way she needed and continued not to see her emotional needs, Ana began to negotiate an adult relationship with her parents and siblings. Respectfully and lovingly, she began to ask what she needed from them. To her surprise, her parents expressed their admiration for her independence. Suddenly, she reported, finding a man to give her an accepted identity seemed less important. She felt she had her parents' permission to be an independent adult.

As Ana came to terms with how the history of Mexico and the United States were forever interlocked, she began to imagine what an integrated Mexican American identity would be like for her. The next stage in therapy focused on forging integration of her multiple identities. We utilized the metaphor of midlife and *los cambios que acompañan la madurez* (the changes that midlife brings), that as a woman enters her forties she no longer needs to follow prescribed scripts (Flores-Ortiz, 1994). She could now reauthor her life (White & Epston, 1990). Ana was able to imagine this, as while still a young girl, she had once imagined going to Mexico to become a dancer. While maintaining her day job, Ana concentrated on finishing cooking school and planning a trip to Mexico to visit friends, reconnect with potential business contacts, and assess the feasibility of her plans to attend cooking school in Mexico for a year.

"I noticed lately that people are looking at me more these days," she said one day. "What do you think accounts for that," I asked. She smiled as she replied, "I feel that wherever I am now . . . , I carry home inside me. I don't erase myself anymore. I know who I am. Frankly, I don't care if others want to ignore me. The fact they need to erase me is proof of my very powerful existence."

CONCLUSION

Family therapy can be a powerful vehicle for change. Culturally sensitive and informed interventions can create a safe and sacred space where women can explore the political, historical, and cultural legacies that nurture and bind them. Each woman must decide within this sacred place and time what aspects of her multiple identities must be guarded and protected against racism, marginality, and erasure, and which cultural scripts and family legacies she needs to modify, revise, or integrate. Whether she seeks therapy by herself or brings along those she loves and who cause her pain, the therapist must explore each woman's code of familism in order to support connectedness, justice, and fairness within family relationships. Women need not sacrifice the cultural values they want to maintain in order to gain a greater sense of entitlement.

REFERENCES

Anzaldua, G. (Ed.). (1990). *Making face, making soul = Hacienda caras: Creative and critical perspectives by feminists of color.* San Francisco: Aunt Lute Foundation.

Bernal, G., & Flores-Ortiz, Y. (1984). Latino families: Socio-historical perspectives and cultural issues. *Nueva Epoca, 1*(1): 4–9.

Bernal, G., & Shapiro, E. (1996). *Cuban families.* In M. McGoldrick, J. Giordano, J. K. Pearce (Eds.), *Ethnicity and family therapy.* New York: Guilford Press.

Boszormenyi-Nagy, I. (1987). *Foundations of contextual therapy: Collected papers of Ivan Boszormenyi-Nagy.* New York: Brunner/Mazel.

de la Torre, A. (1993). In A. de la Torre & B. Pesquera (Eds.), *Building with our hands: New directions in Chicana studies.* Berkeley: University of California Press.

Fiol-Matta, L. (1997). Writing *despues de tanto guardar silencio.* In *Latina Feminist Testimonios: Papelitos Guardados.* Manuscript submitted for publication.

Flores-Ortiz, Y. (1993). La mujer y la violencia: A culturally based model for the understanding and treatment of domestic violence in Chicana/Latina communities. In N. Alarcón et al. (Eds.), *Chicana critical issues* (pp. 169–182). Berkeley, CA: Third Woman Press.

Flores-Ortiz, Y. (1994). Chicanas at midlife. In J. Adelman & G. Enguídanos (Eds.), *Racism in the lives of women* (pp. 251–260). New York: Haworth Press.

Flores-Ortiz, Y. (1997a). The broken covenant: Incest in Latino families. *Voces: A Journal of Chicana/Latina Studies, 1*(2), 48–70.

Flores-Ortiz, Y. (1997b). Voices from the couch: The co-construction of a Chicana psychology. In C. Trujillo (Ed.), *Xicana critical theories.* Berkeley, CA: Third Woman Press.

Flores-Ortiz, Y. (1997c). Fostering accountability: A reconstructive dialogue with a couple with a history of violence. In T. Nelson & T. Trepper (Eds.), *101 interventions in family therapy.* New York: Haworth Press.

Latina Feminist Collective (1997). *Latina feminist testimonios: Papelitos guardados.* Manuscript submitted for publication.

Sluzki, C. (1979). Migration and family conflict. *Family Process, 18* (11), 379–392.

Trujillo, C. (Ed.). (In press). *Xicana critical theories.* Berkeley, CA: Third Woman Press.

U.S. Department of Labor, Women's Bureau. (1997). Women of Hispanic origin in the labor force. In *Facts on working women, 97-2*, February 1997, DOC L 36.114/3.

U.S. Department of the Census. (1994). *CPS: Full-time year round earnings of persons by race-ethnicity and sex*. Washington, DC: U.S. Government Printing Office.

Vasquez, M. J. T. (1984). Power and status of the Chicana: A social-psychological perspective. In J. L. Martinez & R. H. Mendoza (Eds.), *Chicano psychology* (2nd ed., pp. 269–287). New York: Academic Press.

Vasquez, M. J. T. (1994). Latinas. In L. Comas-Diaz & B. Green (Eds.), *Women of color: Integrating ethnic and gender identities in psychotherapy*. New York: Guilford Press.

White, M., & Epston, D. (1990). *Narrative means to therapeutic ends*. New York: Norton.

PART II

FOCUS ON THE THERAPIST

4

CULTURE CLASH OR NOT?

GABRIELLE CAREY AND LAURA MANUPPELLI

I want to understand the world from your point of view.
I want to know what you know in the way you know it.
I want to understand the meaning of your experience,
to walk in your shoes,
to feel things as you feel them,
to explain things as you explain them.
Will you become my teacher and help me understand?
—SPRADLEY, 1979, p. 34

The questions surrounding the meaning of culture and its applications in the therapy room have been of concern to family therapists and other mental health professionals for decades. Today, almost every training program contains a course in multicultural counseling and ethnic diversity. Cultural sensitivity is recognized as a necessity for therapists. Clearly, knowledge of culture and ethnicity is needed, but how much knowledge is enough? Our purpose in writing this chapter was to interview therapists about their cultural experiences with Hispanic clients to find how they perceive their successful as well as unsuccessful outcomes. If culture clashes do, in fact, exist, is there a way to avoid them?

CULTURAL AWARENESS

What is culture? How is it defined and studied? Ethnography, the anthropological study of individual cultures, is a method of qualitative research that has been used for several decades. Currently, most ethnographers delimit their explorations to what they call "local culture" (Gubrium & Holstein, 1995). This term refers to "the locally shared meaning and interpretive vocabularies that participants in relatively circumscribed communities or settings use to construct the content and shape of their lives" (p. 50). These smaller communities or groups are diverse and grounded in a contextual setting. The larger sense of culture is more socially encompassing, composed of many local cultures. In order to discuss cultural differences and similarities, we need to define what is meant when we specify Hispanic culture.

Hispanic Culture: A Myth?

On the *NewsHour with Jim Lehrer* (July 10, 1998), President Clinton discussed cultural issues with a roundtable of ethnically diverse community leaders. Richard Rodriguez, a panelist from California, stated, "There is no such thing as Hispanic culture." He pointed out that Latinos are far too diverse a body of people to be clumped into one cultural category. Hispanic culture is really a collective of Latinos from many different nations with many different customs. Despite the variance among generations, geographical sites, levels of education and income, distinct stereotypes concerning "Hispanics" still exist in the United States. Rodriguez strongly objected to "tokenism." In his opinion, affirmative action results in continued marginalization of Latino people and other minorities. The general consensus around the table seemed to be that we should address the discrepancies in educational opportunity at a much earlier grade level, with programs and funding at the elementary school level. What was particularly intriguing about this program was not that the group had reached an answer or made a conclusion considering racism and discrimination in the United States, but that there was an openness to share differing viewpoints and a willingness to dialogue about these very controversial issues.

In the past decade, "Latinos" or "Hispanics" have criticized their panethnic identity (Jones-Correa & Leal, 1996). Not only do the labels imply common geographical origins, but they presuppose that Latino peoples share other cultural commonalities, such as common customs, similar emotional temperaments, common health problems, a single linguistic base, and a shared experience of discrimination in the United States. Critics call for the elimination of such a nonsensical term that homogenizes the differences among the Latino peoples (Calderon, 1992; Oboler, 1995; Shorris, 1992). Clearly, such a broad label serves to stereotype people who came from or live in Latin America.

Despite the critical views of the labels, increasingly "Hispanic" and "Latino" are terms that are embraced by Latinos themselves (Gonzalez, 1992; Oboler, 1995; Trevino, 1987). Embracing a common political identity, *la communidad Latina* or *La Raza* promotes solidarity and representation, and implies some important, internalized beliefs among those who do identify themselves as Hispanic or Latino. This political dialectic illuminates the struggle therapists and others have when working with "Hispanic" families. Educational reading and classroom instruction can provide a knowledge base that broadens common stereotypes, but that alone is not enough for culturally resonant therapy to occur. Training and experiential learning in the therapy room itself is invaluable.

Avoiding the Clash: The Culturally Sensitive Therapist

Developing cultural awareness and sensitivity is a lifelong process and is best accomplished with intentionality, openness, and curiosity. One might argue that every family is, in itself, a culture, and, therefore, it is an impossible task to obtain complete knowledge of another culture. Although in some ways this is true, there are some patterns and similarities worth mentioning. Our investigation of Hispanic cultures is an exploration of both the similarities and the differences among people, including ourselves. Cultural sensitivity requires more than mere knowledge; it requires a desire to appreciate others and an honest, sometimes difficult, observation of one's own presuppositions. Cultural resonance occurs as we become aware of how our own cultural background impinges on our impressions of other cultures.

Within the field of marriage and family therapy there are a multitude of models, theories, and philosophies, but very few addressed the implications of differing cultures in the therapy room until fairly recently. Over time, our research methods have become more culturally sensitive by questioning our dominant discourses, assumptions, and values. Consequently, more culturally friendly, self-questioning, and collaborative models and theories are beginning to develop. The feminist criticism of family therapy helped spark gender-sensitive research (Avis & Turner, 1996) and critical theory research, an overtly political approach developed from three founding principles: spirituality, justice, and simplicity (Rediger, 1996). Family therapy can lead to the raising of consciousness, transformation, and emancipation from human oppression. Although family therapists are beginning to be sensitive to oppression in the lives of their clients, in their own lives, and in the therapeutic process itself, there is a long, challenging road ahead. Rediger (1996) notes:

> One of the greatest deterrents to the acceptance of critical theory in marriage and family therapy lies in the unexamined models, theories, and educational philosophies in the field. Family therapy would benefit from unpacking the hidden values and ideologies in its theories and models. To what aims and purposes do these models aspire? (p. 141)

In order to begin to address this question, we would like to consider some of the suggestions that have been made about working with cultural difference.

McAdams (1993) emphasizes *how* we create and come to *know* our life stories. Over time, we create a sense of identity or personal myth. Sharing our stories with others creates meaning out of our cultural setting and simultaneously constructs the culture.

> The stories we create influence the stories of other people, those stories give rise to still others, and soon we find meaning and connection within a web of story making and story living. Through our personal myths, we help to create the world we live in, at the same time that it is creating us. (McAdams, 1993, p. 37)

McAdams's philosophy of human development is similar in theory to early social constructionism as described by Berger and Luckmann (1966), and to the method of interpretive social inquiry known as the "circle of meaning," or as a return to the hermeneutical circle

(Rabinow & Sullivan, 1979). Amidst the tumultuous chaos of life, we actively construct our stories within our relationships with others in our world to render human existence meaningful and coherent. How similar must we be to create meaningful dialogues and construct or change our worldviews?

Do therapists need matching cultural or ethnic backgrounds to be sensitive to families within a certain culture? Carl Whitaker believed that when working with families of differing ethnicities it was necessary to bring in a cotherapist with an ethnicity similar to the family (Hightower, Rodriguez, & Adams, 1983; Roberto, 1991; Whitaker & Keith, 1986). Are Hispanic therapists or cotherapists helpful or necessary for Hispanic families? Are Mexican American therapists needed for Mexican American families; Puerto Rican therapists needed for Puerto Rican families? There seems to be a general consensus in the therapeutic community that matching ethnic backgrounds is helpful, but as the category Hispanic is extremely broad and diverse, is it possible to match backgrounds? What are the key qualities for success in therapy with Hispanic families? Are these qualities any different than the qualities needed for effective work with families of any ethnicity?

Collaborative language systems and other narrative therapies (cf. Anderson, 1997; Freedman & Combs, 1996; White & Epston, 1990) propose that by listening to client's stories and interpretations, by remaining curious and asking questions, we are able to gain greater understandings of the client and of myself. The client's story is based on a memory of lived experience that is situated in time and place. The interpretations of that memory become the retold story, which helps to affirm the client's experience or to change the understanding of that experience.

Central to the therapeutic conversation or the storied narrative is language. Language is a bridge through which we connect with each other and construct our "reality" or our shared meanings. Milton Erickson suggests that matching the client's language and communication (Rossi, 1980) is essential to the therapeutic process. Client-centered approaches such as solution-focused therapy (de Shazer, 1994; O'Hanlon & Weiner-Davis, 1989); narrative therapies (Freedman & Combs, 1996); and collaborative languaging systems (Anderson, 1997; Goolishian & Anderson, 1994) also incorporate matching language. Using the client's own description of his or her own ethnicity offers a respectful solution to the problem of ethnic labeling. If a client considers herself a Latina, the therapist uses the term Latina when addressing her cultural identity. If a family refers to itself as Cuban, the therapist uses the term Cuban. The use of matching language helps put people at ease and feel understood. For Latinos whose first language is Spanish, the more fluent the therapist is, the easier the process of developing cultural resonance when working with Hispanic families.

Self-in-relation theorists (Miller & Stiver, 1997) emphasize the impact of connecting in relationships and discuss its profundity in the therapeutic alliance. They recognize that "we all know how extraordinarily hard it can sometimes be to connect with another person, and this is especially true when there are differences in power between individuals within a relationship" (p. 12). According to these authors, the critical criterion for therapists is to promote "growth-fostering relationships" by using their power to empower others. Miller and Stiver (1997) refer to this relational interaction as a "power-with" (p. 16), which is a key dynamic in the striving toward mutuality.

Self-in-relation theory proposes that a basic developmental necessity for human beings is to be in connection with others—to be heard and understood as well as to hear and understand others. This sense of connection is essential for sound psychological development, and we believe it is possible to achieve regardless of a person's race, ethnicity, or color. The establishment of an authentic therapeutic relationship is a step toward transcending white privilege and cultural differences. Miller and Stiver (1997) explain the impact of mutual relationships with simple eloquence:

> As we move into authentic connections with the people in our lives, we will find more common ground with them, leading us toward an enlarged sense of community and of possibilities for social change. Making connections has implications for the world, not only for our individual lives. (p. 23)

In discussing culturally sensitive supervision, Breunlin and his colleagues suggest using an integrative or metaframeworks approach (Breunlin, Rampage, & Eovaldi, 1995). The metaframeworks approach to therapy provides a way to put on six different "lenses" to view a case on multiple levels: (1) internal family systems, (2) patterns and sequences of interaction, (3) organizational, (4) developmental, (5) cultural, and (6) gender.

> *Each lens examines the problem from a different angle or has a different focal point, but the lenses are ground from the same piece of glass so they are highly compatible. In fact several of them can be used simultaneously. (Breunlin, Schwartz, & MacKune-Karrer, 1992, p. 7)*

For culturally sensitive therapy, the supervisor directs therapists to consider their cultural fit with their clients. Therapists and supervisors reflect on the cultural fit of the therapeutic system and the supervisory system. This reflection involves considering one's own beliefs, presuppositions, and cultural heritage as well as diversity and the dominant discourses.

On Difference and Clash: Exploring White Privilege

It is essential to address the issue of White privilege when studying the concept of culture clash between therapists and Hispanic clients. We believe that exploration of what it means to be White in America must be undertaken by every therapist who works with a multicultural population, because presuppositions and epistemologies are buried under the surface of this issue.

The issue of White privilege is pervasive and exists regardless of a therapist's level of awareness of it. Actually, it seems that White privilege is a phenomenon of which we say we are aware, although our awareness remains too often at a superficial level. Similar to death, we are aware of it, yet we continuously strive to push our awareness outside of consciousness due to the complex, confusing, and uncomfortable emotions that accompany awareness; and we have been conditioned not to question such precarious and ubiquitous issues because they seem to be so insurmountable. In addition, confronting these issues reifies the potential losses that will ensue. More so, the issue of White privilege and racism have become so deeply ingrained in our culture, our world view, and our identities that the existing questions often do not even occur to us.

In *Killers of the Dream,* Lillian Smith (1949) references our immersion into a racist culture:

> *"You have to remember," I said, "that the trouble we are in started long ago. Your parents didn't make it, nor I. We were born into it. Signs were put over doors when we were babies. We took them for granted just as we took heat and sandspurs and mosquitoes. We worried about things close to home but I don't think we noticed the signs. Somehow we seemed always to walk through the right door. People find it hard to question something that has been here since they were born." (Smith, 1949, p. 57)*

Living White has historically meant that privileges were awarded to us at birth based solely on the color of our skin. Socially, politically, and culturally, we have been taught that being white skinned is preferred as it accesses opportunities and power that persons of color have been denied. The White dominant culture has perpetuated this belief system in the interest of maintaining this hierarchy of power.

Silence about racial and ethnic clashes or melds results in a problematic society. The ensuing problem has been the sustaining of segregation in our society, a problem that creates disruption in our ability to relate authentically and universally among others in our world. And if we raise our consciousness to realize this profound relational problem we have created, we necessarily confront a social-existential dilemma against which we have been defending. Awareness of White privilege creates a dilemma for the culture: Although awareness is the first step necessary toward an ameliorative process, awareness creates emotional discomfort and threatens the status quo from which we have reaped our benefits. However, similar to any therapeutic process, change comes through challenging the status quo and grappling with the pain and suffering in the interest of healing and positive growth. In order for significant change to occur, the dilemma of White privilege and the ensuing discomfort must be confronted. We need to recognize and process the pain that White privilege has created; otherwise, we will continue to live in a world where segregation and discrimination promote unhealthy competition, unfairness, and disharmony in our lives.

Smith (1949) addresses segregation as "a word that is both symbol and symptom of our modern, fragmented world . . . [a problem that has] split the human experience" (p. 21). She states, "Man is a broken creature, yes; it is his nature as a human being to be so; but it is also his nature to create relationships that can span the brokenness. This is his first responsibility; when he fails, he is inevitably destroyed" (p. 21).

Judith Katz (1978), in her book *White Awareness*, refers to racism as the White person's problem; and, in fact, she identifies racism as a "psychological disorder" that actually destroys rather than enhances the freedom of white-skinned people. She believes that White people are imprisoned by their conscious and unconscious views about people of color, and this imprisonment results in themselves being oppressed. The oppression stems from a lack of awareness of their own White identity—of their own exploration of their Whiteness and the privileges that accompany their skin color. As a result, world views are tunneled through White views, thereby stunting relational capacities. The ability to experience humanity on a universal level is limited because White people have learned to respond only to that which is salient in their environment; and the White dominant culture teaches importance in terms of the color of one's skin.

Katz (1978) attributes the belief that "White is Right" to much of the confusion of White's identity development. She discusses the fact that since White history is taught as American History, we are miseducated about Whiteness at a very young age. She states:

> It is clear that racism has severely hindered White people's psychological and intellectual development. In psychological terms racism has deluded Whites into a false sense of superiority that has left them in a pathological state. In intellectual terms racism has resulted in miseducation about the realities of history, the contributions of the Third World people, and the role of White people in the present-day culture. The intellectual perspective and growth potential of Whites [have] been severely limited owing to racism. (Katz, 1978, p. 15)

Katz (1978) discusses that since racism is a White problem that "Whites created through the establishment of policies and practices that serve to their advantage and benefit" (p. 10) and is supported by a White dominant culture that promotes the "economic, political, and social power to enforce discriminatory practices on every level of life" (p. 10), then it is within the power of White people to begin a process of resolving the problem. The process begins with increasing our awareness of the issue.

The issue of awareness is prevalent across the literature on White privilege. In a working paper from the Center for Research on Women at Wellesley College, Peggy McIntosh (1988) parallels White privilege with male privilege. She states, "We are kept ignorant about white privilege and are ignorant about this ignorance" (p. 2). She believes that Whites are taught not to recognize White privilege in the same way that males are taught not to recognize male privilege. She points out that one of the reasons it is difficult to confront the "invisible package of unearned assets which [we] can count on cashing in each day, but about which [we were] meant to remain oblivious" (p. 1), is that we are then placed in a position of accountability—an accountability that requires us to relinquish some of our power.

In her paper, McIntosh (1988) constructed an expansive list of ways in which she has enjoyed the power associated with unearned skin privilege and concluded that we "have been conditioned into oblivion about its existence, unable to see that it put[s us] 'ahead' in any way, or put [our] people ahead, overrewarding us and yet also paradoxically damaging us, or that it should or could be changed" (p. 4). Her list included such reflections as, "I can easily buy posters, postcards, picture books, greeting cards, dolls, toys, and children's magazines featuring people of my race" (p. 7) or "I can choose blemish cover or bandages in 'flesh' color and have them more or less match my skin" (p. 9). These are privileges we take for granted, and without any reflection, we remain in the oblivion of thinking that these privileges are accessible to everyone when they are not. It is this oblivion into which we were conditioned that McIntosh (1988) asserted is the root of our own destruction.

Like Katz (1978), McIntosh (1988) questions whether Caucasian people realize that "so-called [White] privilege [is actually] a deficit" (p. 4). Because we take our daily experiences of White privilege for granted, we fail to provide a just society for everyone and we "give license to be ignorant, oblivious, arrogant, and destructive" (p. 10). It prevents us from having to be angry or guilty, which necessarily prevents us from being authentic. She remarks, "We were given cultural permission not to hear voices of people of other races, or a tepid cultural tolerance for hearing or acting on such voices" (pp. 11–12). She mentions that although White privilege has protected us against "many kinds of hostility, distress, and violence, [we have been] subtly trained" (p. 12) to turn these injustices back on people of color. She believes that because the dominant White system serves to overpower certain groups, then the word "privilege" is misleading, because "such 'privilege' may be widely desired without being in any way beneficial to the whole society" (p. 12).

White privilege is destructive because the unearned advantages create a power over distribution that results in the impediment of our moral development. Since we are taught to be entitled without regard to how this entitlement affects others, we have fallen short in our ability to unite with humanity as a whole. We are not placed in a position to struggle with who we are as human beings and therefore have not developed some of the moral strengths and resiliencies we see in survivors of oppression. McIntosh (1988) explains, "Power from unearned privilege can look like strength when it is in fact permission to escape or to dominate" (p. 13). She makes a critical distinction about the advantages and disadvantages of White privilege, however, by emphasizing that we *are* in a position of power to initiate changes in our unjust system. She concludes:

> It is an open question whether we will choose to use unearned advantage to weaken hidden systems of advantage, and whether we will use any of our arbitrarily-awarded power to try to reconstruct power systems on a broader base. (McIntosh, 1988, p. 19)

For therapists, awareness of White privilege is critical for transcending power differences in the psychotherapeutic process. In order for us to achieve an authentic connection with our clients, we must be aware of the cultural presuppositions and implications that White privilege has formulated for us and our clients. In fact, an amelioration to the problem of White privilege can begin with the therapeutic relationship.

INTERACTIVE ETHNOGRAPHIC INTERVIEWS

Incorporating the tradition of ethnography (Geertz, 1973, 1983; LeCompte & Preissle, 1993; Spradley, 1979), we approached our interviewees as coresearchers, hoping to elicit their stories and to learn from them. Rather than creating broad generalizations about working with an extremely diverse culture, we wanted to create a "thick description" (Geertz, 1973). Hispanic culture is a global term. To begin to understand its diversity, we need a broader depiction of each of the varied local cultures defined within. We set out to interview many different family therapists to ask about their lived experience while working with Hispanic people. The result is a rich tapestry of many stories and suggestions from many different perspectives. With our diverse collection of descriptions, we hope to break down many of the stereotypical notions that may fill the minds of those who have little knowledge of Hispanic cultures. While the therapists we questioned raised many similar issues and concerns, each voice brought something new, something unique to the discourse.

Our findings are grounded and presented to you in the actual dialogue we cocreated with the family therapists we interviewed. Although our inquiry is not a formal research project, we obtained written consent from each participant. The interactive interviews (Baszanger & Dodier, 1997; Holstein & Gubrium, 1997; Kvale, 1996; Rubin & Rubin, 1995) were informal, audiotaped, one on one, chats of approximately one hour in duration. We asked broad general questions about each therapist's personal and professional background and experiences with ethnic awareness. More specific questions emerged from the dialogue and we remained open to where our co-researcher's memories would take us. This style of interviewing is similar to the therapeutic conversations created in collaborative language systems (Anderson, 1997). "In this view, the systems with which we work in therapy are the products of the linguistic domain of existence, and they exist only in our descriptions, only in our language. They are the narratives that evolve through conversation" (p. 72).

One of our beliefs, shared by postmodern social constructionists, is that people create and maintain meaningful worlds intersubjectively through language (Berger & Luckmann, 1966; Crossley, 1996; Dawson & Prus, 1993; Gergen, 1994; Kvale, 1996). The stories we collected represent voices of therapists with various ethnic backgrounds, of different ages and genders. While all of the therapists interviewed were currently presiding and working in San Antonio, the diversity of opinion casts some light into the question of culture clash in therapy. The knowledge contained in the final narrative, this chapter, is a product of those voices resonating with our own. We, as interviewers, are inextricably implicated in the meanings we created from the interviews (Cicourel, 1974). We were not neutral bystanders passively collecting objective data; we were actively participating in the interview and the knowledge it produced.

> *Respondents are not so much repositories of knowledge—treasuries of information awaiting excavation, so to speak—as they are constructors of knowledge in collaboration with interviewers. Participation in an interview involves meaning-making work. (Holstein & Gubrium, 1997, p. 114).*

Our conclusions are based on our own perceptions, as well as in time and place. We filter the voices of our interviewees with our own biases. The culture in which we find ourselves immersed is like water to a fish. It encompasses us and we take it for granted, unable to take a metaperspective to see ourselves within the fishtank or ocean. Sharing our stories with others creates meaning out of our cultural setting and simultaneously constructs the culture. "The stories we create influence the stories of other people, those stories give rise to still others, and soon we find meaning and connection within a web of story making and story living. Through our personal myths, we help to create the world we live in, at the same time that it is creating us" (McAdams, 1993, p. 37). The first step in ethnographic interviewing is to examine one's own assumptions and presuppostions about the culture one is exploring by looking at one's own personal myths. Therefore, we begin the exploration with our own stories. Then we will present our findings and discuss them in light of the current literature and in the words and sentiments of the therapists we have interviewed.

THE AUTHORS SHARE SELF-NARRATIVES

> *If you want to know me, then you must know my story*
> *for my story defines who I am. And if I want to know*
> *myself, gain insight into the meaning of my own life,*
> *then I, too, must come to know my own story.*
> *—McADAMS, 1993, p. 11*

We are both considered "White/Non-Hispanic" or "Anglo," and although we have experienced working with Hispanic families and befriending Mexican, Cuban, Puerto Rican, Portuguese, Central and

South American Hispanics, this particular project was a learning experience for us. We began our experience with the knowledge that facing our own biases would likely be difficult. We approached our self-observations and the project as a whole with a profound respect for other lives that would be different from our own. We also held an expectation that we could learn to be better therapists by exploring the cultural interface between ourselves and others. During the exploration, we not only dissolved some of our own assumptions, we were forced to examine the process of developing cultural sensitivity in our own lives. Both of us would describe ourselves as having once had some prejudiced opinions that we worked through, and we suspect we still entertain some prejudices and stereotypical assumptions even if we are not aware of them.

We met while in the doctoral program in counseling at St. Mary's University in San Antonio. We were both born in 1959 and soon gravitated toward each other, becoming good friends. Gabrielle entered the program with an M.A. in marriage and family therapy, and Laura entered with an M.A. in clinical psychology. Currently, we are employed as therapists at the Marriage and Family Institute in San Antonio, but there the resemblence ends. Laura has 15 years of clinical experience in a wide variety of settings, such as schools, hospitals, and clinics, and Gabrielle entered the program immediately following her Master's work. Gabrielle has four years of experience as a therapist in addition to seven years experience as a former middle school teacher and two years in cancer research. She has been married for 14 years and has two daughters.

Gabrielle's Story

I moved to San Antonio in 1981, fresh out of Smith College with a Bachelor's degree in biological sciences and entered the field of cancer research at the local medical school. Considering myself liberal and open-minded, I was idealistic in believing the politically correct dominant discourse that encouraged acceptance of others, regardless of race, gender, ethnicity, sexuality, or religion, was the norm for the majority of the people in the United States. In practicing acceptance of others and pointing out injustices, I believed I was doing my part in creating a better society. I was glossing over the reality of prejudice that existed in the United States, lulling myself into believing that all was well. Adopting this attitude prevented me from taking a more painful, but honest consideration of my memories. It created a silence that hid the reality of prejudice behind the veil of political correctness. I believed that prejudice was wrong and hateful and did not admit that I was prejudiced, ever. This fear of admitting or even refusing to consider that one might have held some prejudiced feelings and might still, silences authentic dialogue. I now believe that this dialogue is essential to the healing of racism and other forms of discrimination.

When I first moved to San Antonio, I felt as though I was visiting a foreign country. I was entranced by the Tex-Mex cuisine, the Spanish billboards, the fiesta atmosphere, the warmth and *bienvenidos* of the Latinos and non-Hispanic Texans. Although I was occasionally teased about being a "Yankee," I felt accepted. My best friend at work was Mexican American, which was an unusual pairing as most of the social circles at the Medical Center seemed ethnically segregated.

Although my friend was in her late 20's and had a Master's degree in Biochemistry, she lived at home with her mother and her chihuahua. I was curious about why she would choose to continue to live at home (I knew that I could never live at home again—and maintain my sanity). She invited me to a family gathering during the holiday season. The tiny houses were decorated with festive lights and statues of Jesus, the Holy Family, the *Virgen de Guadeloupe*, and various other saints. My husband, whom I was dating at the time, said, "San Antonio, the place where the slums have front and back yards!" I remember being shocked by his use of the word "slum." Having grown up in the suburbs of New York City, I thought a slum was a crime-ridden place full of abandoned tenements and dangerous people. I looked around and noticed that the neighborhood streets were filled with potholes, as the city did not bother to pave the poorer sections of town. My friend told me later that her street was often the sight of gang shootings and drive-bys. Again, I wondered why they continued to live there. Her mother was comfortable in her neighborhood and many of the old families were still there. Despite the poverty, there was a warmth, an inviting, cozy feeling to her home and her family that felt very different from my family's home.

As time went by, I could not help but notice a rift between the Mexican American and "Anglo" American populations in my new city. My husband's friends were Anglo and openly labeled themselves "rednecks." They would often joke using racial, ethnic, female, and gay slurs. Although it was in jest, I found it somewhat offensive and hypocritical of me to listen without pointing out the injustices. I became especially vocal about the male "chauvinist" attitude of many of my husband's friends. I'd like to believe our conversations raised our consciousness and made us aware of what it might be like not to be a privileged White person. In retrospect, I was quite hostile to some and lost some friends. The anger was yet another block to enriched dialogue.

Because of my belief in the acceptance of others, I was at ease with the African American, Asian American, German American, and Latino Americans that I met. I rarely felt any accusations of discrimination from those who were different from me. When I was accused of cultural insensitivity, I argued rather than listened. However, I was always conscious of difference. I seemed to focus on difference more than on similarity. Getting to the place where one invites critical dialogue is a necessary step in developing cultural sensitivity.

When my family first moved from Albany to the Boston area, I knew only people like me. At age seven, I had no sense of difference among individuals or families. We lived in Boston for about two years. It was here where I began to develop a sense of identity and difference that included the knowledge and pride that I was Roman Catholic and Irish American. My parents encouraged me to believe that I was capable of becoming whatever I wanted to be. I was imbued with a sense of confidence that I might not have been able to internalize if I had been a person of color. The sense of well-being that is instilled in childhood is so important to the future. Prejudice creates a poison that can ruin this sense of self-acceptance and appreciation of others.

Our neighborhood was inhabited by many Jewish families. One of my best friends was an Orthodox Jew, who was nicknamed "kitten," in Yiddish. I remember calling for her to play on Saturday and being turned away, because it was her Holy Day. I wondered what the family did all day if they could not play. Later that year, I was invited to join the family's Passover celebration. Before the ceremonious meal, Kitten and I and her cousins gathered in her bedroom. I was told about the restrictions of being kosher and Orthodox. I examined her brother's yamulke and marveled at the restrictions against pork and the need for separate dishes. It was such a wonderful introduction to an ethnicity foreign to my own. When I heard her family did not drive or use the telephone or electricity on the Sabbath, I teased Kitten by pretending I was going to switch on the light. I never understood all of the rules, but their traditions fascinated me. I remember the tone of the feast changed from an atmosphere of solemn prayer to joyous merriment. Although my memory of being a guest at their religious banquet is sketchy at best, it is a treasured memory.

We moved to New York when I was eight. In Sleepy Hollow, everyone knew everyone's ethnicity. The founding fathers were Dutch with names like Van Tassel and Phillipse. People's ethnicity was in part determined by their last names. We learned early to recognize Gilligan, Moran, and O'Connor as Irish; Waterhouse and Elliot as English; Johnson and Armstrong as common African American names; DeLuca, Bucci, and Biritella as Italian; Goldberg, Mendelowitz, and Perlman as Jewish; and Cortez, Hernandez, and Pinon as Hispanic names. When we encountered a surname we did not recognize, we inquired as to their country of origin. We became very specific in our ethnic identities.

When I lived there, Sleepy Hollow, or the Tarrytowns, as the villages were known, had a large ethnic population of Italian Americans who were full of pride in their identity. The Italian delicatessens, ristorantes, and pizzarias were superb! What I found most interesting was the sense of community. It seemed that all the Italian families knew one another and celebrated their togetherness. Most of the popular kids in high school were of Italian descent; it was almost a clique. In retrospect, I think I was accepted on the basis of my similarities to the majority population.

Despite a sense of similarity there were obvious differences. More than any other factor, socioeconomic status determined one's acceptance. But even that status was by nature ethnic. As each flood of immigrants entered the community, voluntarily seeking financial gain or freedom from oppression, they were met with some hostility and discrimination. Most entered the workforce at the local auto factory as unskilled labor, who represented the lowest economic levels. Over the generations, with education, time, and connections in the United States, ethnic groups moved up the socioeconomic ladder, gaining acceptance along the way. The most obvious exception was the African Americans, who were "imported" here as slaves, against their will and who could not blend as well because of their skin color. Another exception was Cuban immigrants, who were often highly educated professionals and assimilated quickly into the middle classes.

Before the sale of our new house was completed, we had to spend the summer months living with my mother's parents. My grandfather was my most beloved relative and he had great pride in his Irish ancestry. Unfortunately, he was discriminatory in his views about "Coloreds" and "Puerto Ricans." Instead of easing my worries about being the new girl, he inadvertently heightened them by encouraging a fear of others. He pointed out the Black neighborhoods and the Puerto Rican barrios. He referred to Italian Americans as "Eye-talians," in a derogatory ethnic slur. Likewise, he made fun of the British aristocracy and the crowd at the "Waspish" country club. My parents disliked his prejudices and tried to counteract them but I was still affected.

Consequently, I entered my third-grade year in fear of those who were different from me. Although my parents and my church told me to love everyone and accept others who were different because in essence we are all human, I harbored a distinct fear of others who appeared different from me. I believe this fear of the other manifests itself as prejudice, as we cling to those most like us and build barriers against the unknown.

As I developed friendships on a one-to-one level in the classroom and on the playground, I began to see how misdirected my fears were. As my fears of African Americans dissipated, so did my ethnic and racial tensions. I remember when our textbooks were revised to include an ethnic and racial variety of children. Although at first it seemed so foreign, it soon became familiar and I knew in my heart it was right. Realizing how wrong it was to discriminate against any other group of people, I joined the ranks of the politically correct. For me, this was a first step toward cultural acceptance and embracing cultural diversity.

In retrospect, the fact that I used to be prejudiced of other human beings, to fear other children, is abhorrent. It fills me with disgust, shame, and sorrow. It is not a part of my past that I want to examine, but I think that we must admit these fears if we are to understand them, work through them, and eradicate them. As a therapist, it helps to understand the "fear of the other." I am not quite so quick to condemn those who hate; instead, I know that it is a symptom of fear. I also know that it does not have to continue. It is possible to learn to love others and to embrace difference and variety among the human community. Every so often, a hate crime is committed so offensive that we all rise in indignation and horror. And yet, ironically, we continue to reside in virtually segregated neighborhoods. We avoid looking too closely at how our complacence feeds the hatred in society. Hiding behind our shields of political correctness, we prevent honest dialogue and perpetuate the status quo.

As a fledgling marriage and family therapist in San Antonio, I embraced Native Americans, Latinos, White non-Hispanic, Asian, and African American clients equally, or so I thought. Establishing rapport and comfort in the therapy room seemed to come easily to me, but I was troubled when my efforts to join were unsuccessful. Most of my clients were of Mexican American backgrounds. As my clinical experience grew, so did my awareness of Latino culture, the diversity within that culture, and the need for cultural sensitivity.

In gathering stories, I hoped to find some information that might be useful to the process of developing cultural resonance when working with Hispanic families. Greg Sarris (1993) stated that learning by gathering stories is a dialogue of discovery that increases knowledge of the self and the other.

> *In understanding another person and culture you must simultaneously understand yourself. The process is ongoing, an endeavor aimed not at a final and transparent understanding of the Other or of the self, but a continued communication, at an ever-widening understanding of both.* (p. 6)

Although I do not share the exact experience as my clients, I may find similarities to my own life stories. If I do not remain open to being educated by my clients in a way that entails a constant questioning of my own experience, I cannot learn or rise above my biases and presuppositions. Part of becoming sensitive to gender and cultural issues in therapy is being able to recognize how one's own assumptions may cause a distorted or misinterpreted view.

Laura's Story

I grew up in Alamo Heights, a small elite suburban area of San Antonio. Materialism was expected, and entitlement ran rampant. The neighborhood and the schools were predominantly White even though the overall population of San Antonio always exceeded more than 50% Hispanics, primarily of Mexican descent. But *they* lived in the *other* neighborhoods—the less prestigious neighborhoods where funding for streets and schools was anemic. They lived in *their* part of town where privilege was scarce and crime was high. They wore clothes that were not like mine and my brothers. They had distinctive accents when they spoke. Their bicycles were rickety—not like the shiny, new designer bikes that were parked in front of our homes and schools. The Hispanic children were not like me, and the differences were perpetuated and continuously discriminated by the dominant White culture. And this discrimination was particularly bred, distributed, and maintained within the privileged community of Alamo Heights. *They* were *they* and *we* were *we*, and integration did not seem to occur to anyone despite the fact that there were some exceptions to the rules—that there was in fact a Mexican subculture that lived in Alamo Heights.

Within the Alamo Heights school district was an expansive cement factory that was known as Cementville. Within its gates lived the families who worked for the factory, and their children went to the Alamo Heights schools. These families were almost all Hispanic, and besides a handful of other Mexican families who typically lived in a poorer section of the district, the Hispanics from Alamo Heights lived and worked in Cementville. Or maybe they didn't; but the stereotypes and presuppositions deeply ingrained in the narrow world view of Alamo Heights promoted the assumption that if you are brown-skinned with a Mexican surname, then you must live in Cementville. The prejudice in Alamo Heights certainly did not stop there. You could be white-skinned with a Jewish or Italian surname, which generally subjected you to discrimination, but not to the degree to which the Mexican families were subjected. There was a hierarchy of status that existed among the Whites, and it depended largely on socioeconomic standing—or more accurately, on *perceived* socioeconomic standing *and* to one's connection within the radically elitist San Antonio Country Club culture, the latter against which I rebelled relentlessly. And one could be quite certain that one would not find an Hispanic member in the Club, and almost as likely to find someone of Jewish or Italian descent.

I was born in 1959, the youngest of three children, to Lauretta Buschell and Frank Manuppelli. Both of my parents were of Italian descent and third-generation Italians. My mother was a native of New Jersey whose familiarity with Italian culture came primarily through food traditions alone. She remembers that her grandmother spoke only Italian; however, English was the sole language spoken in her home. Although not practiced directly, my mother had an affinity for Italian history and culture, as she identified with both as a result of inherited experiences. My mother brought these experiences with her to San Antonio in 1951 when she married my father whom she met while he was an FBI agent in New York City.

My father is a native San Antonian. He grew up on the west side of town, which was predominantly populated with Mexican Hispanic families. He played, schooled, and worked with Hispanics his entire life. Although differences were noted between his Hispanic companions and himself, his childhood experiences with Hispanics carried vast qualitative differences from mine. His environment allowed for diversity and integration; Alamo Heights did not. And although I never harbored the hostile, somewhat supremist attitudes toward Mexicans that I observed in my schoolmates, I was still a product of a culture that viewed people of color as underprivileged, unassimilated, and different. Whites and Hispanics generally remained segregated.

The Hispanic children that attended Alamo Heights worked, played, and gathered among themselves. There was little interaction between the Hispanic and White children. Since they were brown-skinned with Hispanic surnames, they did not have a chance from the start of joining the complex social climbing dance of the Whites; their outer appearances automatically excluded them. The White culture kept them in a one down position. Even the handful of acculturated, assimilated Hispanics who more freely associated with the less elitist Whites were nevertheless viewed differently because of their minority status. We were not taught cultural diversity, we were only taught difference; and the difference we were taught was consistent with the White dominant culture that privileges white-skinned people with WASP surnames and discriminates against nonwhite people.

So I grew up with profound influences that encompassed political, socioeconomic, cultural, and social-elitist views about Hispanics.

By the time I entered college at the University of the South in Sewa-
nee, Tennessee, I had not experienced Hispanic culture and an understanding of its people anymore than someone from Mobile, Alabama.
I had been sheltered by layers of social illusions and cultural norms
that prevented even mere reflection of what it meant to grow up Hispanic inside America. Although, as I am reflecting now, I remember
an exercise we were assigned in junior high school, where we were
asked to imagine being anything we wanted to be with an ensuing explanation. I think some of the recognized winners offered such trite
and ostensibly clever analogies as, "I wish I were an arrow because an
arrow always has somewhere to go" or "I wish I were a new sports
car because I would always look cool and fun." Well, I made the mistake of wishing to be a half-breed adopted by an Indian tribe because
I was intrigued by the culture within their reservations, their protection of one another, and the pride they took in community and tradition. The teacher threw my submission out of the contest and scolded
me for being so unrealistic. I guess I had more chance of being an
arrow than a person wanting to assimilate and acculturate into another culture. So this is the environment from which I was nurtured
and educated. This is the environment that not only condescended to
people of color, it shamed Whites for expressing interest in cultural
sensitivity.

I graduated from the University of the South with a B.A. in psychology and returned to San Antonio to complete a master's program
in clinical psychology at St. Mary's University. It was not until I entered the job force in 1984 that I came into direct contact with Hispanic families and their culture.

My presuppositions about Hispanics were challenged when I
was placed in the role of a therapist. The fact that these people were
coming to me for help evoked my humility and changed the way I
viewed difference in them. I became "familiar" with the difference
that necessarily altered my perceptions and slowly began a process of
transcending my prejudices.

After many years of working closely with Hispanics of all socioeconomic levels, "familiarity" began to acquire new and more profound meaning. To become familiar is to become family. As we
developed strong therapeutic bonds, I found that people from the
Hispanic culture embraced me—they brought me gifts they had

handcrafted, they lit candles and prayed for me when I was sick, they let me into their lives in a way that incorporated me into their family system. This therapeutic relationship was the essence of what constituted positive change—not only for them, but for me as well. We taught each other from initially separate perspectives, which eventually became one perspective, a perspective we constructed together within the therapeutic process that provided us with shared meaning. A deeply human bond was constructed that surpassed skin color or culture clash.

Cultural differences do not constitute clash. There is only culture clash when there is resistance to difference, when we buy into the White dominant culture as a translation of truth, when we are threatened by familiarizing ourselves with diversity because we somehow believe that our identities will be negatively altered or, worse, that we may lose some of the privilege that has been bestowed on us by the nature of our white skin. Yes, we come from different worlds with different traditions; but the similarities inherent in being human, of having shared experiences of pain and suffering, of bonding at an authentic and empathic level overwhelm any cultural differences that exist.

I do not want to appear to be taking a naive Pollyannic view on the subject of cultural differences between therapists and our clients. I know that several extenuating factors played into my experiences in bonding with persons of Hispanic culture in therapy. First of all, I look like them. I have dark hair, dark eyes, and olive-complected skin. The initial visual image that I presented to them on our first meeting was not a foreign one. I could have been their sister, or cousin, or aunt; a familiarity was already present. Second, while I grew up in San Antonio with all of our fiestas, meriendas, and pinatas at every birthday party, I never pretended to act like I understood their culture. Rather, I took a stance of not knowing; so that whatever meaning and knowledge transpired between us was a result of our relating and sharing openly within the therapeutic relationship. Perhaps my having similar features facilitated our ability to bond in this way—I don't know. What becomes evident to me is that we cannot generalize and absolutize the concept of culture clash because everyone's experiences are different. I did not bond with all of my Hispanic clients any more than I did with all of my White clients. However, I do not believe that predominant cultural issues were the impediments to bonding. An unwillingness to familiarize oneself with diversity creates culture clash. An openness and willingness to meet people at a purely human level, a level that transcends color and culture, promotes therapeutic bonding, healing, and positive growth.

THERAPIST NARRATIVES

The therapists, whose voices you will hear, are of many different backgrounds and ethnicities. We traced each therapist's development in terms of ethnic awareness to see how that awareness factors into cultural sensitivity. We sought to find the stories of what worked well with Hispanic families and what situations to avoid. Each voice told of a unique life growing up among people and learning to relate to others. For each, there was a choice to enter the helping profession, many experiences leading to that choice, and a technicolored fabric of experience as a therapist.

Language

Every therapist we interviewed mentioned the importance of language. On a surface level, the importance of linguistic similarity to communication seems so obvious it might not even be worth mentioning. However, it is critical. We wanted to know what was it about language that was so important in preventing cultural clashes.

A Spanish surname was considered an asset by many of the Hispanic therapists. One therapist explained that it acts as a filter. The people who would not be comfortable seeking help from a Hispanic do not call me. Yet, the ones who want a Hispanic call me. That may be one factor why I rarely experience discrimination or cultural clashes in therapy.

Another therapist who values her Spanish name, Leticia Cortez, moved from Ohio, where she spoke English but listened to Spanish at home, Eagle Pass, a Texas border town where almost everyone can speak Spanish fluently.

If we hadn't moved, I bet I would have lost my Spanish. Down there you never have to speak English; everyone speaks Spanish. I am so thankful I speak Spanish! I always have plenty of clients because there is no one in my office who is bilingual except me. And I kept my own name Cortez to maintain my Mexican identity, because my husband is Anglo. With my Hispanic families I speak Spanish to those who prefer to speak Spanish, and English to those who prefer English. It drove my co-therapy team, behind the mirror, in graduate school crazy. Often I would be speaking Spanish to the parents and switching to English to speak to the children. My team called it therapy in "Spanglish." But it helped put everyone in the family at ease.

One therapist mentioned that language structures the way we create our reality. This is a common refrain among narrative theorists (Bakhtin, 1991; Bruner, 1989), philosophers (Ricoeur, 1974; Wittgenstein, 1953), social constructionists (Berger & Luckmann, 1966; Gergen, 1994), and family therapists (Anderson, 1997; de Shazer, 1994; Freedman & Combs, 1996; White & Epston, 1990). But we wanted to expand the definition to what it looks like in the session when an Hispanic family meets with a therapist.

According to one professor of family therapy, Randall R. Lyle, language is the bridge that joins people in the cocreation of meaning. When one is fluent in a language, one actually thinks in that language. One of his students was from Mexico and had many clients who spoke Spanish. She conducted her sessions in Spanish and he supervised her in Spanish. One day, he overheard her tell a fellow Latino doctoral student, "He's a totally different person when he speaks Spanish. He's a lot more fun when he speaks Spanish."

Randall realized that his easygoing manner while speaking and thinking in Spanish was part of his experience in developing a bicultural identity. While living in Argentina, he had immersed himself in the Spanish language and the culture of the Argentines. At first, he was frustrated by their sense of time, finding himself waiting for hours. He found himself in awe of the lack of punctuality of the Argentines. Soon he realized that the Latinos of Argentina were operating on "people-centered time," while he was operating on "clock time," where cost and efficiency were the bottom line. After the first year, he adapted to the slower pace:

You always have time to stop and have coffee, because the emphasis is on the person. I relaxed, changed my priorities, and enjoyed living the Argentine way. . . . Joining with a person and sharing his or her language is a way of showing respect. Language communicates more than mere lexical meaning, more than just words. "It speaks understanding; it speaks appreciation; it speaks acceptance."

One Mexican American therapist and professor of family studies helped elaborate this larger sense of meaning in language. While working with a Cuban couple, they shared a common language, but very different backgrounds. The common language was a bridge, another bond to strengthen the therapeutic connection. In addition to adding to the therapist-client fit, language is the conveyor of key concepts or key constructs. Some words carry meanings in Spanish that are hard to describe in English, because there is no word to describe the concept. The concept is something part of an Hispanic culture but not in an Anglo culture. One example is the number of words and phrases in Spanish that are used to describe feeling badly about oneself. These words would play a critical role in the therapeutic process of someone from a different culture.

One therapist described his work with a Spanish-speaking psychoanalyst when he was on the other side of the couch, in the role of the client. The therapist/client had a basic working knowledge of Spanish and the analyst had only a basic knowledge of English. The therapist admitted that perhaps the therapeutic process was enhanced by the care taken to tease out each other's meanings. There was less room to assume shared meaning, more space to define the interpreted meaning.

However, the therapeutic process would naturally be slower than when one has a better idea of shared meanings and more familiarity with the language. It also depends on the individual therapist and the client's background. One Hispanic female therapist and professor stated, being bilingual "gives you a sense of knowing where the other person is coming from when you're able to relate key terms to key concepts." She described her work with a woman in the process of divorcing her highly successful Anglo husband. The couple had shared social circles that were far removed from the wife's background. Although she was equally if not more successful than her husband, the divorce had brought back a lot of her old struggles. The client admitted that, once again, she was "feeling like a young girl from the South

Side. I am amazed at his [her husband's] lack of *respeto*." The term *respeto* has a much broader, different meaning in Spanish compared to in English.

> It's not just respect of you, or of the other, as in English. Showing a lack of *respeto* takes away your own self-worth. In Spanish the word goes beyond the meaning in English, it is also showing bad manners. The worst insult in Spanish is to accuse someone of not having *respeto*, of having "a lack of education." It does not mean you did not go to school, it means you do not have good manners and it lowers your value as a human being. You were not raised properly and so your family's value also suffers a drop in value. It is such an insult—to the very core of you—the worst insult!

One Hispanic therapist described her experience of working in a very poor school district in San Antonio with children who had very different upbringings than what she had experienced as a child of the middle class with two successful working parents. Nevertheless, the shared language and the shared memories of her extended family enhanced her ability to connect with the children, to love the children and her work. Her knowledge of Spanish provided an entry into a culture that was different yet similar.

> *I didn't pretend to know what their experience was, but language gave me an entree into their world. There was enough commonality that we connected, but there was an open space to describe what their experience was.*

The concentration on similarity, finding ways to be alike, is also part of the therapist's ability to connect.

Albert Valadez held on to his Hispanic heritage and identity through the Spanish language; it is through language that he connects with his emotionality. Since language represents meaning and essence through symbol and metaphor, he believes he connects at a deeper emotional level with his Hispanic heritage through the Spanish language. Therefore, emotionality and therapeutic bonding with other Hispanics are facilitated by a profound understanding of the symbols that are attached to the Spanish language and culture. Similarities of identity development are shared at a symbolic, emotional, intersubjective level. Albert believes that it is when a person is unwilling or unable to compromise his or her language that a culture clash presents itself. Differences become heightened, and bonding between a Hispanic client and a White therapist will become less likely to encounter culture clash.

Acceptance versus Discrimination: Focusing on Similarities

One theme we heard echoed in some of the Anglo and Hispanic therapists' narratives was the focus on similarity rather than difference. Language can be one of the similarities, but there are others with which to work. One therapist spent his summers living on his grandfather's farm in Nebraska. Nearby the house where his grandparents lived, across the ditch, was the shack where the illegal migrant workers lived. Although he was aware of the differences in the two homes, the shack had no plumbing and dirt floors; that was not important. As there were no other children for miles around, he would go over to play with the Mexican children or they would wander over to play with him. He describes his early childhood experiences as important to the development of an attitude of acceptance that celebrates diversity.

> They spoke Spanish; I spoke English, but we communicated. I wasn't searching for how we were different, but for how we were similar. My grandfather was very prejudiced, but for some reason I never paid attention to his rantings and ravings. My mother had rejected his prejudiced views. For me, I think there was this notion from those early days that they were just people and their culture was okay. Later, I let my grandfather know I didn't appreciate his prejudice, but that didn't affect my love for him.

The therapist believed that the attitude of acceptance and the search to find similarities were critical in his later work with other Hispanics. This attitude is necessary for bicultural awareness. When working in Hispanic communities or countries, the therapist must go out and seek to understand the culture by mingling with the people.

If a therapist only knows the community from his or her clinic office, the kind of cultural understanding that is gained while interacting on many levels in the neighborhood will not develop.

Nan Smith, a graduate student in family therapy, grew up in Edinburg near the border of Mexico in the Rio Grande Valley. Although she has bright red hair, blue eyes, and an obvious Anglo appearance, she claimed she never thought of herself as different from her Hispanic friends while growing up. In fact, one of her grandfathers was Spanish, with ancestors who had immigrated from the Canary Islands.

> *We lived the same way. When I went to their homes, they looked the same inside. They ate the same foods that I did. In retrospect, I suppose that was because we ate Tex-Mex foods too. I just thought of it as food. When we went out to eat we ate "Mexican food" at the restaurant.*

Nan's father spoke fluent Spanish and both of her parents were careful to bring up their children with an attitude of acceptance of people. She was forbidden to play with one Hispanic family, not because they were Hispanic, but because the parents smoked marijuana and let the children run wild and play in the drainage ditch. She did not think about race or ethnicity until she moved to San Antonio and went to high school where she heard ethnic slurs.

Jeannette Caballero admits she rarely experienced discrimination here in San Antonio. The first time she encountered blatant discrimination was during her sophomore year while sitting in on her sorority's membership meeting during rush week. Her sorority sisters were discussing the pledges and deciding who to offer acceptances or who to reject. Jeannette had befriended one of the pledges, a bright Hispanic woman named Maria, who was also from the Valley. Jeannette was one of two members who were Hispanic; the others were Anglos. When Maria's name came up, one of the sisters objected to her because "She was too Hispanic." Jeannette was shocked by the comment, and turned to the other Hispanic member for support, but instead of support, she was nodding her head in agreement with the anti-Hispanic sentiments.

> *I just stood up. They didn't realize how awful their judging was! I said, "I will not be a part of this if this is what joining and accepting*

*is all about. This is a Catholic University. It is so wrong to judge
people on how pretty, well-dressed, or rich they are, or on their ethnic background!" I fought for Maria's acceptance and she got in.
They finally agreed with me, but if I had not stood up and showed
how highly I valued my culture, the sorority would probably still be
all Anglo. Now, I think it is about 50% Hispanic.*

Jeannette expressed how amazed she was that other Hispanics
bought into the idea that Hispanic was of lesser value than Anglo. She
commented, "But that girl was White-oriented, from a rich family in
San Antonio. She thought it surprising that I spoke Spanish!" The author questioned how she felt while she was standing up for her friend
and her cultural heritage. "All that was going through my mind was
how proud my parents and grandparents would be if they could see
me. I thought, 'I can do this. I'm not going to let anyone stop me.'"

Jeannette feels strongly in taking pride in her Hispanic traditions.
In therapy, she will ask parents, "What kinds of things are you doing
to show your children, not just that you accept them as they are, but
that you accept the culture that they're from?" Jeannette brings her
Hispanic culture into therapy with her Hispanic clients, "Sometimes
we'll make tortillas or pinatas together in session. Sometimes we'll go
to Spanish mass together." She believes that part of the acculturation
process for Hispanics involves developing pride for oneself and pride
for their cultural heritage.

Julius Lundy describes the first moments of a therapy session as
the time when therapeutic magic can happen, "I'm Black, you're Hispanic and then we blend." Clients can feel his acceptance of them, his
genuine authentic way of being. He puts his cards on the table, "I am
a family therapist and I honestly want to know you." As the session
goes on, differences continue to meld, to blend together. Soon, we no
longer see each other's color or differences. We are being ourselves.

*I never label my clients. I used to prepare to meet an Hispanic but
now I don't prepare. There are too many books on how we are supposed to act; we have too many presuppositions. I grew up in Ohio
and the Hispanics there were mostly Puerto Rican. The Hispanic
presuppositions I grew up with didn't fit my Mexican American
clients here in South Texas. So now I just approach everyone with a
deeply humanistic approach.*

However, another African American therapist, Thomas Johnson, has not felt that sense of "blending" of color. Although all African Americans and Hispanics experience some degree of discrimination in the United States, the experience is qualitatively different. Thomas grew up in Maryland during the 1960s and had no contact with Hispanics, until later in life.

It's much easier for Hispanics to blend into American society than Blacks. After a few generations, Hispanics mix blood with Whites and they become less distinguishable. African Americans can never blend that way. I was bused to a White high school in a different neighborhood so that I could get a better, more challenging education. I was the only African American in the honors classes. I never really fit in with the other White students, even though we spent a lot of time together at school. I had friends, but I was always aware of being part of the Black minority. And then my neighborhood friends accused me of becoming White—speaking like a White. I did not fit into either world. I still live in two worlds today. So I think I have a greater sense of empathy, or ability to relate to other minorities, or people of color. It's something that's working inside me. I'm more open and understanding and find that similarity useful when joining. We have something in common; it's part of our connection.

Color is an important issue and a source of discrimination in the United States. Although skin color is on a continuum from the palest Albino to the darkest ebony of some African Americans, we continue to categorize people as Asian, Black, White, or Hispanic, or we label with colors. One Hispanic therapist points out that these categories are not useful. It is a question of culture not of color.

What about White people from South Africa who move to the United States. Aren't they African Americans too? What about Latinos who do not have any Native American blood? Aren't they White? Many Mexicans are full-blooded Native Americans, what color are they, Red? There are a lot of Irish or English people that get very dark tan. Do we call them White or Brown? The more I work with Hispanic people and with others in therapy, the more I realize how very unfitting labels can be. There are so many blends of colors and races in the Hispanic people that labels do not apply. Just look at the

*color variations among Whites and Blacks. I don't think the color
blending is as important as the acceptance.*

Discrimination played a role in a female African American therapist's experience. Wynette Hadnott grew up the daughter of a highly
successful, wealthy surgeon. When her father went to medical school,
he had to live alone because the dormitories were segregated.
Wynette's mother and father took great care in protecting their children
from discrimination whenever they could. Her parents moved to a different school district when they heard that the high school their children would attend had sports teams called the Southern Rebels. They
would not send their children to a school that continued to celebrate
the Old South where Black slaves were legal. Wynette commented:

*Money goes a long way in helping minorities fit in. It puts you in a
place where you can be less aware of prejudice. You get pulled into
the dominant White culture, until you get slapped in the face. But
then it gets harder to go back to your own culture for support. They
don't understand. They look at your wealth and can't feel sympathy
for you.*

When Wynette was in middle school, shortly after she and her family had moved to Alamo Heights, someone painted "NIGGER" across
their front fence with black paint. Instead of quickly painting over it
and hiding its ugliness, Wynette's parents decided to leave it there for
a few days for all the neighbors to see. Many of the people in the neighborhood were as outraged as the Hadnotts. It was a way of showing
pride and of pointing to the fact that prejudice was alive and well.

Although Wynette also experienced the sense of two worlds, she
believed it gave her a better understanding of both cultures. Many of
her current clients are African Americans because they feel more comfortable working with her than with interns of other ethnicities.
Wynette admits that similar ethnicities or skin colors may enhance
the therapeutic relationship at first, but the quality of the relationship
is based on much more than color.

*It might be important for some Hispanics to see Hispanic therapists,
but it is not necessary. The issues are much bigger; that's not what*

people seek therapy for. If therapeutic bonding was not able to be es-
tablished because people can't get past the color issue, then therapy
could not occur.

Albert Valadez alluded to the issue of color blending and acceptance in his discussion of skin color discrimination. Despite his growing up in the Rio Grande Valley, where 90% of the culture was
Hispanic (Mexican), the power, money, and land were owned by Anglos, and the schools were therefore controlled by the dominant
Anglo American culture. Hispanic children were judged by their
Spanish surnames as well as by the darkness of their skin. Those with
the darkest skin were often the children of transient migrant workers
who had an array of difficulties getting an education. In school, children with Spanish surnames were automatically placed in lower
reading, English, and math groups. Complicating the dominant
White cultural presupposition that Hispanic children had lesser academic ability was the assumption that darker Hispanic children were
less acculturated and therefore less likely to succeed in an Anglo
American school system.

Albert's mother, who was an academic diagnostician, had Albert
complete a battery of diagnostic tests, which indicated his high level
of intelligence and academic aptitude. Presenting the results to the
school, she fought hard to advocate for appropriate scholastic placement of Albert within the basic curriculum. To prevent further discrimination of Albert, she forbade him from playing in the Texas sun
as to avoid the darkening of his skin color.

Albert remembers that subtle messages of inferiority like these
were continuously being sent to him because of his Hispanic heritage.
He explained that in order to excel in the White culture, the Hispanic
part of him became lost; with every step toward assimilation came a
compromise. A part of the self was lost to the letting go of Hispanic
traditions. As a result, identity formation was encumbered. To avoid
discrimination, the Hispanic person must transcend significant por-
tions of his or her roots in the development of his or her identity.

In contrast to Albert's experience, Nan, whose ancestors were
Irish, English, Scottish, and Spanish, had a very different experience
growing up in the Rio Grande Valley. Whereas Albert was intensely aware of difference as one of the marginalized group, Nan

was virtually unaware of difference. She knew that the Anglos were in all of the positions of power in town, but she felt she fit in. Everyone knew her family. Her parents embraced the Spanish culture, and her friends were Mexican American and Anglo. Ironically, as she became aware of prejudice against African Americans and Hispanics, she experienced discrimination of Anglos.

The racial prejudice was worse when I went to college. Maybe because it was in El Paso, I don't know. Some people had a very strong prejudice against Anglos. One time I went to apply for a job at this store where all of the other employees were Hispanic. After I filled out the application the manager and assistant manager were going to interview me. While I waited they started speaking Spanish. They automatically thought that because I was White, I could not understand. They said some derogatory things about me and Anglos in general. But, it didn't strike me as discrimination until later. I just remember thinking they were very rude people. Sometimes it helps in therapy to put discrimination in the perspective of just plain rudeness. Not to make light of it, but it is ignorance—lack of respect for other human beings. I think we need to welcome our differences, celebrate them.

Another therapist explained acceptance by wondering what would happen if her Mexican American family moved to live next to a family of Scandinavian descent. She thought it would be easy to be friends and accept each other on an individual level. Yet, proximity raises acceptance to a whole new level. Could she accept a Norwegian American son-in-law?

Would we socialize? Would we want our children to date or to marry? As we socialize, we move closer together. People go for preferences. Hispanics prefer Hispanics. If I get a hint that you're having a party and you are not going to invite me because I'm Hispanic, then I've already learned something about you. And if I'm going to have my family reunion and I'm not going to invite you, it says something about me . . . why I don't want you there. For some reason we are excluding each other. Hispanics will look for discrimination on the part of their therapist [as will any person who feels oppressed]. If they find it, they will not return to you. If they don't they will bond.

The Extended Family

Traditionally, Hispanics have maintained strong ties with all of their relatives. One of the major and perhaps most threatening challenges facing Hispanic families in the United States today is the loss of the large close-knit family. All of the Hispanic therapists we interviewed mentioned that as part of their upbringing, a highly valuable experience. Therapists can view the maintenance of these extended ties as one of the strengths and beauty of the Hispanic culture. One Hispanic therapist born and raised in San Antonio said, "Hispanics just like each other. We like to get together and just enjoy each other's company. We need to live close to each other."

Jeannette Caballero, an Hispanic counselor who works in a clinic that serves low-income Hispanic families, describes her experience while growing up. She grew up in the Valley, in Westlaco, Texas. During the seventeen years she lived there until she left home for college, she cannot remember experiencing any form of discrimination, only acceptance.

> *It was like a big extended family. Everybody is related to everybody. I'm told whoever is Caballero, I'm related to. Everybody is really close. Everybody knows everybody, so reunions are really fun! My Dad, although he left school at 13 is a really intelligent man. He works for the school district and he knows everything there. Everybody knows "Chatto" and loves him there. Everybody knew me as Chatto's daughter.*

Leticia Cortez describes her experience growing up as the daughter of Mexican immigrants. She spent her first eight years living in Ohio. It was a bicultural experience. At school, she and her brother spoke English, but at home they spoke Spanish. She remembered Ethnic Day at school when the children celebrated their heritage with traditional foods and reports. There were other Hispanics in Ohio, but everyone had an ethnicity and was encouraged to be proud: Italian, Irish, African, Puerto Rican, and, of course, her own, Mexican. The author asked if she ever felt discrimination, "No. There were all kind of jokes. Actually, we discriminated against Polish people!" Leticia laughed and continued with her story.

> *You know, my brother and I answered my parents in English. They would speak to us in Spanish and we completely understood, but we would answer in English. Guess it was a sort of rebellion. We moved to Eagle Pass when I was eight. I did not want to move, but my mother was scared to stay. Our neighborhood was getting vandalized. Our car was vandalized by an African American gang and my mother became afraid of African Americans. My Dad drove his own truck to Mexico to buy goods and together they ran an imports business. He was gone a lot and my mother wanted to be closer to her family. Both my parents had lived in Eagle Pass before they moved to Ohio.*
>
> *When we moved, I had a hard time fitting in. It was such a small town and everyone had known each other since they were babies. All the families knew each other and I was a stranger. There was an understanding that you can only gain by being part of the culture. I understand the older generations and their rigid traditional values as well as the younger more rebellious generations.*

Leticia Cortez believed that it was an asset to know the Hispanic culture in therapy with Hispanic families.

The author was curious about Leticia's difficulty fitting in with the Mexican American children in the border town.

> *Well, my parents would always say, "Why do you need friends? Play with your brother." And my parents were very protective of me. Before I could play with anyone, my parents had to know their parents. It is a common thing in Mexican families. It's like a sense of pride in your family. The family can take care of all its own needs. Some of my friends could not sleep over at anyone's house or go to slumber parties. It's like, "Why do you have to sleep at her house? You have a bed!" It's a tradition passed down through generations, "We took care of our own. We are competent. You don't need to go over to anyone else's house; you have a house. You have food!"*

Another therapist mentioned a similar gender rift in her family. Her parents were strict with their two daughters, expecting them to do chores around the house and in the garden. The two boys were never asked to help with anything.

I actually used to love to mow the lawn. We had a riding lawnmower and my Dad used to ask me to mow. One day, I was a senior in high school and I had things I wanted to do. I said, "Dad, why don't you ask Tony? He's your son and he should be out here helping you." But instead of asking him, my Dad would do it himself if I had papers or homework, or something to do. I really think that was part of the reason he got into drugs. My bothers are never disciplined or allowed to take the consequences. My father bails them out every time they get in trouble. The last time my brother went to jail, I told my Dad not to bail him out. This time he just looked me right in the eye, and I knew I had pushed him too far. It was as if he was saying, "Please don't say anymore. He is my son." No matter what my brothers do . . . I think he just loves them too much. My Dad is so embarrassed by his sons. At first we tried to keep it a secret, just in our family, but after my brother started getting arrested, everyone knew. I know it's killing my Dad.

I asked how this was useful in terms of therapy. "Well, I do a lot of work with kids." When children come to the session, the therapist plays with and focuses on them. She believes that once you join and win over the child, the parents are sold. "Mexican Americans, probably all Hispanics, are very child-centered. The children always come first."

The older generations have more closed boundaries than the younger ones. There were tight boundaries around the families, and around Leticia's neighborhood and city as well. However, it would be a mistake to assume that all Hispanics have extended networks of helpful relatives. Economic realities are forcing families to limit their size. With fewer children there will be fewer relatives in the future. Women have more reproductive freedom, which allows more to enter the workforce. Many factors can cause ruptures in the typical extended family structure. Gangs, teen pregnancies, drug abuse, sexual abuse, incest, divorce, and spousal abuse are among some of these factors. Therapists should carefully assess the family of origin to ascertain what support networks are in place, as they can be powerful tools in creating therapeutic solutions.

Gender and Family Roles

Leticia described herself as very independent and rebellious because her parents wouldn't let her be independent. They would not let her date, except to attend her Senior Prom. There was a double standard in her home, because her brother had much more freedom. Rather than be angry, Leticia describes being perplexed.

Leticia's mother had attended school until the sixth grade and then lived at home. All of the other children married and left the house. Her mother took care of her invalid father after her mother died. It was not until her father died that she married Leticia's father. She was in her thirties. In Mexico, the only acceptable way to leave the home for a woman was to marry. Leticia fought to attend college in San Antonio; they finally agreed as long as she called home every Sunday at 2 P.M. Another girl in her dormitory was picked up by her father on Friday and driven back to the Valley every weekend. Leticia explained they wanted to guard her from "boys."

Leticia's brother could date freely. He was allowed to choose his university and his parents paid in full. Leticia, in comparison, had to beg to go away to school. Most of her friends planned to live at home and commute to junior college. Leticia put herself through school by working full-time. She admits it is a bit unfair that her parents pay for her brother, but not for her. "That was just the way it was. I knew I could not ask them to pay for both of us at the same time."

Leticia commented about working within the family roles and gender hierarchies:

One time when I took my break behind the mirror, everyone told me to get the father involved in the session. He had been sitting in the corner, isolated, not saying anything and not part of therapy. I explained that this was a traditional Hispanic family. The father is part of the power and authority of the family. When they entered the room they shifted power over to the therapist. I'm not going to actively pull them in if they don't want to talk. I don't want to actively challenge their authority. I'm here to know what's going on, take them there. But it's Mom's job to take care of the kids, and the family. Respect is a big part of it. I always respect their structure. I actively listen for their beliefs, but I don't try to change them, just respect them. What most surprises me is the rigid way the older generations think noth-

ing has changed. I had one family whose daughter was pregnant at
fifteen. Her older brother's marijuana abuse was not a problem, but
they forced their daughter to get married. Even though they knew
that the odds of her marriage failing were very high.

Sometimes there can be cultural clashes in therapy even when the
ethnicities are matched. Leticia's values were very different from the
family's, but she worked with them, respecting their goals instead of
forcing hers on the family.

THERAPEUTIC RELATIONSHIP

All the therapists we interviewed spoke expansively on their experiences with the bonding process that takes place within the therapeutic relationship with Hispanic clients. The issue of similarities versus
differences was pervasive among all of the interviews. A predominant theme that emerged was that a blending of the differences must
occur in order for therapeutic bonding to develop. So many variables
to this blending phenomenon existed that most of the therapists
found difficulty in breaking them down into absolute terms. The relationship between the therapist and the client in its totality is where
meaning was constructed, and each therapist addressed his or her
perceptions from individual backgrounds and experiences. We have
chosen to discuss particular issues and experiences of therapists that
have not been directly addressed in other areas of this chapter.

Estela Olivares eloquently described the blending of variables
within the therapeutic process:

Culture is only one dimension because it breaks down the initial
barriers and may contribute to immediate rapport; but there is more
to the therapeutic relationship, and that is sincerity and authentic-
ity. What I do know, however, is that certain Hispanics, like gang
members, would never talk to me if they didn't think I shared simi-
lar cultural and ethnic experiences. So culture is an important as-
pect because what people see when we walk in the room sparks their
presuppositions. But how do I know if I am connecting with a client
because I am Hispanic, or a maternal figure, or lighter skinned, or

middle-aged, or bilingual? I don't know. I do believe that it is the human quality that transcends everything else in the therapeutic relationship.

Julius Lundy speaks of similar experiences. He states that when he walks into the therapy room, he is "Black" and the client is Hispanic for the first two minutes, and then a blending of the relationship occurs.

Color and cultural differences are transcended as the therapeutic bonding process takes place. The two people are connecting at a deeply human, emotional level. What people have in common is their human condition—skin color and culture are secondary. People want to be heard, understood, and nurtured; every human being understands these needs. The cultural connection is only the first layer; therapeutic bonding runs much deeper.

Wynette Hadnott concurs with these perceptions. She says that the initial visual impression of being Hispanic when working with Hispanic clients is important. The Hispanic client already feels understood at a certain level when a Hispanic therapist walks in the room. However,

. . . the issues are much bigger than this initial impression. Often appearances can be misleading. They can feed your presuppositions, and make you jump to conclusions. The first impression of feeling a likeness with one's therapist is not what people seek therapy for. People have a clear therapeutic agenda, well some do, that goes beyond skin color or culture. As long as discriminations and power differentials are not communicated, the cultural issue is not ultimately essential.

A Hispanic family therapist had a different experience. She had developed a very close bond to her clinical psychologist, who was female and White. They had accomplished a lot and the therapist brought up the idea of going on to get her doctoral degree. Without pausing, the psychologist brought up the worst-case scenario, "Well, it is very hard to get accepted."

The therapist experienced a sinking feeling. She thought, "I guess she really doesn't know me, but then again, maybe she is right. Maybe it is very hard for Hispanics to get in. Maybe I'm being unrealistic." In retrospect, the Anglo psychologist had just assumed that Hispanics were not as intelligent as others and discouraged the therapist from attempting. The therapist worked a while longer with the analyst, delayed her graduate plans for a year, and then applied and got accepted easily. The analyst was not even aware of the effect of her words and her presuppositions. From the moment of that critical point, the therapist no longer had the same therapeutic bond with the analyst. She realized on some level, "She can never really understand me and my culture."

Delilah Trevino says there is an inherent understanding among Hispanics "because you've been there. You can't ignore the similarities because they are obviously there." By the same standard, one cannot ignore the differences either. She explains:

> Being exposed to diversity makes one more amenable to understanding various cultured people. Becoming familiar with the difference facilitates therapeutic bonding. Being Hispanic, however, feeds the motivation to give back to one's culture. It is not necessary to be Hispanic in order to achieve therapeutic bonding, but it somehow enriches the experience be it because of brownness, language, culture, or whatever.

Jeannette Caballero says the key to working with Hispanic clients is to encourage respect. It is important to make clients feel comfortable in order to establish rapport. People have more similarities than differences regardless of their coloring. It's the matching of human similarities that matter in therapeutic bonding.

What becomes apparent in these therapists' stories is that the blending of similarities and differences is what constitutes therapeutic bonding. One's presuppositions about difference, whether the difference is related to culture, gender, geography, skin color, and so on, must be explored and acknowledged when working with diversity. We cannot assume to know another based on our perceptions of what it means to be Hispanic. A willingness and openness to blend our differences with our clients' differences, not impose our values and presuppositions on others, are the essential ingredients for establishing therapeutic bonding. Similarities facilitate initial warmth and familiarity, however, the therapeutic relationship is grounded in a deeper shared human condition. Positive change in therapy is acquired through shared meaning, connection, and mutuality, all of which are constructed through authentic relating. Being real, not pretending to know another based on his or her cultural background, and the sharing of being human in the therapeutic relationship are nestled in the bedrock of the bonding process.

CONCLUSIONS

Culture clash is a significant concept of which therapists working with diverse populations must be aware. Clearly, there is a general consensus that cultural sensitivity and knowledge of ethnicity are essential for practitioners; however, the issues that emerged from our interviews suggest that culture clash does not exist as a product of a therapist having a different cultural background from the client. Most of the therapists interviewed saw the same cultural backgrounds as a facilitator in the initial bonding process, and considered language as a factor that enriches and expedites the therapeutic process; however, culture clash does not necessarily present itself as a result of diversity. Rather, culture clash seems to evolve from resistance to diversity and an unwillingness to explore one's own presuppositions about other races and cultures.

Culture clash does not exist independently; it is generated by an unwillingness or ignorance to understand one's self and another vis-à-vis cultural difference. Our psychological development is influenced by culture. It's inescapable. The culture(s) to which we were exposed molded our epistemologies. Therefore, since diversity is ubiquitous, it is a part of the therapeutic arena whether it is manifested through gender, race, ethnicity, language, or culture. What is critical for the therapist is to explore and acknowledge the presuppositions that resulted from his or her own development, and acknowledge how these presuppostitions impact on the therapeutic process. We need to recognize which of our presuppositions must be transcended in order to bypass discriminations of which we may have previously been unaware. How do we view difference and, more importantly, how do we facilitate therapeutic bonding in the face of difference?

The results of the interviews indicated that therapeutic bonding may be facilitated when the therapist shares the same culture as the client; however, cultural similarities were viewed as only one factor in the bonding process. Most of the therapists agreed that therapeutic bonding runs much deeper than the sharing of a culture, and that culture can indeed be transcended in the development of the therapeutic relationship. Bonding takes place when the therapist and client are able to relate authentically with one another on a deeply sincere level. Our "humanness" surmounts our "cultureness." As stated earlier, culture clash does not exist on its own. An unwillingness to familiarize oneself with diversity creates culture clash. An openness and willingness to explore one's own presuppositions and to meet people at a purely human level, a level that transcends color and culture, promotes therapeutic bonding, healing, and positive growth.

REFERENCES

Anderson, H. (1997). *Conversation, language, and possibilities.* New York: Basic Books.

Avis, J. M., & Turner, J. (1996). Feminist lenses in family therapy research: Gender, politics, and science. In D. H. Sprenkle & S. M. Moon (Eds.), *Research methods in family therapy.* New York: Guilford Press.

Bakhtin, M. (1991). *The dialogic imagination: Four essays by M. M. Bakhtin.* M. Holquist (Ed.), C. Emerson & M. Holquist (Trans.). Austin: University of Texas Press.

Baszanger, I., & Dodier, N. (1997). Ethnography: Relating the part to the whole. In D. Silverman (Ed.), *Qualitative research: Theory, method and practice* (pp. 8–23). Thousand Oaks, CA: Sage.

Berger, P. L., & Luckman, T. (1966). *The social construction of reality.* Garden City, NY: Doubleday.

Breunlin, D. C., Rampage, C., & Eovaldi, M. (1995). Family therapy supervision. Toward an integrative perspective. In R. Mikesell, D. Lusterman, & S. McDaniel (Eds.), *Integrating therapy: Handbook of family psychology and systems theory* (pp. 547–560). Washington, DC: American Psychological Association.

Breunlin, D. C., Schwartz, R. C., & Mac Kune-Karrer, B. (1992). *Metaframeworks: Transcending the models of family therapy.* San Francisco: Jossey-Bass.

Bruner, J. (1990). *Acts of meaning.* Cambridge, MA: Harvard University Press.

Calderon, J. (1992). "Hispanic" and "Latino": The viability of categories for panethnic unity. *Latin American Perspectives, 19*(4), 37–44.

Cicourel, A. V. (1974). *Cognitive sociology: Language and meaning in social interaction.* New York: The Free Press.

Crossley, N. (1996). *Intersubjectivity: The fabric of social becoming.* Thousand Oaks, CA: Sage.

Dawson, L. L., & Prus, R. C. (1993). Interactions, ethnography and postmodern discourse: Affinities and disjunctures in approaching human lived experience. *Studies in Symbolic Interaction, 15,* 147–177.

De Shazer, S. (1994). *Words were originally magic.* New York: Norton.

Freedman, J., & Combs, G. (1996). *Narrative therapy: The social construction of preferred realities.* New York: Norton.

Geertz, C. (1973). *The interpretation of cultures.* New York: Basic Books.

Geertz, C. (1983). *Local knowledge: Further essays in interpretive anthropology.* New York: Basic Books.

Gergen, K. J. (1994). *Realities and relationships: Soundings in social constructionism.* Cambridge, MA: Harvard University Press.

Gonzalez, D. (1992, November 5). What's the problem with "Hispanic"? Just ask a "Latino." *The New York Times,* p. E6.

Goolishian, H., & Anderson, H. (1994). Narrativa y self: Algunos dilemas posmodernos de la psicoterapia [Narrative and self: Some postmodern dilemmas of psychotherapy]. In D. F. Schnitman (Ed.), *Nuevos paradigmas, cultura y subjectividad* (pp. 293–306). Buenos Aires: Paidos.

Gubrium, J. F., & Holstein, J. A. (1995). Biographical work and new ethnography. In R. Josselson & A. Lieblich (Eds.), *Interpreting experience: The narrative study of lives* (Vol. 3, pp. 45–58). Thousand Oaks, CA: Sage.

Hightower, N. A., Rodriguez, S., & Adams, J. (1983). Ethnically mixed co-therapy with families. *Journal of Family Therapy, 10,* 105–110.

Holstein, J. A., & Gubrium, J. F. (1997). Active interviewing. In D. Silverman (Ed.), *Qualitative research: Theory, method and practice* (pp. 113–129). Thousand Oaks, CA: Sage.

Jones-Correa, M., & Leal, D. L. (1996). Becoming "Hispanic": Secondary panethnic identification among Latin American-origin populations in the United States. *Hispanic Journal of Behavioral Sciences, 18*(2), 214–254.

Katz, J. (1978). *White awareness.* Norman: University of Oklahoma Press.

Kvale, S. (1996). *Interviews: An introduction to qualitative research interviewing.* Thousand Oaks, CA: Sage.

LeCompte, M. D., & Preissle, J. (1993). *Ethnography and qualitative design in educational research* (2nd. ed.). San Diego: Academic Press.

McAdams, D. P. (1993). *Stories we live by: Personal myths and the making of the self.* New York: Guilford Press.

McIntosh, P. (1988). White privilege and male privilege: A personal account of coming to see correspondences through work in women's studies. In *Work in Progress No. 189.* Wellesley, MA: Stone Center.

Miller, J. B., & Stiver, I. (1997). *The healing connection.* Boston: Beacon Press.

The NewsHour with Jim Lehrer. (1998, July 10). New York and Washington, DC: Public Broadcasting Service.

Oboler, S. (1995). *Ethnic labels, Latino lives: Identity and the politics of (re)presentation in the United States.* Minneapolis: University of Minnesota Press.

O'Hanlon, B., & Weiner-Davis, M. (1989). *In search of solutions: A new direction in psychotherapy.* New York: Norton.

Rabinow, P., & Sullivan, W. (Eds.). (1979). *Interpretive social science: A reader.* Berkeley: University of California Press.

Rediger, S. L. (1996). Critical theory research: The emancipatory interest in family therapy. In D. H. Sprenkle & S. M. Moon (Eds.), *Research methods in family therapy.* New York: Guilford Press.

Ricouer, P. (1974). *The conflict of interpretations: Essays in Hermeneutics,* D. Ihde (Ed.). Evanston, IL: Northwestern University Press.

Roberto, L. G. (1991). Symbolic-experiential family therapy. In A. S. Gurman & D. P. Kniskern (Eds.), *Handbook of family therapy* (Vol. 2, pp. 444–478). New York: Brunner/Mazel.

Rossi, E. (1980). *Collected papers of Milton Erickson on hypnosis.* New York: Irvington.

Rubin, H. J., & Rubin, I. S. (1995). *Qualitative interviewing: The art of hearing data.* Thousand Oaks, CA: Sage.

Sarris, G. (1993). As cited in J. A. Holstein & J. F. Gubrium. (1997). Active interviewing. In D. Silverman (Ed.), *Qualitative research: Theory, method and practice* (pp. 113–129). Thousand Oaks, CA: Sage.

Shorris, E. (1992). Latinos: The complexity of identity. *NACLA: Report on the Americas, 26*(2), 19–26.

Smith, L. (1949). *Killers of the dream.* New York: Norton.

Spradley, J. (1979). *The ethnographic interview.* New York: Holt, Rhinehart & Winston.

Trevino, F. M. (1987). Standardized terminology for standardized populations. *American Journal of Public Health, 77,* 69–72.

Whitaker, C. A., & Keith, D. V. (1986). *Conversation hour on co-therapy.* Annual meetings of the Association for Marriage and Family Therapy, Orlando, FL.

White, M., & Epston, D. (1990). *Narrative means to therapeutic ends.* New York: Norton.

Wittgenstein, L. (1953). *Philosophical investigations.* Oxford: Blackwell.

5

SUPERVISION AND CONSULTATION WITH LATINO THERAPISTS

GONZALO BACIGALUPE

Que todo el mundo sepa que el sur tambien existe.
—MARIO BENEDETTI

As Latinos become the largest nonmainstream ethnic and racial group in the United States, new ideas arise that are necessary to understand our practices as family therapy supervisors and supervisees. In this chapter, I sketch some themes that emerge from my practice of integrating collaborative and postcolonial perspectives to inform the work of supervisors and consultants. Similarly, Gonzalez (1996) integrated a postmodern affirmative epistemology with cross-cultural sensitivity, advocating for a critical perspective on the effect of modernism on Latino experience. Gonzalez remains skeptical about the significance of postmodern ideas in the therapeutic and supervisory process of Latinos. I would argue that the postmodern sensibility questions the expertlike position that professionals in Latin

America and in the United States assume when speaking of Latinos and in particular Latinos from nondominant groups. Cross-cultural and postmodern approaches emphasize integration, exemplified in family therapy by the need to use a both/and approach rather than a selective one that chooses modernism or postmodernism.

Interestingly, it is the both/and approach that characterizes the third wave of family therapy theories that emerged in the mid-1980s and that continue to be embraced by authors of different perspectives. In this chapter, I embrace this principle as sustaining a more emancipatory and collaborative approach in supervision. This approach prioritizes high levels of reflexivity to prevent supervision from becoming just a functionalist exercise in adapting new practitioners to models of family therapy solely based on general systems theory (McLean, 1986). To assume that Latino societies are premodern and that by implication would not benefit from a postmodern critique succumbs to a particular set of historical stages defined by the Western industrialized world.

The dominant Western discourses define what is normal, developed, most advanced, and most relevant. They also define the criteria by which ways of knowing are to be accepted as natural. Mignolo, a historian, makes the case for conceptualizing epistemology in the Third World in radically different ways. He suggests, "exploring new ways of thinking about what we know [rather] than to accumulate new knowledge under old ways of thinking" (Mignolo, 1995, p. xv). We may benefit by exploring the spaces in between produced in the interstice created by different ways of knowing. The modernist and postmodernist schools of thought arose in the Western nations during the last few centuries. They are specific in time and place and may not apply to other cultures around the world.

Supervision is about the encounter of epistemologies and ontologies about relationships, ways of construing the other, and taken-for-granted assumptions about expert knowledge. Consultation and supervisory encounters are part of wider social relationships that frame the supervisory context. As consultants and supervisors, we may strive to be "neutral," but we are positioned by our particular values and social location. Our conversations with supervisees are framed in the context of our location in the world and our perennial position as outsiders to the clients' world (Bacigalupe, 1998).

Despite Latinos' capacity for agency, we are commonly known through the discourse of others, with little control over the discourses that define our social identities. Knowledge, then, becomes situated knowledge (Lal, 1996; Lather, 1991). A useful compromise may be found in the proposal to construe the supervision and consultation encounter as one between the native and the ethnographer in postmodern anthropology (Clifford & Marcus, 1986). Postmodern family therapists have often described supervisors, therapists, and clients as equal participants in the telling of stories, as if by entering therapy or supervision sessions they all become equal coparticipants in the storymaking (Anderson & Goolishian, 1988; Anderson & Swim, 1995). These ideas, however, may confuse the need for equality in professional relationships with the constraints of therapy (Golann, 1988) and supervision as potential sites for unjust power arrangements since supervision has been defined generally as a hierarchical relationship.

If the basic practice of supervision is constructed through conversation, it is of essence that supervisor and supervisee have a voice in the construction of the conversation. To achieve this, the participants would have to engage in joint action, "a situation in which *I* feel I have made *my* contribution, and in which *you* can feel that you have made yours" (Shotter, in press).

POSITIONING MY THINKING AND UNDERSTANDING OF FAMILY THERAPY

Like many others who have been captivated by the narrative and collaborative developments, I have navigated the challenging waters of systems and cybernetics theories and, later, those of the evolving story (Freedman & Combs, 1996; Hoffman, 1993, 1998; Roberts, 1994; Weingarten, 1998). My initial training, in the mid-1980s, made me sensitive to communication patterns, interactions, processes, relationships, ecology, and constructivism.

I have also experienced a "parallel" life as a political activist, a participatory action researcher in my country of origin, and later on as an immigrant in the United States. Besides formal training in family therapy, I worked as a participatory researcher and popular educator in Chile. In training as a family therapy supervisor in the United States, I became keenly aware of how the therapist and supervisory roles are framed by social discourses about gender, class, culture, race, and the varied forms in which those identity markers are construed or marginalized from supervisory conversations. These themes were not novel in the political and educational endeavors I experienced in my work with community and grassroots organizations that fought to reestablish democracy in Chile. However, the introduction of family therapy ideas followed closely the model developed in the United States and thus conflated with a general silence about issues of social justice and a lack of critical analysis in the newly developed family therapy trainings (Bacigalupe, 1998). Despite the marginalization of minority discourses, when I conceptualized systems, they included a social conflict dimension. My U.S. colleagues conceived systems in a functionalist manner, that is, as well-lubricated mechanisms by which social structures are maintained (i.e., families or therapeutic systems). My U.S. colleagues and I were speaking of different constructs. In my opinion, families in the family therapy paradigm were contained by a rigid, ecological discourse in which every person played a defined role within a whole and any deviation from the role was seen as dysfunctional and in need of repair.

Along with many others in the field, I started to realize the contradictions between these paradigms. My reflection led me to focus on the importance of supervisory processes as value laden in which a moral stance was always at stake. This stance was associated with a general distrust of family therapy proposals that construe Latinos as a homogeneous group that fits within the confines of a conceptual model of family therapy, that is, structural (Minuchin, 1978) or intergenerational (Boszormenyi-Nagy, 1987). The appeal of postmodern approaches, with their focus on conversations as political encounters and a reflexive framework that critically questions itself on a continuous basis (Erickson, 1988; Schon, 1983; Tomm, 1988), has facilitated an integration of systems ideas with a more critical undertaking. All in all, the ideas that emerge from this work are not postulates for an orthodox approach to supervision. It is only part of a contribution to advance a more just, emancipatory, and participatory approach in supervision and consultation. I am particularly sensitive to the appropriation of emancipatory epistemologies by mainstream researchers (cf. Piercy & Thomas, 1998) who present them as "new developments" when, in fact, they were part of the tools that lesser known scientists and practitioners had used in nonindustrialized countries for years. In this chapter, I use my experiences with Latino therapists as templates for practices beyond the work with Latinos. The reflections emanating from this position are amenable to applications across the borders that divide Latinos from non-Latinos or from those that place Latinos on one side of the fence.

CONSULTING AND SUPERVISING COLLABORATIVELY

Despite the similarities among therapy, supervision, and case consultation (Fine & Turner, 1997; Gardner, Bobele, & Biever, 1997; Piercy & Sprenkle, 1986; Roberto, 1997; Todd, 1997a; Wynne, McDaniel, & Weber, 1989), and the fact that the lesson that follows could be applied to any of them, as supervisors, we are called to distinguish these various conversations based on ethical and legal grounds (Sand-Pringle, Zarski, & Wendling, 1995; Stewart & Amudson, 1995; Storm & Haug, 1997). This is a continuous struggle because the development of genuine dialogue to enhance creativity and the development of local knowledge may be endangered by the accumulation of responsibilities linked to our expertise. It becomes visible in the context of taking a nonexpert position as a clinical supervisor—an approach that encourages curiosity and true respect for the clinicians' stories (Anderson, 1997; Dyche & Zayas, 1995; McGoldrick, Giordano, & Pearce, 1996).

It is important to carefully delineate the responsibilities I share with the therapist. When I am hired as a consultant and do not have any direct administrative responsibility, supervisees feel free to explore the institutional underpinnings of their work without feeling trapped by potential conflict of interest between my role as clinical consultant and my role as administrator. This is not always easy to delimit, as in the case of an organization that hires a supervisor as consultant, unless the clinician establishes a private contract with her supervisor. In this case, I try to facilitate a dialogical agreement concerning the ways supervisees and supervisors frame the supervisory relationship vis-à-vis the therapeutic one. These conversations about our conversations are particularly important not only for ethical and legal reasons, but because there are strong social expectations on the part of supervisees and supervisors about who is responsible for therapeutic success. As a Latino supervisor working with Latino supervisees, this dialogue must include the ways in which Latinos are perceived, construed, and their roles defined in mental health organizations, as well as the level of respect and trust demonstrated in the work they pursue with clients and colleagues. This conversation includes, paraphrasing Anderson (1997), rejecting the "accepted culturally ascertained meanings of therapy that decry remedial treatment designed or serving to bring about social compliance" (p. 265).

Listening Contexts

How we listen to clients and how we listen to each other in supervision legitimizes or marginalizes these stories. Listening plays a bigger role in these conversations than talking (Andersen, 1992; Anderson, 1997; Echeverria, 1994) because the stories told by participants in the clinical context are stories told in particular "listening contexts." As a supervisor, I consider my role to be that of continuously listening and evaluating the limits and scope of each supervisees' responsibilities to establish a form of contextual and systemic accountability. This listening should provide a safe context for therapists in supervision to approach clients professionally while choosing a therapeutic perspective with which they are comfortable. I point out potential ethical, legal, and personal problems that may appear as the therapist engages clients within a particular approach. I suggest relevant literature that complements or contradicts my own perspective and let the therapists decide on the best approach to the case. Most academic writing depicting Latinos is dominated by a discourse of deficit; however, supervisees and supervisors can enrich their wealth of knowledge with literature that reaches beyond clinical descriptions to elicit descriptions that are closer to the experience of Latino families.

Writing, Wording, and Documenting

An important element in my supervision work is the emphasis I place on the words we use to record in the form of clinical records and supervisory notes the conversations that take place during sessions. Documenting has always been intrinsically connected to labeling and the creation of static identities for clients and therapists. However, writing can play an important role in aiding clients, therapists, and supervisors to include multiple voices and diverse positions in their communications. In narrative therapy, writing has been used to help clients distance themselves from problem-saturated descriptions, mobilize multiple meanings and voices, and further the dissolving of their dilemmas (White, 1997; White & Epston, 1990).

In a reflecting format, written communication can be an invitation to a reflexive conversation, a direct intervention in the search for change, or both. The use of writing in therapy is not based in the concept that the whole universe is determined by language, but on the notion that words have a strong effect on how we constitute the social world. Words, languages, texts, and realities are interconnected and inform each other constantly.

Progress Notes

The following questions (Bacigalupe, 1996) are used to call therapists' attention to the link between writing procedures and treatment decisions. The questions highlight writing as a medium to deconstruct oppressive practices through an extensive revision of how we proceed with documentation in the clinical settings. As therapists begin to see how notes can oppress, they begin to create more culturally respectful progress notes.

> *How would your clinical practice change if you were not to take notes during or after the therapy session? If you were given time to review the previous session, how would your practice be different if you had access to a transcript of each session?*

To address issues of empathy, respect, and the client-therapist relationship, clinicians can explore the oppressive dimensions of case documentation and issues of power, such as the distance created between the experience of client and clinician.

> *If you were your client, would you like to be pictured in the text as you represented your client? In the case of a letter written to a family,*

how would you react if you were a member of that family? If your clients were to read your files, reports, or any written communication about them, would they understand the contents and intentions of your writing? Would the writing reflect the ways in which the conversation switches and combines Spanish and English?

Exploring the degree to which the client participates in treatment decisions may show the link between institutional practices that disempower or keep secret forms of alienation and colonization.

How would you describe the level of access to their files that you give your clients? What are your thoughts about your clients' participation in the documentation and design of their therapy? What would be the issues in the therapeutic relationship if the documentation of therapy were kept in the clients' home instead of the clinic?

The world and experiences of Latinos are inscribed in oppressive ways within agencies and organizations that attempt to serve them. More often than usual, Latino therapists are trapped within the same oppressive relations as their clients in clinics and other service providers. Institutional values and organizational preferences frequently limit the perspectives clinicians may have and may determine the process, duration, themes, and assumptions underlying the therapy. To expand the limits imposed in a particular context to the therapeutic process, it is important to clarify the institutional context in which clinicians work. The following questions foster clinicians' awareness of their internal dialogue and to whom they respond in therapy.

How much of your writing is done having in mind insurance companies, journal review board members, administrators, supervisors, colleagues, clients, etc.? If you were presenting the "case" in the context of a conference or journal publication, what would your clients' reaction be if they were spectators or readers? Do you imagine clients or their relatives requesting to read the files to reconstruct their past?

Clinicians agree that the progress note should give a sense of what has transpired during the session (Reynolds, Mair, & Fisher,

1992). Progress notes, which are considered clinical writing per excellence, have been dissociated from the therapeutic process itself although they can be a productive part of it. The progress note can be reflective of the elements and the rationale underlying the clinical work. They can also suggest which voices continue to have a life beyond the therapy session. How do we encourage supervisees to write meaningful progress notes for themselves, their clients, and other constituencies like the courts and managed care institutions?

Mindful professional progress notes do not to obliterate or make invisible the thinking, feelings, or intuition attached to the decision-making process embedded in the session. Like any human activity, neutral writing is impossible. Succinct progress notes need not silence important issues for the therapist and the client; it is important to introduce our rationale underlying our questioning and interventions. From a legal standpoint, this stance may make sense; ethically, we need to be as truthful as possible with regard to the thinking process at the time of the session. This position in the writing process may acknowledge all participants (multipartiality or multipositionality), but the progress note will also (or may) have to take a multipositional approach in relation to its potential audiences.

Therapists are accountable to an extended audience. Family therapists—as well as other clinicians—write for a diverse constituency in the present and to their clients in the future. Working with a family increases the level of complexity because therapy participants may have a diverse perspective on what needs to be recorded. Then we can ask, "How can clients participate in the process of construing the progress note?" In sum, to include the diverse perspectives also means to include context, process, and meaning in the progress notes. A process is more than simply accounting for some of the contents offered by the client during a particular session. It includes the writer and its potential audiences.

There is the potential for therapists as well as clients to construe their lives as an evolving text. The following questions are useful in encouraging therapists to review the influence clients have had on them:

> *If you were to write a novel of your life, what would the title be? In that novel, what chapter(s) would include your clients? If you were to ask your clients, what chapter(s) would you occupy in their*

novel? What have you learnt from this client and previous ones? How would you write about the experience of learning from clients?

The task of mapping the clients' effect on the therapist is relevant, particularly when working with supervisees who work with Latino survivors of abuse, violence, and trauma.

Expectations and Outcomes: Thinking Reflexively

"Am I helping to produce 'reflective practitioners' or school specific clones?" (Gurman & Kniskern, 1991). From a reflexive and collaborative perspective, therapists and supervisors are experts in interviewing, asking, reflecting, and relating to diverse constituencies. Accordingly, I start supervisory sessions by asking therapists about their thoughts regarding what they would like me as the supervisor to help them with as well as the process that would lead to a successful interview. Supervisees take responsibility for their own learning process and focus it on their specific needs; this is isomorphic to the question that clients can be asked in therapy:

> *What would you like to do today? How would you like me to approach the session? It is easy for us as Latinos to just start talking and forget we need to achieve some goals. What is the kind of conversation that will invite you to explore what you have in mind thoroughly? Can I suggest the following . . . ?*

Supervisees are asked to provide questions they have about their own behaviors and what they would like to learn from the supervision session. These are ways of engaging supervisees in dialogue that deviate from the notion that they are unable to create innovative and helpful ideas in the session.

Certain organizational contexts may make these interventions difficult to enact and the supervisor is restrained from a more egalitarian relationship. Institutional contexts that foster one model or gloss over unjust patterns make these kind of relationships difficult for Latino supervisors and supervisees who may be the minority constituency in that setting. Thus, the supervisor needs to have support to pursue an approach that fosters criticism of dominant dialogues and is free to name injustices.

In live supervision, I always ask supervisees how they would like me to intervene during the session in the form of some of the following questions.

> *Do you want me to call you on the phone? Is there a limit on the times you would like me to call? Would you like me to go in? Would you like to use the reflecting team as part of the supervision [Biever & Gardner, 1995; Prest, Darden, & Keller, 1990]? Are there any specific aspects you would like me to observe today? Are there any stories or words you would like to address today? What kind of feedback do you want from me today? If I say something, should it be before, during, or after the session? My mind is wild sometimes. Should I restrain myself or can I ask for your permission to say things we did not know would come up? How would you like me to relate with your client? What should I do if I change my mind about the ideas we have discussed today? Should we switch from Spanish to English in particular ways if ever?* ¿Estamos preparados para esto? *(Are we ready for this?)* ¿Que necesitamos para estar preparados? *(What do we need to do to be prepared?)*

If the supervisee is being observed by other trainees, I also ask them to collaborate with feedback, which expands the pool of practical questions and interventions, rather than striving for elaborated assessment during the live supervision breaks. Questions about their cultural background may be interspersed at this point to contextualize observations within cultural beliefs and biases. These questions help clinicians explore the impact of their cultural value system on clinical decisions and make explicit the ethical aspects and biases involved in systemic work.

In sum, I envision a supervisory relationship in which we can keep a "constructionist mind" that balances responsibility, accountability, transparency, cooperation, participation, and sharing various forms of expertise. This is not what non-Latino administrators may expect from Latino therapists, who are frequently overwhelmed by requests to intervene for Latino families due to the high demand for and lack of resources to hire bilingually and biculturally competent therapists in community mental health agencies. In my experience though, I have noticed that Latinos tend to accept higher levels of ambiguity and may present less dissonance about problems that seem without resolution. Within agencies, there is an underlying expectation that Latino therapists should quickly help resolve the needs of families from the same ethnic background and to quickly start with new "cases."

In the two examples that follow, there is no attempt at defining a specific Latino therapist identity or a Latino supervisor identity that can be captured by a group of discrete variables as often has been the case in ethnic-related research. This is not to say that therapists who work with Latino families create, recreate, use, and promote certain discursive practices that lead us all to characterize ourselves as fixed within certain characteristics, that is, being more centered on the relationship rather than the product. From a critical and postmodern perspective, a more useful exercise is to analyze what are the characteristics expressed by Latino and non-Latino mainstream colleagues. Some of these characteristics may restrain our development and thus marginalize us from full participation in the definition of our heterogeneous identities as Latino supervisors and clinicians.

SUPERVISION IN A TRAINING CONTEXT

The following analysis corresponds to a description of supervision work with a Latino family therapist. I supervised Juan weekly at a family therapy clinic using a one-way mirror and did case consultation based on videotapes and case notes. I was also available to meet with him at other times or to speak on the phone in the case of an emergency. Special supervision times were scheduled when he needed to write a report for the court or community agencies. Juan had some information about my theoretical and clinical background. He chose me as his supervisor because he wanted to learn about narrative and reflecting approaches in family therapy. He also wanted to be supervised by a bilingual supervisor who could also observe him working with families that needed a Spanish-speaking clinician.

Many of the families that request help at his clinic were recent immigrants from South America who had little knowledge of English.

We had lengthy discussions of what could be helpful to clients, and I made efforts at integrating not only the collaborative-reflexive ideas into the supervision, but other concepts that were useful to empower clients within a multicultural and systemic framework. Family therapy and social sciences are suggested as useful notation and exploratory tools in supervision meetings. Examples abound in the form of genograms (McGoldrick & Gerson, 1985), variations of them (Hardy & Laszloffy, 1995; Kelly, 1990), circular and future questions (Fleuridas, Nelson, & Rosenthal, 1986; Penn, 1985), appreciative inquiry (Bushe, 1995; Hammond, 1996), ethnographic interviewing (Agar, 1986), and conversational analysis (Gale & Newfield, 1992).

Sharevision

In the first session, we shared some characteristics of each other since our respective "locations" in the world certainly would affect the supervisory relationship even though an outsider could easily describe us as "Hispanic." We spoke about our own family histories and how they fit with our shared expectations about the supervision. In this regard, the genogram as a cultural story aids me not only in the work with clients, but also in the process of knowing supervisees.

Juan was thirty-two years old at the time of the supervision. He trained as a pastoral counselor and was pursuing a doctoral degree in family therapy. His parents and sister emigrated from Cuba three decades ago and live close by. He was raised in Puerto Rico in a middle-class environment, and as an adolescent, experienced many of his peers joining a gang at the age of fifteen. He had been married for only a couple of years. To support himself, he worked as a mental health clinician in a traditional residential treatment unit for adolescents.

Juan was uncomfortable about his previous professional training within a pathology-based framework because it restrained his creativity and resource-oriented approach with couples and families. In subsequent sessions, he told me of his frustrating experience as a family therapist because families stopped coming back after a first session. However, he thought that he joined well with families. As a result, he wanted to reflect on the process of engaging with families and "to be more effective and relaxed." He also wished to "listen more" and "be open to the observations of others." He made a special request from me to provide honest and open feedback (*hablame sin pelos en la lengua*).

As in other supervision experiences, listening to family stories is done with the understanding that no one would be forced to disclose information they would feel uncomfortable sharing at a particular time in the supervisory context. I also describe my own immigration and family history and invite supervisees' questions. I usually start by talking about my arrival in the United States from Chile and some experiences in South America. In these conversations, I found that the term "immigrant" does not describe well my experience or that of many others. We often feel as if we are from many places at the same time and thus I describe myself as a *transmigrant*. This term accounts for some of the ambiguities of being in the "land of others," the border, and the memories and connections with the place where I came from. I also talk about my middle-class background, about my working professional parents who lived in a country other than where they were born, and about my siblings who live in Chile. I also describe my struggles with the English language and my difficulties at understanding xenophobia and racism in this country. I usually explain how I became a family therapist and my present theoretical choices, choices that I consider as valid as the ones Juan may want to pursue. This sharing is connected with the possibilities and dangers of a psychotherapy approach grounded in diversity. This conversation leads to an ongoing discussion about making these issues visible, about respecting clients' construction of reality, and about the dilemma of appreciating difference in context. This kind of storytelling leads to a form of supervision that could be renamed as "sharevision."

A Bilingual Process

A typical supervision session included evaluating together previous family therapy sessions and planning the next, the live supervision, and a discussion of the process. We spoke alternately in English and Spanish, checking on the nuances of language to enrich the content and context of clients' stories and the ways clinicians listen to them. Juan and I evaluated what would be the goals for a particular live supervision session and how they connected with the family's expectations. I considered his ideas and shared my own expectations, negotiating on particular goals or supervisory format for that occasion.

Juan also appreciated watching segments from videotaped sessions. Several questions were asked during intermissions, and as in an ethnographic interview, I was interested in understanding more and attended anew to what he and his clients were saying and/or doing.

Whose story are you paying attention to? What did you find fascinating and intriguing from your intervention? What were you thinking at the moment of saying that to the family? In what ways were your questions congruent with your body posture and that of clients? What potential stories or openings could you have explored during that specific interaction? How could you use those openings in the next session? What are other questions or ways of asking that may empower the client to find solutions or resources within their own family? How does each family member make sense of their own telling?

It has been a long-standing tradition in several family therapy models that in live supervision the supervisor calls-in (Colapinto, 1988; Montalbo & Storm, 1997; Pirrotta & Cecchin, 1988; Schwartz, Liddle, & Breunlin, 1988; Todd, 1997b). Juan and I experimented with the idea of having him call me rather than having me interrupt him, changing the traditional call-in into a more flexible tool that later on some families found they could try. We both found out that this way of communicating during live supervision fostered a better alliance and a productive reflecting process. Soon, we agreed that we could both "call each other." On several occasions, I went inside the therapy room and carried on live case consultations in the presence of the family. Most of the time, I talked with him using the reflecting team format. After the reflections, I left or stayed with the family to ask questions.

Let Me Think

As in the cases of many Latino therapists working in community mental health agencies, many of Juan's clients were court-referred families. I provided him with feedback concerning his wish to engage clients quickly in an assessment of the situation without letting the clients fully express their concerns. Sometimes, his eagerness to "fix the case" interfered with progress because he could not think of new ideas. I suggested that he refrain from saying anything by telling the family: "I'm going to think for a couple of minutes." He described the experience of staying silent as feeling like he was carrying out a "reflecting team conversation within himself." Then, he shared his thoughts with his clients, or he phoned me to share his ideas and questions in front of the family. He repeated this exercise many times and found that clients also started to utilize his behavior. We called this the *Let Me Think Exercise.* This process was effective at empowering both Juan and his clients to think anew in the context of highly complex situations, including the diffusion of potentially violent interactions in the session.

Sensitivity to Multisystemic Perspectives

A strong sensitivity toward the larger system and how it intertwines with the family's concerns was also a subject to which I paid special attention. Making a larger system analysis brought him to reconsider the question of who is the client (Imber-Black, 1988). To answer that question, Juan needed to engage as many participants as possible in the conversations. Aware of the larger system includes discussion of the way Juan addressed family members during the interviews. Since my approach also focuses on how we script the therapeutic events, I suggested a review of the clinical files to check on what would be the reaction of the clients and other potential constituencies to the notes (insurance companies, attorneys, courts, etc.). This activity was helpful in bringing forth issues of liability and accountability.

Latino immigrants are highly sensitive to issues of social class, race, ethnicity, gender, and sexual orientation. Supervisors need to help supervisees become aware of how these issues affect their work. I provided feedback concerning three ways in which Juan was recreating traditional gender stereotypes. First, he spoke and listened more often to men than women in families and couples' sessions. Second, he often treated women in families as if their only role was to be mothers by calling them "mom" or by asking questions that only privileged that role. Finally, he also thought of girls as fragile and in need of protection, less able than boys to behave actively, or described them using only traditional stereotypes of how a woman should look or behave. He explained this bias as part of what he considered normal cultural values, but he started to recognize the disempowering effect of a belief that defines women solely in the role of mothers.

We explored alternative ways of conceptualizing women's work by discussing the fact that most women without income work at home without pay. Specific, concrete, and timely feedback was given during live supervision, tape reviews, and case consultations; at times ironic remarks or predictions were made regarding what other patriarchal practices could emerge in a family therapy session or in supervision. Juan was able to observe the way his own socialization as a male kept him and indeed all of us, from looking at those issues critically. My own supervisor at that time mentioned to me the occasions in which I may have inadvertently acted in the traditional stereotypical way, a behavior that could undermine a positive supervisory relationship when the supervisor is a woman and the supervisee is a man, or vice versa. The same process can be applied when we address issues of racial or ethnic diversity and social injustice.

Juan and I evaluated his clinical work using a format developed in the context of a training institution (Flemons, Green, & Rambo, 1996) to evaluate advances and potential areas in need of development. Before we discussed the evaluation and the sharing of my opinion as a supervisor, I asked Juan to self-evaluate and to fill out the form, too. Later, we discussed his self-evaluation and my evaluation. Juan wanted to continue in supervision with me, but I encouraged him to find another supervisor to solidify the skills he had learned and to observe from another perspective his accomplishments during the time I supervised him. Overall, Juan became confident working in situations with high levels of ambiguity. He was also able to listen to his clients more carefully without having to intervene until they were prepared to listen to new ideas or until after a thorough exploration led to an understanding of his clients' perspective.

SUPERVISION AND CONSULTATION WITH EXPERIENCED SUPERVISORS

Marta is an experienced Latina therapist who has been working toward becoming an approved supervisor (American Association of Marital and Family Therapy, 1997). She works in a multicultural community mental health agency within an African American and Latino community while continuously attending trainings on different theoretical orientations. Supervision sessions with Marta are a combination of theoretical conversations, review of specific interventions, use of self and self-disclosure, and the search for universal aspects in work with highly complex situations that frequently involve drug addiction, poverty, trauma, and clients' interaction with protective and/or judicial systems. Several supervision sessions incorporate the use of videotape and audiotape. I am frequently invited to consult with her and her clients, which gives me the opportunity to use collaborative reflecting techniques within different variations: reflecting team and reflexive conversations, documentation, and ethnographic questioning. Through careful planning on her part, all of these tools are used, depending on the client's situation. For instance, we always evaluate if it is appropriate to have me as a guest of her clinical and supervisory work. The following are excerpts of conversations addressing different dilemmas that she faces as an experienced supervisor who is focusing on developing her own unique supervisory and therapeutic approach.

Marta's Developmental Dilemmas

While Marta was writing a brief philosophy statement as required by AAMFT, we had an opportunity to reflect on the connection between theory and practice.

S: If you were to watch a tape of your supervision with the eyes of someone who knew about writing, do you think that you would be able to see and describe what it is that you're doing?

M: I have difficulties reproducing this nice lavish description. You know, when I read these descriptions in the literature . . .

S: Can you give me an example of a lavish description?

M: There is an example in the book that describes, mentions all these models, all these influences, different concepts and models . . .

S: So, you mean, to integrate different concepts and models . . .

M: Yeah, these models have been described and I have such an intuitive way of working that sometimes I don't know where it all comes from. Sometimes, really, I can't tell where it comes from. That's how it feels.

S: When you check the videotape afterwards, do they still remain in that—quote—"intuitive stage"?

M: There are pieces like that.

S: There are moments when you're observing yourself doing that work in which you go beyond that intuitive here and . . .

M: Do you mean after?

S: Yeah, when you're observing the tape.

M: No. I could say, "Well that was successful or helpful" or "That wasn't helpful," and I could see how it began and could see how it was helpful and where it was going and . . .

S: So you can make a description after all, "this is this and that is that. . . ."

Language Hurdles

Capturing the experience and the theory emerging from practical work in the context of English as a second language is difficult; Latino supervisees, for whom English is not their first language, confront serious challenges, believing in their capacity to create theory in connection with their clinical experience.

M: It's acceptable and meets the criteria for a beginning supervisor. . . . But I don't think that gives justice to who I am. I always feel like I am not there.

S: In between . . . Who you are feels much more complex than the way you describe it. . . .

M: What you just said sounds like the best suggestion because that would describe my work. I have these sayings and things when I am working with clients that look very simple but they have tremendous meaning. . . . They cannot realize that they have all this knowledge, because it was put there in such a simple way. I will tell my clients the work they have done is like books and books and books. And how they make progress—they overcome the problem but they have been very concrete.

S: ... your experience tells you that there are clients who tell their stories or their experiences in such a rich way, in comparison to the words you find in chapters in books or in papers ... and at the same time you want for your own writing to be very "complex."

M: Yeah, because I never see, in all the things I read, I never see this trouble that I have, or this way of reading or working. There isn't a piece that describes what I do.

S: That's it, that's how you start—there is some need for it.

Encouraging New Stories
Stories evoke stories. I would tell a story about my daughter, and that would evoke the telling of a story about Marta's daughter and the development of a metaphor that could lead her out of a theoretical or practical muddle, our muddle. Mirroring through our own personal stories as we relate with clients' stories is a common feature in my work with advanced Latino therapists. This sharing allows the more pragmatic aspects of the supervision to resolve quickly and problems to dissolve without much discussion as new possibilities emerge in the sharing of stories embedded in the process of discussing complex problems. This sharing highlights the importance of listening, listening to their stories, to your stories, and realizing their interconnectedness. Thus, the relevance of silence as an important part of the therapeutic tool box.

Listening to the client after exploring an idea is harder for less experienced clinicians who may desire observable results despite the complexity of clients' stories and the linkage to larger systems. Sometimes they expect results from a particular question as suggested by the team or the supervisor. Similarly, supervisees may sometimes insist too much on the supervisor's idea, losing track of the clients' needs. Supervisors can encourage supervisees to ignore a supervisor's directive if a client seems to reject it. More experienced clinicians may be willing to experiment with a more intensive use of the self rather than a particular technique. When working with clinicians with diverse experiences in training contexts, trying new ways of using the self requires protecting supervisees from destructive interactions emerging from team members. In agency contexts, safety precautions should be taken to protect Latino supervisees from destructive forms of marginalization when they try new ways of connecting and listening to clients. For instance, clinicians' ability to disclose without fear their stream of thoughts to clients may require more experience in trusting a reflexive stance. It may also mean acknowledging how "wrong" we could be at different moments.

CONCLUSIONS

My supervisory role provides me with a surprising amount of influence on the work of clinical practitioners. Besides listening attentively, supporting, and validating, I am always confronting and deconstructing. How can I use this influence that is inherent to the supervisory relationship and combine it with the creation of a dialogical interaction? Through focused and tentative questions that test the limits of any taken-for-granted assumption in the clinical context, supervisees' knowledge is shaped, mobilized, and given credit within a frame that is respectful of the clients' needs. In a collaborative postmodern framework, ideas about social justice and care are to be dialectically incorporated. Incorporating justice and care is needed to prevent us from embracing a skeptical postmodern posture that abandons the potential for making clients and supervisees the participants of knowledge creation through committed conversations.

In this chapter, I have outlined a series of experiences and concepts that were helpful in the work with Latino therapists. I have used a collaborative-reflexive approach that distances itself from attempts at defining the identity of Latino supervisees or Latino families as fixed and monolithic. Several family therapy ideas can serve the purpose of deconstructing a monolithic view and aid in embracing a complex and evolving one if supervision becomes a more exploratory, curious, and collaborative enterprise. Latino supervisees and their clients are in a continuously evolving process of self-definition. Supervision is an opportunity to help shape clients' and practitioners' Latino identities through professional and personal self-definition. Structuring the lives of Latinos without engaging them in dialogue will help only to continue their colonization and to inhibit self-determination as individuals, families, and communities.

REFERENCES

Agar, M. H. (1986). *Speaking of ethnography.* Beverly Hills, CA: Sage.

American Association of Marital and Family Therapy. (1997). *Approved supervisor designation.* Washington, DC: Author.

Andersen, T. (1992). Relationship, language and pre-understanding in the reflecting processes. *Australian & New Zealand Journal of Family Therapy, 13,* 87–91.

Anderson, H. (1997). *Conversation, language, and possibilities: A postmodern approach to therapy.* New York: Basic Books.

Anderson, H., & Goolishian, H. A. (1988). Human system as linguistic systems: Preliminary and evolving ideas about the implications. *Family Process, 27,* 371–393.

Anderson, H., & Swim, S. (1995). Supervision as collaborative conversation: Connecting the voices of supervisor and supervisee. *Journal of Systemic Therapies, 14*(2), 1–13.

Bacigalupe, G. (1996). Writing in therapy: A participatory approach. *Journal of Family Therapy, 18*(4), 361–375.

Bacigalupe, G. (1998). Cross-cultural systemic therapy training and consultation: A postcolonial view. *Journal of Systemic Therapies, 17*(1), 31–44.

Biever, J. L., & Gardner, G. T. (1995). The use of the reflecting team in social constructionist training. *Journal of Systemic Therapies, 14*(3), 14–25.

Boszormenyi-Nagy, I. (1987). *Foundations of contextual therapy.* New York: Brunner/Mazel.

Bushe, G. R. (1995). Advances in appreciative inquiry as an organization development intervention. *Organization Development Journal* (Fall), *13*(3), 14–22.

Clifford, J., & Marcus, G. E. (Eds.). (1986). *Writing culture: The poetics and politics of ethnography.* Berkeley: University of California Press.

Colapinto, J. (1988). Teaching the structural way. In H. A. Liddle, D. C. Breunlin, & R. C. Schwartz (Eds.), *Handbook of family therapy training and supervision* (pp. 17–37). New York: Guilford Press.

Dyche, L., & Zayas, L. H. (1995). The value of curiosity and naivete for the cross-cultural psychotherapist. *Family Process, 34*(4), 389–399.

Echeverria, R. (1994). *La ontologia del lenguaje [Ontology of language].* Santiago, Chile: Dolmen Ediciones.

Erickson, G. (1988). Against the grain: Decentering family therapy. *Journal of Marital and Family Therapy, 14*(3), 225–236.

Fine, M., & Turner, J. (1997). Collaborative supervision: Minding the power. In T. C. Todd & C. L. Storm (Eds.), *The complete systemic supervisor: Context, philosophy, and pragmatics* (pp. 1–16). Boston: Allyn & Bacon.

Flemons, D., Green, S., & Rambo, A. (1996). Evaluating therapists' practices in a postmodern world: A discussion and a scheme. *Family Process, 35,* 43–56.

Freedman, J., & Combs, G. (1996). *Narrative therapy: The social construction of preferred realities.* New York: Norton.

Gale, J., & Newfield, N. (1992). A conversation analysis of a solution-focused marital therapy session. *Journal of Marital and Family Therapy, 18,* 153–165.

Gardner, G., Bobele, M., & Biever, J. L. (1997). Postmodern models of family therapy supervision. In T. C. Todd & C. L. Storm (Eds.), *The complete systemic supervisor: Context, philosophy, and pragmatics* (pp. 217–228). Boston: Allyn & Bacon.

Golann, D. (1988). On second-order family therapy. *Family Process, 27,* 51–64.

Gonzalez, R. C. (1996). Postmodern supervision: A multicultural perspective. In D. B. Pope-Davis & H. L. K. Coleman (Eds.), *Multicultural counseling competencies* (pp. 350–386). Thousand Oaks, CA: Sage.

Gurman, A. S., & Kniskern, D. P. (Eds.). (1991). *The handbook of family therapy* (Vol. II). New York: Brunner/Mazel.

Hammond, S. A. (1996). *The thin book of appreciative inquiry.* Plano, TX: CSS Publishing.

Hardy, K. V., & Laszloffy, T. A. (1995). The cultural genogram: Key to training culturally competent family therapists. *Journal of Marital and Family Therapy, 21*(3), 227–237.

Hoffman, L. (1993). *Exchanging voices: A collaborative approach to family therapy.* London: Karnac Books.

Hoffman, L. (1998). Setting aside the model in family therapy. *Journal of Marital and Family Therapy, 24*(3), 145–156.

Imber-Black, E. (1988). *Families and larger systems: A family therapist's guide through the labyrinth.* New York: Guilford Press.

Kelly, G. (1990). The cultural family of origin: A description of a training strategy. *Counselor Education and Supervision, 30,* 77–84.

Lal, J. (1996). Situating locations: The politics of self, identity, and "other" in living and writing the text. In D. L. Wolf (Ed.), *Feminist dilemmas in fieldwork* (pp. 185–214). Boulder, CO: Westview Press.

Lather, P. (1991). *Getting smart: Feminist research and pedagogy with/in the postmodern.* New York: Routledge.

McGoldrick, M., & Gerson, R. (1985). *Genograms in family assessment.* New York: Norton.

McGoldrick, M., Giordano, J., & Pearce, J. K. (Eds.). (1996). *Ethnicity & family therapy* (2nd ed.). New York: Guilford Press.

McLean, A. (1986). Family therapy workshops in the United States: Potential abuses in the production of therapy in an advanced capitalist society. *Social Science Medicine, 23,* 179–189.

Mignolo, W. D. (1995). *The darker side of the Renaissance: Literacy, territoriality, and colonization.* Ann Arbor: University of Michigan Press.

Minuchin, S. (1978). *Families and family therapy.* Cambridge, MA: Harvard University Press.

Montalbo, B., & Storm, C. L. (1997). Live supervision revolutionizes the supervision process. In T. C. Todd & C. L. Storm (Eds.), *The complete systemic supervisor: Context, philosophy, and pragmatics* (pp. 283–297). Boston: Allyn & Bacon.

Piercy, F. P., & Sprenkle, D. H. (1986). Supervision and training. In F. P. Piercy, D. Sprenkle, & Associates (Eds.), *Family therapy sourcebook* (pp. 288–321). New York: Guilford Press.

Piercy, F., & Thomas, V. (1998). Participatory evaluation research: An introduction for family therapists. *Journal of Marital and Family Therapy, 24*(2), 165–176.

Pirrotta, S., & Cecchin, G. (1988). The Milan training program. In H. A. Liddle, D. C. Breunlin, & R. C. Schwartz (Eds.), *Handbook of family therapy training and supervision* (pp. 38–61). New York: Guilford Press.

Prest, L. A., Darden, E. C., & Keller, J. (1990). "The fly on the wall" reflecting team supervision. *Journal of Marital and Family Therapy, 16,* 265–273.

Reynolds, J. F., Mair, D. C., & Fisher, P. C. (1992). *Writing and reading mental health records.* Newbury Park, CA: Sage.

Roberto, L. G. (1997). Supervision: The transgenerational models. In T. C. Todd & C. L. Storm (Eds.), *The complete systemic supervisor: Context, philosophy, and pragmatics* (pp. 156–172). Boston: Allyn & Bacon.

Roberts, J. (1994). *Tales and transformations: Stories in families and family therapy.* New York: Norton.

Sand-Pringle, C., Zarski, J. J., & Wendling, K. E. (1995). Swords into plowshares: Supervisory issues with violent families. *Journal of Systemic Therapies, 14*(3), 34–46.

Schon, D. (1983). *The reflective practitioner: How professionals think in action.* New York: Basic Books.

Schwartz, R. C., Liddle, H. A., & Breunlin, D. C. (1988). Muddles in live supervision. In H. A. Liddle, D. C. Breunlin, & R. C. Schwartz (Eds.), *The handbook of family therapy training and supervision* (pp. 183–193). New York: Guilford Press.

Shotter, J. (In press). The social construction of our "inner" lives. *Journal of Constructivist Psychology.*

Stewart, K., & Amudson, J. (1995). The ethical postmodernist: Or not everything is relative all at once. *Journal of Systemic Therapies, 14*(2), 70–78.

Storm, C. L., & Haug, I. E. (1997). Ethical issues: Where do you draw the line? In T. C. Todd & C. L. Storm (Eds.), *The complete systemic supervisor: Context, philosophy, and pragmatics* (pp. 26–40). Boston: Allyn & Bacon.

Todd, T. C. (1997a). Privately contracted supervision. In T. C. Todd & C. L. Storm (Eds.), *The complete systemic supervisor: Context, philosophy, and pragmatics* (pp. 125–134). Boston: Allyn & Bacon.

Todd, T. C. (1997b). Purposive systemic supervision models. In T. C. Todd & C. L. Storm (Eds.), *The complete systemic supervisor: Context, philosophy, and pragmatics* (pp. 173–194). Boston: Allyn & Bacon.

Tomm, K. (1988). Interventive interviewing: Part III. Intending to ask lineal, circular, strategic or reflexive questions? *Family Process, 27*, 1–15.

Weingarten, K. (1998). The small and the ordinary: The daily practice of a postmodern narrative therapy. *Family Process, 37*, 3–15.

White, M. (1997). *Narratives of therapists' lives*. Adelaide, South Australia: Dulwich Centre Publications.

White, M., & Epston, D. (1990). *Narrative means to therapeutic ends*. New York: Norton.

Wynne, L., McDaniel, S., & Weber, T. (1989). Professional politics and the concepts of family therapy, family consultation, and systems consultation. *Family Process, 26*, 153–166.

6

GROUP PSYCHOTHERAPY: ADOLESCENT LATINOS

CYNTHIA DE LAS FUENTES

> *"Alien!" they shout, and I turn around to see.*
> *Lights blinking at the Migra stop—again.*
> *"Mom," I ask, "Why do they like our food and clothes,*
> *Our land and crafts, but not me?"*
> *Between the Taco Bell and the Cabrito stand,*
> *I am sure I'll find an answer. . . .*
> *What good is an education if there are no jobs?*
> *Another eight hundred dollars cash, a raft trip,*
> *The Coyote can get you there.*
> *—MARIA T. FLORES, VOICES*

Unlike my parents, who were born and raised one and a half blocks away from each other in Laredo, Texas, I was raised in the United States Navy. My father was an officer and our family traveled far and wide. I attended almost a dozen schools in different countries, commonwealths, and continents before returning to the United States to pursue an undergraduate education. During my own adolescence, I lived in Puerto Rico, New Orleans, Louisiana, and Spain. I experienced the challenges of immigration, acculturation and adaptation, racism and discrimination, the loss of nearby extended family, and the discontinuity of friendships during these formative years. My experiences are not unique. From this vantage point, I, therefore, write this chapter for adolescent immigrants and the mental health professionals who can help them uncover sources of strength and resilience to weather life and thrive in *el Norte*.

THE IMMIGRATION EXPERIENCE

Latinos, people whose ethnic heritages have origins in Mexico, Puerto Rico, Cuba, the Caribbean, Central America, and South America, are one of the fastest growing ethnic groups in the United States today. The rate of legal immigration doubled from about 250,000 annually during the mid-half of this century to around 500,000 annually in recent decades (U.S. Immigration and Naturalization Service, 1991). Twenty-five percent of all immigrants and two-thirds of all Latino immigrants arriving since 1970 are Mexican (Rumbaut, 1994). Although Census Bureau estimates indicate there are currently over 22 million Latinos living in the United States, this figure does not reflect the population of undocumented immigrants who have come into this country looking for work and to be reunited with family. Ten million Latinos in the United States are below the age of 18, and most are under age 30. They tend to have large families, thus accounting for the fact that this ethnic population is one of the fastest growing in the United States.

The following sections provide a context for the immigration experiences many adolescents and their families face. This contextualization of the immigration experience is of utmost importance to the provider of psychological and family services in understanding the effects of the historical and sociopolitical nature of immigration on Latino adolescents. It is important to remember, for example, that most immigrants do not come to the United States seeking the American dream. Many are fleeing war, torture, poverty, and political persecution whereas others are seeking economic respite or reunion with their families (de las Fuentes & Vasquez, in press). Regardless of the motivation for immigration, these families must leave behind their home, country, language, culture, and family. For the adolescent immigrant, who may not have had equal decision-making power regarding immigration, this transition is often very difficult.

Impact of Immigration on Families

To understand the psychological sequelae of immigration on adolescents, it helps to know the experiences of the family who immigrates. Even when the goal of immigration is a positive one, such as family reunification, immigration still involves major changes in the physical, cultural, and social contexts within which families have learned to function (Strier, 1996). The process of immigration engenders a variety of feelings, including loss of shared experiences with former peers, alienation from new peers, stress, exhaustion, and confusion from trying to understand and cope with cultural differences, and a sense of inadequacy resulting from an inability to function as effectively in the new culture as one did in the home culture (Espin, 1997).

For adolescents, the adjustment presents particular challenges since they are in the process of developing their identities (Espin, 1997). Because adolescent identities are not yet determined, it may be easier to adjust to the new way of life. However, the relative speed of their acculturation may also create stress and conflict with parents, who may not transition as quickly, or who may resist challenges to their values.

Motives for Immigration

The reasons for immigration are as varied as the families themselves. Some come to the United States seeking hopeful futures such as career advancement and family reunification, whereas others are fleeing their countries due to war, torture, and poverty. To illustrate, career advancement appears to be a motivating factor for those immigrating from South America as many South American immigrants are in professions such as medicine, engineering, and science, and others are students seeking professional degrees in American universities. Such is not the case for many other Latino immigrants. Political persecution was a grave problem in the Americas in the 1970s and 1980s, and half of the victims of war in Guatemala and El Salvador during the early 1980s were children, thousands of whom immigrated with their families to North America during the 1980s (Ronstrom, 1989).

The motivation for immigration is an important indicator of adjustment and coping to a new culture (Strier, 1996). For example, if the reasons for immigration were positive, that is, a desire to improve one's socioeconomic situation, to advance a career, or to reunite with family, then immigrants tend to have optimistic outlooks and be more flexible in their adaptation to the new culture. On the other hand, if reasons for immigration were negative, that is, immigration was forced in order to escape from physical danger or political oppression, then outlooks may start out more distressed, and families will tend to strengthen their values and traditions from further threats to the integrity of family functioning (Strier, 1996). As mentioned before, however, these efforts to preserve the family can create stress between adolescents and their parents due to differing rates of acculturation and resulting emerging identities.

THE EXPERIENCE OF ACCULTURATION

Acculturation is the process whereby the attitudes and behaviors of individuals from one culture are modified as a result of contact with a different culture; as such, there is no singular acculturation process among children and adolescents (Kopala, Esquivel, & Baptiste, 1994). However, certain factors, such as age, language fluency, education, previous contact with the new culture (Chiswick, 1977), family structure, cultural similarity (Hirschman, 1982), and the motivation for immigration, influence acculturation. For example, older adolescents or those who have had lengthy separations from their parents tend to have a more difficult time adjusting to their new lives (Bagley, 1972).

Identity Development

One of the most important and challenging tasks for Latino adolescents is the development of a positive ethnic identity (de las Fuentes & Vasquez, in press). The ability to do so is an indication of well-being. A positive ethnic identity can give a person a sense of belonging in a community that has a past, present, and future. This is a basic psychological need (McGoldrick & Giodano, 1996). Events experienced during adolescence, such as immigration, thus have enormous power in shaping identity.

Since gender, ethnic, and racial factors are core to one's identity, racism, sexism, discrimination, and oppression, both in U.S. society as well as in the culture of origin, can complicate identity development in adolescents. Inclusion and exclusion issues are major challenges for adolescents and can be particularly poignant challenges for immigrant adolescents who risk rejection by virtue of being different (de las Fuentes & Vasquez, in press). The pernicious cost of racism and discrimination is evident in that having been discriminated against results in significantly elevated depressive symptoms, and the anticipation of discrimination is significantly associated with both increased depression and decreased self-esteem (Rumbaut, 1994).

Acculturative Stress

Among immigrants, acculturative stress is considered to be a significant factor contributing to complications in adjustment and other psychosocial problems, including disordered eating patterns (DiNicola, 1990; Mumford, Whitehouse, & Platts, 1991), lower self-esteem and higher depression (Rumbaut, 1994), and parent-child conflicts (Rumbaut, 1994; Sue, 1981; Wakil, Siddique, & Wakil, 1981; Yau & Smetana, 1993).

Rumbaut (1994), in a broad multiethnic study, found that the strongest predictor associated with lower self-esteem and higher depression in second-generation adolescents was parent-child conflict, disproportionately affecting adolescent females. He also found that other significant correlates to increased depression, decreased self-esteem, and increased parent-child conflict included the adolescent's perception that their immigrant family's economic situation compared to five years before had worsened; paternal unemployment and low education; the absence of the father from the home; the absence of a significant person to help the adolescent with school work; and the adolescent's feeling of being embarrassed by his or her parents (Rumbaut, 1994). Conflict with parents significantly increased when the adolescent preferred to speak in English, had a poor command of the parental native language, spent a greater number of hours watching television, spent fewer hours on homework, attained a lower academic grade point average, and maintained lower educational aspirations (Rumbaut, 1994).

Traditional Values at Risk:
Gendered Expectations

As Latino families acculturate the dominant U.S. culture, issues be-tween first-generation adolescents, especially girls, and their parents emerge. One of these issues is the loss of the preeminence of the pa-triarchal hierarchy because children tend to learn the English lan-guage at a faster rate and often become the family's "culture brokers; parents become dependent on their children to negotiate with the outside world" (Hernandez, 1996). This experience can serve as a threat to parents' traditional authority.

Acculturating daughters presents the greatest dilemma as they challenge their parents' values and restrictions on their behaviors while they attempt to develop new identities in accordance with their new American peer group (de las Fuentes & Vasquez, in press). This is especially difficult for Latino parents because of the beliefs they hold for proper and appropriate behaviors for girls (de las Fuentes & Vasquez, in press). The fact that daughters of immigrant parents are more likely than sons to participate in parent-child conflict illustrates a contrast between traditional parental attitudes about sex roles and dating and the adolescent girl's developing identity in the American culture.

Education

Fortunately, investigations are emerging that demonstrate strengths and resiliencies among immigrants in their adaptation to the United States. For example, children of immigrants perform better and have lower dropout rates in public schools than American-born students; they learn English quickly, and their grades are higher than their American peers' grades (Rumbaut, as cited in the Associated Press, *Los Angeles Times*, June 16, 1997).

Fluency in the English language and educational success are sig-nificantly and positively related to self-esteem and psychological well-being. Specifically, the better the English fluency and the higher the academic grade point average, the higher the self-esteem and the lower the depression score (Rumbaut, 1994).

Unfortunately, Rumbaut (as cited in the Associated Press, *Los Angeles Times*, June 16, 1997) also found marked dissimilarity in career goals among various ethnic groups. Only 24% of Mexicans said they would like to earn an advanced degree, compared to 52% of non-Mexican Hispanics. He also suggested that American culture may erode the work ethic of immigrant children because the longer they lived in the United States, the less time they spent on homework.

STRENGTHS AND RESILIENCE IN FAMILY AND COMMUNITY

Challenging the assumption that differences and struggles result in long-standing maladjustment of the immigrant child and family, research is beginning to identify strategies that families develop to cope with the challenges of immigration (Strier, 1996). Although the development of resilience is influenced by various factors, children's resilience is greater when they have access to at least one caring parent or another supportive adult in their extended family or in their social world (Walsh, 1996). The relatively new focus on resiliency and healthy adaptation in the study and treatment of immigrant families proposes that although the individual and family are stressed by immigration, a systemic view helps assess the strengths and resources of the family as well as the environment, resulting in an appreciation of "hardiness" for weathering the challenge of acculturation (Hawley & DeHann, 1996; Strier, 1996; Walsh, 1996).

The most resilient factor common to all Latinos is the identification with family and community. Latino families provide strength and resources for adolescents struggling with the challenges of uncertainties, conflicting expectations, and rejection based on skin color, language, and social economic class. In fact, parent-child conflict is significantly reduced in families in which parents and siblings are relied on as main sources of support (Rumbaut, 1994).

Large extended families have also been a source of strength and resilience for Latinos, and close friends are often considered part of this extended family network (Ginorio, Gutierrez, Cauce, & Acosta, 1995). Those families able to convey warmth, affection, emotional support, and reasonable structure and limits serve an important protective factor for resiliency in adolescents (de las Fuentes & Vasquez, in press). Relationships with older siblings, grandparents, and extended family, as well as friends, neighbors, teachers, coaches, clergy, and mentors, can provide that support (Walsh, 1996).

In summary, the family is the basis of identification and a source of strength for Latino adolescents. A strong, persistent, familistic, and community orientation is a source of resiliency for adolescents and may provide "inoculation" against the pain of marginality in the new culture (de las Fuentes & Vasquez, in press).

Extending Family and Community: Group Psychotherapy

For the purposes of this chapter, I will assume that the group psychotherapy practitioner most likely to work with immigrant Latino adolescents will also be working in the school setting. Groups in schools are primarily designed to deal with students' educational, vocational, personal, and social concerns, and, as such, the immigrant Latino adolescent may be considered a good candidate for this type of intervention.

Group counseling has preventive as well as remedial goals and tends to be growth-oriented, focusing on discovering resources and strengths (Corey, 1995). The group provides empathy and support, through which an atmosphere of trust facilitates sharing and exploration. The role of the group facilitator is to foster interaction among the members, help them learn from one another, assist them in establishing goals, and encourage them to translate their group learning experiences to their outside communities (Corey, 1995). One factor making group counseling particularly valuable to immigrant Latino adolescents is universality. In a group, these young people learn that they are not alone in their struggles, whether they are in a mixed group with mainstream adolescents struggling with independence and interdependence, or whether they are in a group with other immigrants struggling with acculturation, discrimination, and loss.

In general, group counseling is especially suited for immigrant Latino adolescents because it gives them a place to express frustrations and explore conflicting values, an opportunity that may not be afforded at home. In the group, these adolescents can learn to communicate and develop friendships with their peers. Another value of group counseling for adolescents is that it gives them the opportunity to assist in the growth and development of their peers.

Group psychotherapy with immigrant Latino adolescents must consider the complex contextualism for understanding the effects of culture, ethnicity, race, gender, and class as these factors represent critical influences on socialization and identity development. Group therapists should be sensitive to the challenges and risks of immigration and be able to identify the varieties of healthy adaptation strategies that these adolescents and their families develop while they cope with acculturation and adjustment to the United States. The values of Latinos emphasize the cultural context. Their communitarianist world view stresses interdependence over independency, affiliation over confrontation, and cooperation over competition, values that facilitate the development of group cohesion and strength.

The group facilitator should also be familiar with issues and skills that include identifying the strengths of the family and facilitating strategies for dealing with potential discord as adolescents acculturate the mainstream culture; developing healthy multiple, or bicultural, identities; focusing on prevention efforts, healthy choices regarding sexuality, using contraceptives, and practicing safer sex; and career development.

Case Study: The Immigrants

Eight young people were sitting around chatting, glad to be out of class. Each student was referred to group therapy for assistance in adjusting to school, classmates, or the curriculum. A few were considered "troublemakers." All were immigrant youths, three girls and six boys. We had other groups that were mixed immigrants and U.S. citizens, and some that were composed of all U.S. citizens.

The school population was approximately 90% inner-city Hispanics. Group dynamic exercises were introduced with the specific purpose of creating a safe environment in which they learned to talk and listen to each other discussing topics of interest. Prearranged topics ranged from what could make school more interesting, to favorite sports and books, to conflict skills and self-esteem. Family and personal matters were introduced slowly. Personal matters and cultural issues took on a more lively discussion than other topics.

Tomas was the most vocal and seemed to have the group's respect. He was slender and wore baggy pants. Later he shared with the group that he wore baggy pants because they were hand-me-downs from his older brothers. He was surprised that baggy pants were popular because if he had a choice, he would wear something else. Tomas had been identified as a possible gang member because of his attire. Tomas had golden brown skin and a mischievous twinkle in his eyes when he smiled. He was from Mexico and could switch languages with ease. He would make jokes using both languages to create a relaxed atmosphere. All would laugh and begin sharing in both English and Spanish. A level of trust and interchange took about two months to establish in this group and Tomas helped it happen.

Juan and Carlos seemed to agree with everything Tomas did and said. For these two boys, being connected to Tomas changed their entire attitude, for they now belonged. Jimmy and Jesse had their independent ways. Jesse was the only one in the group that had been in trouble with the police: He had been caught stealing cars for joy rides. Jimmy was rebellious. He did not like school or the teachers or the facilitator of the group very much. He was often sullen. Jimmy was smart and witty, but often in a cruel way. He and Tomas became good friends after they fought over Jimmy's constant "put-downs" of anyone he considered weaker than himself. Jimmy broke down one day and admitted his "put-downs" were simply a means of defending himself from the fear of others attacking him. Of all the adolescents in the group, Jimmy changed and grew the most. He became a very kind person.

Gloria was a quiet adolescent who spoke little English. She had big brown eyes with long, straight, black hair that hung to her shoulders. The group became for her a place where she could belong and a place where she could express her ideas. She was skilled in language without lessons. The group had no trouble translating for her. There was never an appointed translator. All basically took turns though Jimmy and Maria were the best at translating. At other times, Spanish was used throughout the session. Maria and Ana were more interested in the boys than on working on issues. With time, however, they both became vocal and active in expressing their opinions and thoughts. Ana had a very serious home situation that needed family intervention that was acted on by the therapist.

The issue concerning culture was constantly in play. Cultural topics were formally introduced by the group facilitator. Identity formation was addressed: How could they fit into the neighborhood, the school, or their new country? What did they like or dislike about the United States? What did they miss about their former country?

One of the toughest issues addressed was Maria's shame over her parents being treated so poorly by school officials and neighbors.

Maria was ashamed when she had to translate for her parents. Her relationship with Gloria helped her to resolve her language dilemma and shame with her parents. Gloria suggested it was not shame at her parents' inability to speak English, but her reaction to ignorant people who did not show her parents proper dignity or respect. Maria reclaimed Spanish for the beautiful language it is and felt reconnected to her parents. Others shared their experiences over the shame issue and reclaimed their own dignity as well (M. T. Flores, personal communication, 1998).

CONCLUSIONS

This chapter focused on key parameters for understanding the unique experiences for the identity development of the immigrant adolescent Latino: the challenges due to economic stresses, acculturative challenges to traditions, consequences for parent-child relationships, educational challenges, and challenges to ethnic identity. I have striven to identify sources of strength for immigrant Latino adolescents, including the values related to identities based on family. As group facilitators, we must remember that no single coping response is invariably most successful. At each developmental stage, the abilities of any individual or family will shift to manage stressful changes. At times, more vulnerable responses may be expressed while, at other times, these responses may enhance resilience. Nevertheless, a basic assumption is that cultural practices associated with community and family bonding generally serve as protection and "innoculation" to some of the insidious effects of discrimination and prejudice. At other times, however, parental and extended family expectations may clash with those of the acculturating adolescent and may introduce other sources of stress and challenge. The group psychotherapist must remain sensitive to these changes and adaptations.

REFERENCES

Bagley, C. (1972). Deviant behavior in English and West Indian school children. *Research in Education, 8,* 47–55.
Chiswick, B. (1977). Sons of immigrants: Are they at an earnings disadvantage? *American Economic Review, Papers and Proceedings, 67,* 376–380.

Corey, G. (1995). *Theory and practice of group counseling* (4th ed.). Pacific Grove, CA: Brooks/Cole.

De las Fuentes, C., & Vasquez, M. J. T. (In press). Immigrant adolescent girls of color: Challenges and resiliences. In N. G. Johnson, M. Roberts, & J. Whorell (Eds.), *Adolescent girls: Strengths and stresses.* Washington, DC: American Psychological Association.

DiNicola, V. F. (1990). Anorexia multiforme: Self-starvation in historical and cultural context. Part II: Anorexia nervosa as a culture-reactive syndrome. *Transcultural Psychiatric Research Review, 27,* 245–286.

Espin, O. M. (1997). Crossing borders and boundaries: The life narratives of immigrant lesbians. In B. Greene (Ed.), *Ethnic and cultural diversity among lesbians and gay men* (pp. 191–215). Thousand Oaks, CA: Sage.

Ginorio, A. G., Gutierrez, L., Cauce, A. M., & Acosta, M. (1995). Psychological issues for Latinas. In H. Landrine (Ed.), *Bringing cultural diversity to feminist psychology: Theory, research and practice* (pp. 241–264). Washington, DC: American Psychological Association.

Hawley, D. R., & DeHaan, L. (1996). Toward a definition of family resilience: Integrating life span and family perspectives. *Family Process, 35,* 283–298.

Hernandez, M. (1996). Central American families. In M. McGoldrick, J. Giordano, & J. K. Pearce (Eds.), *Ethnicity and family therapy* (2nd ed., pp. 214–224). New York: Guilford Press.

Hirschman, C. (1982). Immigrants and minorities: Old questions for new directions in research. *International Migration Review, 16,* 474–490.

Kopala, M., Esquivel, G., & Baptiste, L. (1994). Counseling approaches for immigrant children: Facilitating the acculturative process. *The School Counselor, 41,* 352–359.

McGoldrick, M., & Giordano, J. (1996). Overview: Ethnicity and family therapy. In M. McGoldrick, J. Giordano, & J. K. Pearce (Eds.), *Ethnicity and family therapy* (2nd ed., pp. 1–30). New York: Guilford Press.

Mumford, D. B., Whitehouse, A., & Platts, M. (1991). Sociocultural correlates of eating disorders among Asian schoolgirls in Bradford. *British Journal of Psychiatry, 158,* 222–228.

Neruda, P. (1986). *100 love sonnets: Cien sonetos de amor* (S. Tapscott, Trans.). Austin: University of Texas Press. (Original work published 1959.)

Ronstrom, A. (1989). Children in Central America: Victims of war. *Child Welfare, 68,* 145–153.

Rumbaut, R. G. (1994). The crucible within: Ethnic identity, self-esteem, and segmented assimilation among children of immigrants. *International Migration Review, 28*(4), 748–794.

Stewart, A. J., & Healy, J. M. (1989). Linking individual development and social changes. *American Psychologist, 44,* 30–42.

Strier, D. R. (1996). Coping strategies of immigrant parents: Directions for family therapy. *Family Process, 35,* 363–376.

Sue, D. W. (1981). *Counseling the culturally different: Theory and practice.* New York: Wiley.

U.S. Immigration and Naturalization Service. (1991). *Statistical yearbook of the Immigration and Naturalization Service, 1990.* Washington, DC: U.S. Government Printing Office.

Wakil, S. P., Siddique, C. M., & Wakil, F. A. (1981). Between two cultures: A study in socialization of children of immigrants. *Journal of Marriage and the Family, 43,* 929–940.

Walsh, F. (1996). The concept of family resilience: Crisis and challenge. *Family Process, 35,* 261–281.

Wong-Reiger, D., & Quintana, D. (1987). Comparative acculturation of Southeast Asian and Hispanic immigrants and sojourners. *Journal of Cross-Cultural Psychology, 18,* 455–462.

Wu, E. P. (1997, June 16). School success of immigrants' children tracked. *Los Angeles Times,* p. A1.

Yau, J., & Smetana, J. G. (1993). Chinese-American adolescents' reasoning about cultural conflicts. *Journal of Adolescent Research, 8,* 419–438.

PART III

CLINICAL ISSUES:
HEALING RELATIONS

7

THE HISPANIC COUPLE IN THERAPY

THELMA H. DUFFEY

The quest for marital intimacy and satisfaction by couples is well documented in the research literature. According to Timmerman (1991), the search for marital intimacy is the leading reason reported by individuals for seeking psychotherapy. Contemporary couples attend marriage-enrichment seminars, seek counseling services, and invest in a plethora of books in an attempt to deepen and enrich their marriages. Indeed, an increasing number of couples desire and expect marriages of depth and substance, intimacy and friendship. Yet, the very real task of maintaining depth, generating intimacy, and enjoying friendship with a person who has needs, desires, thoughts, and feelings separate from our own is a challenge at best.

As a psychotherapist in private practice and professor of counseling, I have had many opportunities to work with couples as they develop their relationships and deepen their attachments to one another. For as far back as I can remember, maintaining relationships has been a primary value of mine. As a little girl, I experienced the comfort, safety, pride, and at times confusion in my own family's expressions of love for one another. It was through their example that I learned of the joy, loss, forgiveness, and ultimate reconciliation that is inherent in any truly intimate relationship. I believe that relationships provide a context in which we increase our levels of awareness, sensitivity, and strength. It is in the love we receive from those who matter most to us that we learn to truly appreciate ourselves; and it is in our losses in love that we are invited to learn the true meaning of self-acceptance. I have learned, as a member of my closely bonded, traditionally Hispanic family, the value and the challenge of relating authentically, lovingly, and intimately. And it is this process of developing intimate and long-lasting relationships between couples that I will address in this chapter.

INTIMACY DEFINED

The word "intimacy" is conceptually defined as a quality of a relationship characterized by emotional closeness, trust, self-disclosure, and reciprocity (Timmerman, 1991). Erikson (1963) first conceptualized intimacy as a positive consequence of a developmental crisis, referring to a person's capacity to commit oneself to close relationship with another. Markus and Wurf (1987) further established that we gain self-awareness, self-acceptance, and crystallize our identities through our intimate relationships. Miller and Stiver (1994) further report that we develop as human beings within the mutuality expressed in our growth-enhancing relationships.

Given that a person must be in a relationship with another to experience intimate behaviors, intimacy is conceptualized as a quality of a relationship rather than as an individual characteristic (Timmerman, 1991). Both partners must have a capacity for intimacy if it is to thrive within the relationship. Intimacy, then, may be distinguished from the quality of love, which need not be reciprocated to exist. In fact, couples in relationship are disillusioned when they feel love for their partners but find that their relationships have not grown or developed into comfortable, intimate connections.

Waring (1988) describes four basic aspects of a well-integrated intimate relationship. He states that "The behavioral aspect of intimacy is predictability; the emotional aspect is a feeling of closeness; the cognitive aspect is understanding through self-disclosure, and the attitudinal aspect is commitment" (pp. 38–39). Couples seeking intimate connections must incorporate these aspects if intimacy is to be sustained.

Indeed, many couples enter into a relationship with hopes and expectations for sharing a fulfilling life. Although initial dreams are often realized, the high incidence of divorce suggests that some fundamental factors must be in place if couples are to become intimate and realize their mutually agreed-on long-term hopes and expectations. Among these factors are a high degree of clarity, commitment, education, and skill. Partners must be clear about their hopes, needs, and desires. Couples must also be committed to deepening their understanding of the hopes, needs, and desires of their partners. In effect, for intimacy to develop and be sustained, partners must be committed to becoming honest with themselves, to taking into account the world view of their partners, and to negotiating their positions as an expression of good will.

Societal Challenges and Intimate Connections

Maintaining intimacy and satisfaction in a marriage is, at best, a formidable task. Society's changing mores present special challenges to couples seeking to maintain their marriages. Along with the challenges faced by couples within a changing society, unique issues arise when one or both partners in the couple seeking therapy belong to a minority culture. In addition to understanding the needs of contemporary couples, the therapist must be aware of the basic values, beliefs, and mythologies held by the cultural group of each member of the couple. The therapeutic needs of the couple must be examined within the context of the dominant culture and the social cultures of their respective families of origin.

In this chapter, I will delineate some traditional values of the Latino culture, including Mexican, Cuban, and Puerto Rican Americans, as they relate to marital relationships. I will also include some corresponding values of the dominant Anglo culture, particularly the prevailing gender-related norms existing within the middle-class professional culture. Using a clinical case study, I will cite reported conflicts that may arise, while outlining processes for conceptualizing salient multicultural issues within a professional couple context.

It is important to note, when examining cultural values, Friedman's (1988) position that not all members within a cultural group hold the same opinions regarding the validity of the values and customs of their heritage. Nor do they all wish to be identified with the ethnic groups with which people would identify them (Jalali, 1982). Moreover, therapists must be familiar with the range within cultures and the dimensions of multiculturalism. Most cultures divide into subgroups of social and economic class structures. Therefore, in considering the cultural implications within a couples context, the therapist must consider the cultural heritage of each member of the couple, their respective socioeconomic status, levels of acculturation, and traditional versus contemporary attitudes. In this chapter, I address specific needs of middle-class professionals in which one or both partners have acculturated into the mainstream dominant culture.

The Relevance of Adlerian Concepts with Latino Couples

I use relevant constructs from the Adlerian Family Therapy model as a structure for exploring the relational needs of this multicultural population. Adlerian theory is a systems theory that examines the patterns of interactional relationships within the systems and among the systems. The context of the family, both historically and in interaction with its culture and community, is specifically addressed (Sherman & Dinkmeyer, 1987). A basic premise of Adlerian theory is that we are social beings who create a philosophy of life, vis-à-vis lifestyle, based on the meaning we prescribe to our personal experiences and our subjective perceptions of these experiences. Our interpretation of these experiences provides us with a framework for relating to others. We use our personal philosophies and world views as backdrops for establishing life goals. These goals, which are often unconscious, motivate our behaviors. Our behaviors, in turn, are designed to help us reach our two most driving needs as human beings: to enjoy a place of significance and a feeling of belonging within our social groups.

The Adlerian principles of examining the philosophies and world views of couples within a counseling context dovetail with Torrey's (1986) and Ibrahim and Schroeder's (1990) positions that a significant variable in establishing trust in cross-cultural relationships and communication is a shared world view. World view, in this context, refers to the values, mythologies, and basic assumptions that propitiate the communication, relational, and conflict resolution strategies inherent in any relationship.

CLINICAL IMPLICATIONS

Ibrahim and Schroeder (1990) postulate the use of psychoeducational interventions in couples counseling to enhance communication skills and increase multicultural awareness. Such awareness facilitates the expressions of closeness, reciprocity, self-disclosure, and trust, four key components of Timmerman's (1991) operational definition of marital intimacy. Couples wishing to increase levels of intimacy must identify the values inherent in their respective cultures that may be at odds with the cultural values of the other. The process of clarifying world views allows each person to gain awareness of the cultural precepts of the other, to understand how these conflicting values contribute to the dynamics of the relationship, and to accept each other as cultural beings (Ibrahim & Schroeder, 1990). Such acceptance facilitates closeness and sensitivity while setting the stage for negotiation and mutuality within the relationship.

Discovering Difference

Acceptance of differences is always a primary goal in couples therapy, as it is the only means by which partners can experience safety and closeness in a relationship. Couples may enjoy compatibility on many levels, only to find that they stand on uncommon ground on some values basic to their personal and cultural world views. When assessing the strengths and limitations of a couple seeking intimacy development, it is important that the therapist explore the personal and cultural positions and feelings of each partner in relation to the following dimensions:

- Gender roles and expectations
- Significance of spirituality in each partner
- Role of the extended family
- Expressions of intimacy
- Negotiation of boundaries
- Negotiation of power
- Role of authority figures
- Expression of affection and sexuality
- Parenting styles

Couples may experience problems or exhibit conflicts in one or more of these areas. A therapist sensitive to the distinct needs of each partner can facilitate a process of awareness and discovery, followed by negotiation and integration of values, leading to a newly formed couple-based culture. The process of discovery and conscious choice is often threatening to the partners. However, such an evolving structure can serve to strengthen the individual and couple identities without sacrificing larger cultural values. The following case reflects some common issues faced by professional multicultural couples attending marriage counseling. We will examine this case on three tiers: Western culture–bound implications for counseling, multicultural factors, and Adlerian-based conceptualizations for therapy.

THE CASE OF NICK AND SONIA

Nick and Sonia, married three years, presented for marriage counseling. Nick, 26, a chemical engineer of English and Irish descent, complains that Sonia, 26, an elementary school counselor of Mexican descent, does not spend enough time with him. According to Nick, both partners work hard at their respective jobs. They come home, prepare and share a meal together, quickly followed by Sonia's daily telephone conversations with her mother and sisters. Nick feels disregarded by his wife and impinged on by his in-laws. An introvert by nature, Nick values his privacy, and does not like family or friends to visit their home on weekends. He can accept Sonia's visits to her family home, but wants to protect his space from "an avalanche of relatives." Sonia resents the boundaries he sets, but begrudgingly told her family that they should not come over while Nick was home. She explained that he worked hard and was very tired from his exhausting workweek. She further explained that his own family was not welcomed either. Sonia is embarrassed by Nick's apparent "lack of hospitality" but wants to meet her husband's need for attention. She does not want to "hurt the feelings of her family by making them feel unwelcome" nor does she want to "humiliate them by allowing them to visit a home in which they are not wanted." Sonia reluctantly defers her wishes to Nick, yet resents him for controlling her. She feels caught in a double bind in the relationship, powerless on the one hand, and guilty for creating problems for both Nick and her family on the other. Nick feels frustrated and misunderstood. He does not experience a position of power within the relationship and feels controlled, particularly by Sonia's familial expectations. Both partners report increasing loneliness in the relationship, even though they continue to share common experiences such as enjoying dinner and a movie, visiting mutual friends, and attending church services. The couple reports a decrease in expressions of affection and sexuality.

Negotiating Dominant Discourse

On a dyadic level, this couple experiences issues of gender, power, and boundaries, conflicts commonly reflected in Western culture. Traditionally, men and women have been socialized to defer to men positions of power and authority within family units and in their communities. Current struggles for significance and belonging for both men and women reflect the consequences of this long-standing power differential. Nick and Sonia face the common task of negotiating these differences in their relationship.

Other gender-based relational aspects are also present. Women in Western culture seek and maintain relationships outside the marriage while men tend to focus their relational needs on their spouse (Gilligan, 1982; Gilligan, Rogers, & Tolman, 1991). Further, women have been socialized to please others in their relationships and derive a sense of worth from accommodating another's expectations (Gilligan, 1982). This problem is clearly illustrated in the case of Sonia and Nick. Finally, relational differences also require couples to negotiate boundaries of closeness and distance within the relationship and among members of the extended family. Sonia and Nick currently experience estrangement within the relationship and must negotiate these boundaries in the service of repairing their relationship and increasing marital intimacy and satisfaction.

Multicultural Gender Perspectives

In addition to addressing gender differences common to Western culture, gender values implicit in Sonia's culture are important considerations. For example, a basic value for women in Sonia's culture and immediate family network is the role of *marianismo*, depicted in the Roman Catholic representation of the Virgin Mary as selfless, giving, and self-sacrificing (Collier, 1986; Espin, 1992; Soto-Fulp & Del Campo, 1994; Stevens, 1973). Like their Western cultural counterparts, women in Hispanic cultures have traditionally assumed their place and position by providing nurturance and care for their husbands and children. However, the religious and ethnic components of *marianismo* are reflective of the assumptive Latino cultural value of gender hierarchies.

In addition, Sonia's acculturation into the mainstream culture and her position as an active member of her professional community further complicate her internal value struggle. The dichotomous role of contemporary woman and community leader on the one hand, and dutiful and subservient wife on the other, highlight significant gender and culturally based identity issues within her.

Sonia's acquiescence to Nick's demands seem to make sense to her, in light of her interpretation of her duties as a wife, but are also in direct conflict with her desires to be a competent woman with a voice of her own, whose needs and desires are of consequence to her mate (Gilligan, 1982). Sonia stated she "feels controlled" by Nick's restrictions and resents the position of power he seems to hold over her in the relationship. It is reminiscent of the position of powerlessness she recalls the women in her family to have held. At the same time, Sonia sincerely wants to please her husband, her family, and herself. Undifferentiated, these needs seemed to be irreconcilable.

In addition, another value intrinsic to Sonia's culture is the concept of *familismo* (Soto-Fulp & Del Campo, 1994). *Familismo* reflects the significant role assumed by extended family members in the lives of Hispanic families, and Nick's boundaries threaten this most basic of values. Indeed, Nick's reluctance to entertain Sonia's family threatens the *dignidad* (dignity) of her family and displays *una falta de respeto* (lack of respect), both gross violations of cultural norms.

Nick is not without his own conflicts. He aspires to the role of a loving, doting husband and is perplexed by Sonia's characterization of him as controlling and power yielding. He is further disheartened by his perception of being slighted by Sonia. Not without discomfort, Nick reports a desire to hold a place of significance in Sonia's life, one he believes is reserved for her family. Nick's family, which lives in remote areas of the country, has been disengaged throughout most of his life. Nick devalues the connection between Sonia and her family, referring to her as "dependent and childlike" in relation to them. And yet, there seems to be a wistful longing for such a familial connection within him.

An Adlerian Case Conceptualization

Using the Adlerian model in addressing cultural issues, a therapist is able to assess the world views of the couple, their misconceptions concerning the beliefs and resulting goals of each other, and the boundaries and behaviors that serve to perpetuate goals and philosophies of life. In the case of Nick and Sonia, Nick's cultural framework and interpretation of life experiences lead him to believe on an unconscious level that he must compete for love. Nick is unaware of his unconscious goal to be chosen in spite of his difficult demands. To be chosen under these circumstances would be evidence to him of his place of significance. Nick's behaviors, which include blaming, judging, and being a martyr, are symptomatic of his mistaken beliefs of being unworthy and unwanted. His unconscious goals, if left unexamined, could compel him to act in ways destructive to himself and his marriage. These destructive acts would ultimately threaten his feeling of significance and belonging, which would perpetuate his unfounded belief that he is unworthy, and ultimately unloved.

Sonia's interpretation of life experiences and her cultural background lead her to believe that she must make people happy if they are to approve of her. Her unconscious goal, then, is to be "good enough." Her behaviors, which include placating and pleasing, are symptomatic of her mistaken beliefs that she must be all things to all people. As this is not possible, her belief system consistently leads to disappointment for all concerned and threatens her basic need to be significant and to belong.

Sonia's striving for significance and belonging are further complicated by her minority status. Consistent with the research, the identity of minority individuals becomes an emotional issue when they experience discrimination or have conflicts with others over differences in communication and values (Atkinson, Morten, & Sue, 1989; Ishiyama & Westwood, 1992; Ruiz, 1990). During the course of treatment, Sonia reported such conflicts, citing examples of covert discrimination. Basic to Adlerian theory is the concept of overcoming inferiority, which is relevant in discussing issues of prejudice and racism. Since our search for significance is often characterized by a need to overcome feelings of inferiority, people choose varying means of reaching this goal. Unfortunately, for some, combatting insecure feelings by striving for superiority is initiated at the expense of another. Members of minority cultures are often scapegoats for such compensatory measures. Middle-class professionals bridging two cultural worlds may experience prejudicial treatment in unique ways.

Caught between Two Worlds

Nick and Sonia's case illustrates the subtle implications of being a successful contemporary couple in which one or both partners live in a dominant culture whose values are different from his or her own traditional Latino ties. Aspects of this case are reminiscent of the struggles of other cultural groups negotiating between two worlds. Coner-Edwards and Edwards (1988) report the identity confusion in the context of psychological consequences for African Americans who achieve middle-class status. Achieving African Americans who enjoy aspects of the dominant culture also experience conflictual guilt-laden feelings regarding family members who have not acculturated into the mainstream culture or reaped the benefits of Western culture–based successes (Coner-Edwards & Edwards, 1988). Sonia expressed such ambivalence in her therapy.

Other researchers describe this phenomenon. Hamburger's (1964/1990) concept of "psychic bends," or the transitional stage of moving from one cultural context to another, is one such example. Pinderhughes (1989) describes the concept of biculturality and the challenge of holding on to two worlds while maintaining one's cultural identity and heritage. Watkins and Rountree (1984) discuss the issues of first-generation African American professionals, who, in attempting to negotiate both the white corporate culture and their community, often form an "in-between class." Again, in treatment, Sonia described similar struggles of "in betweenness" as she illustrated her experiences and shared her world view.

A Biculturally Sensitive Therapeutic Process

It is important that Sonia share with Nick her struggles of identity. It is also important for Nick to be invested in seeing Sonia's world view. Nick is Anglo and male, dominant by cultural standards on both counts. He has cultural and societal power to support his world view over Sonia's. They both must feel this differential, albeit unconsciously. Therefore, in the service of their relationship, their bonds of friendship, mutuality, and intimacy, there must be tremendous commitment on both their parts to give credence to Sonia's world view.

Within the context of negotiating world views, therapy focused on two prevailing issues: bicultural implications for the marriage and the established boundary patterns of both Nick and Sonia's family of origin, patterns that affect their personal needs for closeness and distance. The couple was encouraged to share and resolve their different and conflicting needs and desires. Sonia was also encouraged to relate her experience of bridging traditional Hispanic values and beliefs with her contemporary lifestyle.

In therapy, Sonia described initial feelings of embarrassment and shame regarding the prejudicial treatment she received, and Nick was able to provide support and encouragement to his wife. Sonia described hearing both subtle and more obvious expressions of prejudice and racism since childhood. These experiences contributed to some mistaken beliefs, challenged her sense of self, and lead to feelings of inferiority. Sonia reported hearing comments such as, "You're not like the others," or "I couldn't even tell you were Hispanic," or even "Don't worry about it, you're like one of us." Such messages evoked feelings of shame, guilt, and pain, despite the "personal acceptance" from the dominant culture.

A Hispanic middle-class professional such as Sonia is more likely to hear such insulting and confusing messages among people with whom she is closely associated than would her less advantaged counterparts. It was important that Sonia address these experiences if she was to maintain a sense of respect and pride in her own identity. It was also important that she communicate her struggles to Nick, as a measure of self-disclosure in the relationship. Nick, then, would have an opportunity to empathize and provide support and validation for his spouse.

In therapy, Sonia also noted the deep love and affection she holds for her family, and her desire to maintain these family ties while she negotiates her space and time demands. She described the circumstances of her childhood in which she shared meals daily with extended family at her grandmother's home. Sonia recalled the bittersweet feeling of knowing as a child that she was loved and protected by her parents and family. She credits these very important early memories with an inherent sense of confidence and security she holds in spite of any prejudicial treatment.

Along with feelings of comfort and security in recalling important family ties, Sonia expressed sadness when she described the changing roles within her own family that she herself enforced. Her memories of meals with grandparents are central to her identity, and yet the reality of her busy, cosmopolitan world seems light-years away from the close-knit, small-town intimacy she remembers. Still, Sonia feels a deep bond with her family, a bond she fiercely protects and wishes to sustain.

Sonia's attempts to maintain those important bonds while negotiating her needs with those of her husband are noteworthy. Sonia reevaluated the value of *marianismo,* by exploring the means by which she attempted to be "good daughter" and "good wife." She discovered that she has the power to make choices even though they may create conflict within a relationship. Sonia found that she could be "good enough" in relation to the people she loved while at the same time taking note of her own thoughts and feelings. She identified feelings of guilt when she perceived herself as letting someone down, but worked through these guilt feelings by distinguishing between actual versus perceived transgressions.

In negotiating boundaries, Sonia found, to her surprise, that she, too, needed time alone. Sonia noted, "I was always so worried about whether or not Nick had his space that I hadn't discovered how much of my own I needed, too. I seemed to have lost sight of my own comfort level by trying so hard to protect his." Sonia's focus on Nick's needs, coupled with Nick's demands for privacy, had prevented her from identifying her own spatial boundaries.

Nick's insights into his own needs and desires were also enlightening. Nick found that although he valued his time alone, his need for companionship was greater than he had known. He also became aware of the lonely feelings associated with the detached positions held within his family. Nick noted, "In not letting people come over, I can see that I was protecting myself from something I really wanted. I think I was afraid that if I let people come over, they wouldn't go away. I guess in my family I am the one who wants more connection, and, in a sense, that makes it easy. I don't have to worry about getting too much. But it looks like I have kept myself from getting much of anything at all. I guess I have stayed resentful of Sonia and privately blamed her for my bad feelings."

Nick discovered that his twice a year visits to siblings seemed rigidly predictable and lacking in comparison to the spontaneity he witnessed in Sonia's family interactions. Yet, his fears of being overwhelmed kept him in a position of control, which did not allow for a natural flow of give and take to develop. Nick was encouraged to explore the communication and boundary patterns within his family of origin, which led to his alternating feelings of abandonment and engulfment, feelings that contributed to the current problems in his marriage.

Nick's introspection netted interesting findings. First, he realized that his striving to be the "good" husband veiled an unspoken sense of entitlement to Sonia's time, attention, and presence. He identified the "martyr" role as a powerful family pattern, which often resulted in withdrawal and punishment when members of the family were disappointed in one another. Second, Nick identified feelings of isolation within himself that he had expected Sonia to fill. As he became more comfortable with his feelings and with himself, Nick was able to appreciate the differences between Sonia and himself, which significantly diffused the hurt and angry feelings between them.

Sonia also worked toward meeting Nick's relational needs, maintaining her relationships with family and friends, and structuring time for her own activities and leisure. Both people were able to reexamine their culturally based world views, reframe mistaken beliefs, and create a culture inclusive of their relationship, leading to increased empathy, mutuality, and intimacy.

Cross-Cultural Latino Values

The preceding case illustrates the personal, social, and cultural challenges faced by couples negotiating intimacy within their marriages. The role of the extended kin system within Latino families is clearly depicted. The case of Nick and Sonia reflects the challenges faced when one partner is of Mexican American ancestry. Unique difficulties can arise between spouses of different Latino cultural backgrounds as well. Mexican Americans are the dominant Latino group in the United States, followed by Puerto Ricans and Cubans. Although each of these cultural groups have their unique characteristics, Latinos or Hispanics from distinctly different areas share some basic similarities. The case of Nick and Sonia clearly illustrates common issues of gender and extended family ties within cross-cultural Latino communities.

CULTURAL DIVERSITY AMONG LATINOS

As the largest minority group in the United States, Mexican Americans comprise 64.3% of the total Hispanic population. Mexican Americans are a people rich in culture and tradition, represented in a broad range of social and economic classes. Traditionally, Mexican Americans belong to close-knit patriarchal families and extended family systems. Males are the heads of the household, responsible for providing for and protecting their wives and children. Females assume the responsibility to care for, nurture, and provide direction for their families. The elderly maintain a significant place in their family units, often living with one of their children. Spirituality plays an integral role in the traditional lives of Mexican Americans, with many belonging to the Roman Catholic Church. Mysticism also plays an important role with this population, as reflected in the strong belief in *cudanderismo*, or folk healing.

Puerto Rican Americans constitute the second largest Latino group in the United States. Abad, Ramos, and Boyce (1974) describe middle-class Puerto Ricans as family-oriented individuals motivated to improve their social and economic standings. Religion plays an integral role in their lives, and males continue to hold positions of dominance and power in their families. In addition, they (Abad, Ramos, & Boyce, 1974) describe qualities common to Puerto Ricans across cultures. Like Mexican Americans, Puerto Ricans enjoy the deep sense of commitment, obligation, and responsibility within their extended families. And just as Mexican Americans include people outside the family to take on roles such as godfather (*compadre*), godmother (*comadre*), and godchild (*ahijado*) (Soto-Fulp & Del Campo, 1994), Puerto Ricans are also characterized by their value of *comadrago* (godmother), *compadrazgo* (godfather), and close-knit ties with extended kin.

Cuban Americans differ in some respects from Mexican Americans and Puerto Ricans, which could result from their voluntary migration to the United States. Research indicates that issues for members of minority cultures whose land was taken by settlers are distinct from those of members of minority cultures who chose to live in this country (McGoldrick, Giordano, & Pearce, 1982). Cuban Americans who settle in the United States are generally well educated and held positions of authority and status in Cuba. Their migration results in substantial losses of extended family, professions, wealth, and home. However, it could be argued that their intrapsychic beliefs about their worth and value are reportedly greater than their Hispanic counterparts. But like Mexican American and Puerto Rican groups, Cuban Americans enjoy the affection, companionship, and affiliation with their families, and hold values of religion, gender, and hierarchy consistent with the Hispanic mainstream culture. In the context of couples therapy, each of these groups must consider their distinct cultural experiences and world views while examining the prevailing norms of Western culture.

CONCLUSION

Men and women in Western culture each have world views that govern their interactions with one another, constituting separate cultural norms (Miller and Stiver, 1994). Multicultural couples such as Nick and Sonia require further understanding of the cultural implications of their relationship. As partners become more sensitive and aware, they may appreciate the distinct cultural differences within their relationship while reaping the benefits of diverse customs and values. In the case of Nick and Sonia, each partner was able to develop intrinsic qualities that broadened and deepened their relationship. Sonia gained personal power and autonomy, while Nick developed an increased sense of familial connectedness. Sonia came to appreciate her need for some distance or separateness, and Nick understood the value of strong, enduring ties reflected in *familism.* Eventually, Sonia integrated dominant-culture values important to Nick into her world view without sacrificing her deeply held value of relatedness and connection. And Nick eventually learned to value *interdependence,* or the mutual support of one another, without compromising his need for space and autonomy.

Interdependence is closely linked to the Adlerian concept of social interest, which is the ultimate goal for couples wishing to generate greater intimacy, negotiation skills, and cultural adaptivity. As people identify their idiosyncratic philosophies of life, the mistaken beliefs that drive them, and the resulting unconscious goals for living that motivate their behaviors, they are able to overcome feelings of inferiority and enjoy a place of significance and belonging. In that respect, they know they matter. They know they are enough. They are free to give. And they are free to receive. It is at this point that couples are truly able to express care and concern for each other, that they are free to experience loyalty and cohesiveness at its best. They feel their personal power and are willing to share it. And it is in the mutual sharing of that power that couples are equipped to express social interest and enjoy true intimacy and satisfaction. For couples like Nick and Sonia, who choose to live consciously and collaboratively, developing social interest moves them one step closer toward their goal.

REFERENCES

Abad, V., Ramos, J., & Boyce, E. (1974). A model for delivery of mental health services to Spanish-speaking minorities. *American Journal of Orthopsychiatry, 44*(4), 584–595.

Atkinson, D. R., Morten, G., & Sue, D. W. (1989). *Counseling American minorities: A cross cultural perspective.* Dubuque, IA: Brown.

Collier, J. F. (1986). From Mary to marianismo. *American Ethnologist, 13* 100–107.

Coner-Edwards, A. F., & Edwards, H. E. (1988). Relationship issues and treatment dilemmas for Black middle class couples. In A. F. Coner-Edwards and J. Spurlock (Eds.), *Black families in crisis: The middle class.* New York: Brunner/Mazel.

Erikson, E. H. (1963). *Childhood and society.* New York: Norton.

Espin, O. M. (1992). Cultural and historical influences on sexuality in Hispanic/Latin women: Implications for psychotherapy. In M. L. Anderson & P. H. Collins (Eds.), *Race, class, and gender.* Belmont, CA: Wadsworth.

Friedman, E. H. (1988). Systems and ceremonies: A family view of rites of passage. In B. Carter & M. McGoldrick (Eds.), *The changing family life cycle: A framework for family therapy* (2nd Ed.). New York: Gardner Press.

Gilligan, C. (1982). *In a different voice.* Cambridge, MA: Harvard University Press.

Gilligan, C., Rogers, A. G., & Tolman, D. L. (Eds.). (1991). *Women, girls, and psychotherapy.* New York: Haworth Press.

Hamburger, M. (1964/1990). Personal communication. In F. A. Ibrahim & D. G. Schroeder (Eds.), Cross-cultural couples counseling: A developmental, psychoeducational intervention. *Journal of Comparative Family Studies, 21*(2), 193–205.

Ibrahim, F. A., & Schroeder, D. G. (1990). Cross-cultural couples counseling: A developmental, psychoeducational intervention. *Journal of Comparative Family Studies, 21*(2), 193–205.

Ishiyama, F. I., & Westwood, M. J. (1992). Enhancing client-validating communication: Helping discouraged clients in cross-cultural adjustment. *Journal of Multicultural Counseling and Development 20,* 50–63.

Jalali, B. (1982). Iranian families. In M. McGoldrick, J. K. Pearce, & J. Giordano (Eds.), *Ethnicity and family therapy.* New York: Guilford Press.

Markus, T. P., & Wurf, E. (1987). The dynamic self-concept: A social psychological perspective. *Annual Review of Psychology, 38,* 299–337.

McGoldrick, M., Giordano, J., & Pearce, J. K. (1982). *Ethnicity and family therapy.* New York: Guilford Press.

Miller, J. B., & Stiver, I. P. (1994). Movement in therapy: Honoring the "strategies of disconnection." *Work in Progress, No. 65.* Wellesley, MA: Stone Center.

Pinderhughes, E. (1989). *Understanding race, ethnicity, and power: The key to efficacy in clinical practice.* New York: The Free Press.

Ruiz, A. S. (1990). Ethnic identity: Crisis and resolution. *Journal of Multicultural Counseling and Development, 18,* 29–40.

Sherman, R., & Dinkmeyer, D. (1987). *Systems of family therapy: An Adlerian approach integration.* New York: Brunner/Mazel.

Soto-Fulp, S., & Del Campo, R. L. (1994). Structural family therapy with Mexican American family systems. *Contemporary Family Therapy, 16*(5), 349–362.

Stevens, E. (1973). Marianismo: The other face of machismo. In A. Pescatello (Ed.), *Female and male in Latin America.* Pittsburgh: University of Pittsburgh Press.

Timmerman, G. M. (1991). A concept analysis of intimacy. *Issues in Mental Health Nursing, 12,* 19–30.

Torrey, E. F. (1986). *Witches, doctors, and psychiatrists.* New York: Harper & Row.

Waring, E. M. (1988). *Enhancing marital intimacy through facilitating cognitive self-disclosure.* New York: Brunner/Mazel.

Watkins, B. A., & Rountree, Y. B. (1984, April 28). *Bridging two worlds: The Black "in-between" class.* Paper presented at the annual convention of the New York State Psychological Association, New York.

8

LIFE-CYCLE DEVELOPMENT, DIVORCE, AND THE HISPANIC FAMILY

RANDALL R. LYLE AND FLOR FAURE

The very definition of ethics that we have proposed—
living well with and for others in just institutions—
cannot be conceived without the project of living
well being affected by solicitude, both that which
is exerted and that which is received.
—RICOEUR, 1992, p. 330

This chapter is the product of two colleagues who worked for four years in tandem, in a unique multicultural learning process. The first author, a university professor in southern Texas, was a mentor to the second while she perfected her English, "Spanglish," and family therapy skills. He is a marriage and family therapist and an Episcopal priest, fluent in Spanish due to several years of service in Argentina. The second author, a master therapist and citizen of Mexico and Spain, shared her expertise of the Mexican culture, as the two learned to appreciate the many distinctions within the Hispanic populations of southern Texas. Together, they shared their observations with each other and with other students in the clinic.

The chapter reflects the duality of their relationship in that it serves two distinct purposes. The chapter is both theoretical and clinically relevant. In working together, they created a close collegial relationship in which each grew and differentiated individually. The first author, whose work embraces theory and philosophy, offers a dialectical, developmental approach to family therapy that can be used to enhance work with all families, whether Hispanic, Asian, African American, or any minority or majority group. The second author helps us apply the model, illustrating its use with a postdivorce case from her practice, and practical suggestions throughout.

FAMILY LIFE-CYCLE DEVELOPMENT

The conceptualization and use of family life-cycle development has generally proven to be very beneficial for those professionals seeking to assist families through the trials and tribulations of forming, growing, and eventually launching new families. However, significant shortcomings have also been noted. This is particularly the case when we combine a significant nodal event, like divorce, with a fundamental human characteristic, like ethnicity.

Traditional Life-Cycle Models

The first and most significant problem for traditional family life-cycle theory is its assumption of a normative, linear stage model of family development (Carter & McGoldrick, 1980; Haley, 1973; Hughes, Berger, & Wright, 1978; Rhodes, 1977). These models tend to assume a single, monogamous, lifelong, heterosexual union with children. The stages of these models, determined by the individual developmental stages of the children and the tasks of transitioning from one stage to another, are fundamentally related to each family member's needs in relation to the needs of the child. The values underlying the tasks and ideal development have generally been those of the dominant culture. Recent improvements in family life-cycle development models (McGoldrick, Giordano, & Pearce, 1996) have emphasized the need to take into account ethnic variations in family values and structure as well as the addition of new stages of transition when families are reformed as a result of divorce and remarriage (Ahrons & Rodgers, 1987).

However, the elaboration of family life-cycle models to include other ethnicities and alternative family structures has done little to aid the family therapist in learning how to best help these families. Rather, the result has been for therapists to feel that unless they can become expert on the customs and traditions of every ethnic group that comes to see them, they will run the risk of mistreating these clients. This becomes particularly problematic when we are considering a category such as Hispanic, which is a general term for an extremely heterogeneous grouping of ethnic origins.

Since other chapters in this work have addressed the specific concerns of different cultures and traditions within the general category of Hispanic, we will not address those issues here. Rather, our goal will be to offer an alternative life-cycle development model. One that frees therapists from a singular focus on ethnic origin and opens the way for therapists to remain cognizant of concerns with both ethnicity and alternative family structures, such as divorced and remarried families. We now turn our attention to an elaboration of the developmental model that we are proposing. We will conclude the chapter with a case study chosen to highlight how the model facilitates our therapeutic work with Hispanic clients.

The Intimacy-Identity Developmental Model

Our developmental model is based on the work of Rice and Rice (1986). Although the focus of their work was exclusively in terms of understanding and treating divorce, the model serves as an excellent basis for integrating concerns about ethnicity and divorce. The authors point out that a more helpful model of development would be one

> based on the assumption that there are but two key tasks of all human development, and that they recur over and over again, but with different meanings at each period of life. These two key concepts will be labeled intimacy, where the key task is communion,

that is, being able to be close to another individual, and identity,
where the key task is successful separation or individuation. (p. 83)

Deconstructing Stages to Rewrite Cultural Norms

This model offers a significant simplification of life-cycle development compared to such models as Duvall (1971) with eight stages, Rodgers (1960) with twenty-four stages, or Carter and McGoldrick (1980) with six stages. The simplification of the model is important for two reasons. The first reason is that by eliminating the various stages of development, we also eliminate a significant portion of "cultural normativity." A stage model generally implies a linear progression through specific developmental tasks. These tasks are inevitably related to underlying, and most likely unquestioned, cultural norms and beliefs. The end point of the linear progression through the different stages is generally conceived of as an arrival at a place of perfect balance where all of the developmental tasks have been successfully accomplished. What the stage model fails to take into consideration is how the various stages are linked to the values and beliefs of the dominant culture. By shifting our attention away from predefined stages toward the interactive process of human development as understood through the key tasks of intimacy and identity, we free ourselves, as therapists, to become curious cocreators of meaning and normalcy with our clients.

The second reason the simplification of this model is important is the fact that by focusing on the key tasks of intimacy and identity, we are able to turn our attention to the universal elements of human development and how they are systemically integrated into both our inter- and intrapersonal relationships. Intimacy, with its partner communion, and identity, with its partner separation, operate in a recursive pattern of interactions that happens both within the self and between the self and others. As Rice and Rice (1986) state:

At each period of life, these two concepts, intimacy and identity, and
their core tasks, communion and separation, occur again and again,
with different meanings at each period. At each stage they are re-
worked, redefined, and transformed. The adequate solution for one
period of life may not be the best one for the next. Each period of life
can require a redefinition of intimacy, moving from the intense de-
pendency on and love for and from a parent, from selfish love to peer

*love, to committed love for a nonfamilial figure, to generative love
for one's biological children and finally, to a sense of global intimacy,
a feeling of love for the world and the species. (p. 84)*

There is also a third reason for using this model of life-cycle development in relation to multicultural counseling. As Casas and
Pytluk (1995) have noted, ethnic identity development is best understood when we take into consideration both enculturation and acculturation. Acculturation is defined as "the culture learning that occurs
as a result of contact between members of two or more culturally distinct groups" (p. 158). Enculturation "is the socialization process 'by
which developing individuals acquire (either by generalized learning
in a particular cultural milieu, or as a result of specific instruction and
training) the host of cultural and psychological qualities that are necessary to function as a member of one's group'" (p. 272) (Berry, 1993,
as cited in Casas & Pytluk, 1995, p. 158).

The Tasks of Acculturation and Enculturation in Establishing Ethnic Identity

As noted before, the two key tasks of this developmental model are
identity and intimacy. These two key tasks conceptually parallel the
two elements of acculturation and enculturation in ethnic identity
formation. Identity can be fundamentally linked to the process of acculturation. In acculturation, as in identity formation in general, we
formulate our identity in comparison and contrast with others. Identity is "partnered" with separation in the same manner by which acculturation is accomplished by struggling with my "differentness"
from the dominant culture.

Likewise, we can link enculturation with intimacy. Intimacy is
"partnered" with communion in the same way that enculturation is a
result of the closeness and fellowship that I have with significant others who are "similar" to myself. All of us, whether or not we are a part
of the dominant culture, are familiar with the process of enculturation. It happens to all of us. In the clinical setting, this means that we
have already established at least one common starting point in our establishment of a therapeutic relationship. We can already agree that
our family and our social networks have had a significant influence
on how we understand and participate in our world.

The opposite is also true. Each of us is familiar with the experience of separateness, the sense of being different from others. Our identities are forged out of the tension inherent in our experience of being separate from others. Acculturation is the experience of discovering that I am engaged in an encounter with "otherness" in a context in which I need to discover a means of understanding and belonging.

Since development happens in and through time, it has been tempting to develop models of development, which are primarily linear in their thinking. As mentioned earlier, this has led most models of development to describe human self-understanding as a progression through specific stages. Each stage has a predetermined set of tasks, which must be successfully completed before the individual can successfully move forward to the next stage. The failure of the individual to successfully accomplish these tasks is understood to be the source or cause of interpersonal problems: literally, the person is "stuck" in a particular stage. The challenge for multicultural counseling from this model is knowing whether an individual or family from a minority culture is "stuck" in a particular stage or if something totally unrelated is the problem. Therapists may place clients in significant moral dilemmas when insisting they conform to ways that accord with the dominant cultural position.

CLINICAL APPLICATIONS

Working with Hispanic families while using a recursive, nonlinear, developmental model has many benefits. This section of the chapter will compare and contrast the use of the traditional linear stage models with our dialectical developmental model. Two case studies will be presented to demonstrate the flexibility of the dialectic of intimacy-identity in working with families of diverse cultures. The first case, concerns Laverne (Christopher, 1996). We have chosen to highlight this case because it clearly demonstrates many of the moral dilemmas found in bicultural counseling. The second case, that of Rosario, is the actual treatment of a case in which the two authors collaborated. Rosario's story involves a number of sensitive cultural issues that may arise when working with Hispanic families in the stages of divorce. This often leads to therapists placing clients in significant moral dilemmas when they insist that the client act in ways that accord with the dominant culture's position. We hope to illustrate ways in which traditional and dialectical developmental models can aid or hinder the therapeutic process.

Laverne's Loyalties

"Laverne" was a Hispanic woman who sought counseling because she was depressed and anxious (Christopher, 1996). Laverne had been raised within the moral vision of her Hispanic family amidst a small southern Texas town. This moral vision illuminated her primary identity as one fundamentally derived from being part of a large extended family. Moreover, it mandated that her first priority in life was to fulfill her duty within that role assigned by her family. Such an approach to life, frequently called collectivism (Hui & Triandis, 1986; Kim, Triandis, Kagitcibasi, Choi, & Yoon, 1994), emphasizes the virtue of harmonizing one's relationships with one's in-group. Accordingly, sensitivity in understanding and anticipating other's feelings and reactions is cultivated and viewed as a sign of maturity (Markus & Kitayama, 1991). In collectivism, an individual's worth comes from one's ability to excel at specific roles and functions within the social order (Moore, 1968); this stands in contrast to individualism in which an individual is guaranteed a certain amount of dignity and worth simply by being born a human being (Lukes, 1973).

> Laverne's Anglo-American boyfriend, Richard, had a more stereo-typically individualistic moral vision. Richard viewed family ties and obligations as a waste of time, something that got in the way of the true business of life, happiness, and self-fulfillment. He encouraged Laverne to see herself as a unique, autonomous person. Richard also pressured her to seize control of her life by making her own decisions about how to spend her time (assuming, of course, that she would then make him a higher priority in her life). Virtually every weekend Laverne faced a dilemma—should she go home and help her family or stay on campus with Richard? Laverne was virtually paralyzed in deciding what stance to take toward her boyfriend and her family. (Christopher, 1996, p. 20)

Although Christopher focuses primarily on the conflicting "moral vision" in this case example (which we will address later), this case also offers a typical scenario for understanding life-cycle development in relation to multicultural counseling. Laverne's situation provides us with an opportunity to compare how traditional life-cycle development theory and our theory might understand and intervene in her dilemma.

A Traditional View of the Multicultural Dilemma

Before we begin our analysis of traditional family life-cycle development in relation to Laverne's case, it is important to note that even the most ardent supporter of this model acknowledges the need to take ethnic origin and culture into consideration. The challenge, of course, is to know enough about the other culture to be able to modify the model to fit the particular culture that is being presented. This raises the ethical question mentioned before: If I am not well acquainted with the particular culture of the client before me, can I ethically work with them? This points to a related question: How much knowledge about another culture do I need to possess for that knowledge to be considered sufficient? Bearing these caveats in mind, let us proceed with our analysis.

Traditional life-cycle development theory would probably place Laverne in Stage 1, "Leaving Home: Single Young Adults" (Carter & McGoldrick, 1980, p. 15). For the purposes of our analysis, we will limit ourselves to Carter and McGoldrick's model of Family Life-Cycle Development. The key principles of this stage are described as "Accepting emotional and financial responsibility for self" and the changes required to proceed developmentally are "(a) Differentiation of self in relation to family of origin; (b) Development of intimate peer relationships; (c) Establishment of self re work and financial independence."

A therapist working from this model would be inclined to assess Laverne (and perhaps her family) as struggling with her transition from the adolescent stage to the single young adult stage. Her depression and anxiety are symptoms of her difficulty in "accepting emotional and/or financial responsibility" for herself. As Laverne intensifies the "development of an intimate peer relationship" with Richard, she finds the pressure of "differentiation of self in relation to family of origin" to be unbearable. This is probably further complicated by the fact that she is a student and so is becoming emotionally more independent, while remaining financially dependent on her family of origin.

Setting aside all cultural considerations for the moment, the therapeutic goals in this case might be described as supporting Laverne in her transition from adolescence to single young adult. The support would be accomplished through a combination of attentive listening, normalization, and education about the tasks of this transition stage, exploration of feelings about self and family, examination of the various influences of the family of origin across several generations, and encouragement in the completion of the necessary separation from the family of origin.

When we bring the cultural concerns back into the case, we discover that all of the elements mentioned before are still central to our therapeutic goals but now must be tempered by an understanding of how the cultural influences modify the timing and degree of transition. The model takes for granted Laverne's enculturation. The therapeutic task thus becomes one of support, not only of Laverne's differentiation from her family of origin, but also support of her acculturation into the dominant culture. In order to successfully support her acculturation, the therapist needs to be aware of how Laverne's enculturation differs from that of the dominant culture.

Examples of life-cycle differences with Anglo American norms include a longer state of interdependence between mother and children and a more relaxed attitude about children's achievement of self-reliance skills (often mistaken for overprotection); the absence of an independent living situation for most unmarried young adults; the absence of an "empty nest" syndrome, or a crisis and a refocusing on marital issues in middle age; and a continuous involvement, a respected position, and a usefulness of parents and grandparents in the family. With acculturation, these developmental expectations persist alongside the new considerations of individual pursuits and romantic love espoused by the younger generations, sometimes causing intergenerational tensions (Falicov, 1996, p. 178).

This additional cultural knowledge becomes information that the therapist uses to assist the client in determining the pace and degree of differentiation that may be accomplished. However, the emphasis is entirely on the process of acculturation. The model takes for granted that the transition to the dominant culture's stage of "single young adult" is necessary. The only question is how far and how fast, given the cultural exigencies present in the case. As Falicov (1996) states:

> To deal with life cycle dilemmas, the therapist can assume the role of family intermediary. Acting as a "cultural mediator," he or she might encourage conversation between parents and offspring about developmental expectations and their loyalties to both Anglo American and Mexican culture. (p. 179)

Clearly, cultural mediation is not a bad thing, nor is acculturation an unimportant process to be considered in the course of multicultural counseling. However, the singular emphasis on these elements of human development in a multicultural context often leads to the minority culture's expression of frustration with a therapeutic community that "no me comprende." Laverne may well feel that her therapist, if working from this model, simply does not understand how truly painful her dilemma is. She could easily experience the therapist's insistence on identity and separation as the same kind of pressure that she already feels from Richard and the result could be an increase in her depression and anxiety. The therapist's well-intentioned "cultural mediation" may be experienced by Laverne as "binding arbitration" or even "litigation."

An Alternative View: The Dialectical Experience of Intimacy and Identity

The problem with the stage model is not that it is not true or even helpful, but that it tends to be prescriptive in its attribution of specific tasks at particular stages and that these tasks and stages are culturally conditioned. As noted before, this becomes problematical in a multicultural setting. The advantage of the Intimacy-Identity Model is in its application to specific cases. The model provides a theoretical foundation that inclines the therapist to be on the lookout for both commonalties of experience and differences. The key tasks, communion and separation, can be understood to be universal for all cultures. The therapeutic process resulting from this model thus becomes a dialectical process, which is isomorphic to the dynamics of all human relationships. We will now turn to an explanation of what this means and how the model works in the context of therapy.

We find it helpful to think of this model in visual terms. As can be seen in the following diagram, we have mapped the model onto the ancient symbol for infinity:

Intimacy   *Identity*

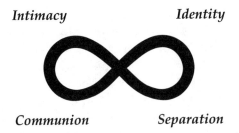

Communion   *Separation*

The symbolism is important. The model presumes that the process of growth and development in human beings is infinite. Unlike the stage models, this model does not assume an end point where all of the tasks of life are completed and where the individual, at least in the ideal, simply ties up a few loose ends associated with generativity and ego-integrity (cf. Erikson, 1963).

The symbol also reminds us that life is dynamic rather than static. The symbol points to the recursive patterns of human experience: the constant flow from emphasis on one side of interaction to the other. That the symbol crosses in the middle reminds us that there are times when we experience our lives to be in balance: an equal choosing of identity and intimacy, communion and separation. Finally, the symbol, taken as a whole, highlights the dialectical nature of human experience: infinite/finite, communion/separation, intimacy/identity (cf. Keeney, 1983). If we accept that theory is what drives our practice and, thus, our interventions and interactions with our clients, then it should be clear that the Intimacy-Identity Model would emphasize very different dimensions of human experience than the traditional life-cycle stage model. It is to those differences that we will now turn.

Bridging the Cultural Gap

The simplest way to examine the differences in the clinical practices that these two models give rise to is to apply the Intimacy-Identity Model to a specific case. The story of Laverne as presented before, will serve this function well. The reader will recall that Laverne found herself caught in a struggle among loyalty to her family of origin, respecting the cultural heritage that the family represented, exploring and deepening the relationship that she had with her boyfriend, Richard, and enriching and exploring her own self-understanding. Her struggle with all of this has been presented to the therapist as resulting in depression and anxiety.

The first thing that our theory is likely to do is to incline the therapist to search for areas of common experience. It is quite likely that the therapist would notice that much of the discomfort that Laverne is experiencing is related to the issue of intimacy and its concomitant task of communion. Laverne desires to continue the intimacy and communion that she has with her family while desiring (perhaps) to increase the intimacy and communion that she has begun to develop with Richard. The search for intimacy is likely to be an experience that the therapist has had as well. The commonality of experience between the client and the therapist can become a foundation of the therapeutic relationship. This may be accomplished by the therapist actually sharing an example of her or his struggle with intimacy/communion or may simply be reflected on by the therapist in such a way so as to facilitate Laverne's sense of being heard and understood.

However, as we noticed in our description of the dialectical nature of the symbol, sameness implies difference. As the therapist notices and highlights the universal nature of the desire for intimacy and communion, the therapist also becomes aware that the exact nature of that experience is different for each individual. The therapist will then begin to explore with Laverne how she uniquely experiences her conflicts around intimacy. Of particular interest to us in the context of this chapter: Does her culture present special concerns and how does she understand these to be influencing her desires and goals? Likewise, due to the dialectical nature of the model, both across the poles (intimacy versus identity) and within the key developmental tasks (i.e., intimacy versus separation; identity versus communion), the therapist is not only an observer of the process. She or he is also a participant in the process of both enculturation, how does Laverne understand herself to be a part of her own culture and thus how do I, as the therapist, understand myself to be a part of my own culture; and acculturation, how do Laverne and I enter into the discovery of each other's culture and select those elements that we want to keep and those that we choose to discard?

Developmental Process

This dialectical process is repeated throughout the model. As each concern related to identity and intimacy, family, boyfriend, school, and so on, is raised, the therapist is encouraged to embrace the broader dialectical tensions of how the experience is both the same and different for him or herself and how the relationship between the therapist and the client is itself representative of the tensions inherent in human growth and development. Culture thus becomes one of the elements of development to be given consideration and exploration. The model allows for culture to sometimes become the primary focus and at other times to flow into the background of the therapeutic conversation, depending on the needs of the various relationships, including the therapist/client relationship itself. The model shifts our attention away from the completion of a particular stage toward the process of development itself. As Rice and Rice (1986) states:

> The interactional process is more important than the task, and the task does not have to be begun in one particular developmental period and worked through in another. The tasks of finding intimacy and identity, of blending communion and separation, are lifetime tasks, to be reworked, redefined, and transformed over and over in the lifespan. (p. 85)

What we have tried to demonstrate in this chapter is that in relation to multicultural counseling, the interactional processes of enculturation and acculturation do not happen exclusively outside of the therapeutic relationship. The Intimacy-Identity Model encourages therapists to understand that the therapeutic relationship has the potential to become a microcosm of the other social relationships where the universal struggle of development is being engaged.

Seeking Oasis from the Aftermath of Divorce

Attaining the knowledge of a specific culture of a certain Hispanic client is a complex task and one that most therapists from the majority culture are unlikely to be able to master for more than just a few of the many diverse cultures that the term Hispanic represents. The following case study will highlight how the traditional developmental model and the Intimacy-Identity Model differ in their approach to a specific problem of divorce adjustment with a Hispanic client family.

Rosario is a first-generation Mexican American. Her parents emigrated to the United States from a little town in the north of Mexico shortly before she was born. Tony, her ex-husband is a third-generation Mexican American. When Rosario divorced Tony, she chose to move in with her parents who live in the same neighborhood.

Rosario sought counseling because her oldest son, 5 years old, had been demonstrating aggressive behaviors at school. In the course of therapy, Rosario stated that she had been divorced for about a year and that her ex-husband Tony would not give her child support until she moved out of her parent's home. She reported that she and Tony would often have arguments in front of the children whenever Tony would arrive to pick up the children. On numerous occasions, Rosario's father would join in the arguments. Rosario asked for help with her son's behavior and for help in ending the ongoing arguments.

Therapy Informed by a Traditional View

From the traditional developmental perspective, the therapist would likely consider this case to be one in which a postdivorce family is experiencing difficulties in the transition to a binuclear family and that the problems are being manifested around issues of money, parenting, and social relationships. Brown (1989) would further refine this transition by examining which of the three phases (aftermath, realignment, or stabilization) the family was experiencing so as to specify the tasks and difficulties that this family will need to resolve.

Therapy from the traditional perspective would likely conceptualize Rosario's family as having inadequately fulfilled the tasks of several family life-cycle stages, especially the tasks assigned to the stage of development at which the divorce occurred, that is, divorce in families with preschool children (Peck & Manocherian, 1989). In this case, Rosario and Tony would be understood as having inadequately separated their parental roles from their marital roles. Likewise, Rosario's wish to continue living with her parents might reflect difficulties in the earlier transition to the stage of "the new couple." Living with the family of origin would not be considered "normal" from the perspective of the dominant culture and would be seen as running the risk of enmeshment and cross-generational boundary confusion if the grandmother begins functioning as the mother of her grandchildren (Brown, 1989).

Ahrons and Rodgers (1987) emphasize the task of finding a method to continue performing childrearing and parenting functions. Based on Minuchin's work, these authors state the importance of clarifying the roles and boundaries between parental and spousal subsystems. The fulfillment of these tasks will depend on a complex interweaving of a variety of factors, including acculturation and family-of-origin issues for each of the former spouses.

From this perspective, the therapist will need to be an expert on specific cultural elements related to this unique postdivorce Hispanic family. Research shows that in the first year after divorce, first-generation Mexican American women remained more kin-oriented than Anglos when looking for sources of support (Wagner, 1987). Knowledge about these specific differences among generations of Mexican American women will be necessary if the therapist is to diminish the risk of mistreating this family.

In Rosario's case, even a therapist considered an expert in Mexican American divorced families would assess this family based on its development through the stages of the family life cycle, looking at what stage the divorce happened, the age of the children, the ethnicity in general, and the degree of acculturation. Because being an expert on a culture different from our own is rare, most therapists will tend to conceptualize the tasks and ideal development of the family based on the values of the dominant culture. Here, the therapist might conceptualize Rosario's choice of moving back into her parents home as a sign of enmeshment and encourage her to become more independent of her parents. Rosario might experience the intervention of the therapist as a judgment of her maturity and feel guilty for not being more adult. Likewise, her parents might feel anger and resentment as Rosario seeks more independence, as they understand her moving away from them as a sign of disrespect and rejection. This is a clear example of how the dominant culture's values of independence and separation are in marked contrast with the Mexican values of proximity, cohesiveness, and respect for parental authority throughout life (Falicov, 1982).

The dominant culture, and with it the traditional developmental model, assumes the value and necessity of separation and independence. As Brown states: "The central dilemma for the mother is how to enlist the help of others without allowing them to take over for her"

(p. 394). The challenge thus becomes how to modify the model so as to fit the particular ethnicity of the specific case. The modifications would only affect the degree and the pace of change, not the assumed therapeutic goals of required development. As a result, it is likely that Rosario will feel as if she is a failure in both worlds and the symptoms already manifest in her family will only worsen as she finds herself less and less able to choose between loyalty to her enculturation and her desire for further acculturation.

Therapy Informed by the Intimacy-Identity Model

By working from this model, it is easy to understand from Rosario's own story how as a first-generation Mexican American woman, she feels the necessity of respecting and obeying her parents. She understands them to be wise and loyal, supportive of her and her children. Tony, on the other hand, as a third-generation Mexican American, sees them as intruders who want to take away his parental rights and authority. He is using child support as a means of forcing Rosario to become more "American" and thus to respect him and his authority. Rosario and her children are caught in the middle. If she accepts Tony's values, she risks losing her family. If she remains loyal to her family, she risks alienating her children's father. This conflict seems to be manifesting itself in the aggressive behavior of her son.

As we noticed in the description of the model, the therapist is an observer and a participant in the process of enculturation and acculturation. The therapist and the client need to understand themselves as part of their respective cultures; and both explore different aspects of each other's cultures and share in the common human experiences of all cultures. As a result of this both/and approach, both Rosario and the therapist may grow in understanding of themselves, each other, and the presenting problem.

In this case, Rosario was able to feel understood and respected by the therapist. She felt free to correct the therapist when assumptions about what she might think did not match her experience. This enabled her to face her own dilemmas with more confidence and self-assurance and the therapeutic process modeled a way of cooperation and collaboration that she was able to incorporate in her dealings with her parents, her ex-husband, and her children. An explicit discussion of the elements of the model, the role of identity and intimacy, helped Rosario to understand that she did not have to choose one or the other. Rather, both are essential to a full life and sometimes we will be developing one more than the other.

Likewise, the therapist using this model was freed from struggling to create interventions that would move Rosario to the "next stage" of development. The therapeutic task became focused on the relationships involved and the cocreation of a way of relating that Rosario felt was comfortable and workable in her life. As a result, both Rosario and the therapist were liberated from the necessity of becoming "experts" on life and were able to recognize that they were fellow pilgrims on the journey of living.

CONCLUSION

As our opening quote from Ricoeur indicates, life and ethics are inextricably linked and it is our belief that nowhere is this clearer than in multicultural counseling. The Identity-Intimacy Model of development provides a way of thinking about and interacting with people of different ethnic groups that we believe honors our differences while acknowledging and affirming our similarities. This not only opens the way for a more "ethical" practice of therapy, it also offers both therapist and client a chance to expand in their knowledge and comfort with diverse cultures and values. Freeing ourselves as therapists from the predeterminative notions of stages and "norms" and opening ourselves to the ebb and flow of the search for identity and intimacy, individually and culturally, encourages us and our clients to strive to "live well with and for others, in just institutions." In particular, for Hispanic cultures with their emphasis on community and corporate living, this model seems to us to provide an appropriate and beneficial way of interacting with and being helpful to our clients.

REFERENCES

Ahrons, C. R., & Rodgers, R. H. (1987). *Divorced families: Meeting the challenge of divorce and remarriage.* New York: Norton.

Berry, J. W. (1993). Ethnic identities in plural societies. In M. E. Bernal & G. P. Knight (Eds.), *Ethnic identity: Formation and transmission among Hispanics and other minorities* (pp. 271–296). Albany: State University of New York Press.

Brown, F. H. (1989). The postdivorce family. In B. Carter & M. McGoldrick (Eds.), *The changing family life cycle* (pp. 371–398). Boston: Allyn & Bacon.

Carter, E. A., & McGoldrick, M. (Eds.). (1980). *The family life cycle: A framework for therapy.* New York: Gardner Press.

Casas, J. M., & Pytluk, S. D. (1995). Hispanic identity development: Implications for research and practice. In J. G. Ponterotto, J. M. Casas, L. A. Suzuki, & C. M. Alexander (Eds.), *Handbook of multicultural counseling* (pp. 155–180). Thousand Oaks, CA: Sage.

Christopher, J. C. (1996). Counseling's inescapable moral visions. *Journal of Counseling and Development, 75,* 17–25.

Duvall, E. M. (1971). *Family development.* Philadelphia: Lippincott.

Erikson, E. (1963). *Childhood and society* (2nd ed.). New York: Norton.

Falicov, C. J. (1982). Mexican families. In M. McGoldrick, J. K. Pearce, and J. Giordano (Eds.), *Ethnicity and family therapy* (pp. 134–163). New York: Guilford Press.

Falicov, C. J. (1996). Mexican families. In M. McGoldrick, J. Giordano, & J. K. Pearce (Eds.), *Ethnicity and family therapy* (2nd ed., pp. 169–182). New York: Guilford Press.

Haley, J. (1973). *Uncommon therapy: The psychiatric techniques of Milton Erickson, M.D.* New York: Ballantine.

Hughes, S. F., Berger, M., & Wright, L. (1978). The family life cycle and clinical intervention. *Journal of Marriage and Family Counseling, 4,* 33–40.

Hui, C. H., & Triandis, H. C. (1986). Individualism-collectivism: A study of cross-cultural researchers. *Journal of Cross-Cultural Psychology, 17,* 225–248.

Keeney, B. (1983). *Aesthetics of change.* New York: Guilford Press.

Kim, U., Triandis, H. C., Kagitcibasi, C., Choi, S.-C., & Yoon, G. (Eds.). (1994). *Individualism and collectivism.* Thousand Oaks, CA: Sage.

Lukes, S. (1973). *Individualism.* Oxford: Blackwell.

Markus, H. R., & Kitayama, S. (1991). Culture and the self: Implications for cognition, emotion, and motivation. *Psychological Review, 98,* 224–253.

McGoldrick, M., Giordano, J., & Pearce, J. (Eds.). (1996). *Ethnicity and family therapy* (2nd ed.). New York: Guilford Press.

Moore, C. A. (1968). *The status of the individual in East and West.* Honolulu: University of Hawaii Press.

Peck, J. S., & Manocherian, J. R. (1989). Divorce in the changing family life cycle. In B. Carter & M. McGoldrick (Eds.), *The changing family life cycle* (pp. 335–369). Boston: Allyn & Bacon.

Rhodes, S. L. (1977). A developmental approach to the life cycle of the family. *Social Casework, 58,* 301–311.

Rice, J., & Rice, D. (1986). *Living through divorce.* New York: Guilford Press.

Ricouer, P. (1992). *Oneself as another.* (K. Blamey, Trans.). Chicago: University of Chicago Press.

Rodgers, R. (1960). *Proposed modifications of Duvall's family life cycle stages.* Paper presented at a meeting of the American Sociological Association, New York (as cited in Carter & McGoldrick, 1980).

Wagner, R. M. (1987). Changes in the friend network during the first year of single parenthood for Mexican American and Anglo women. *Journal of Divorce, 11*(2), 89.

9

THERAPEUTIC SENSITIVITY TO THE LATINO SPIRITUAL SOUL

ROSENDO URRABAZO

The language of our people is not just Spanish, it is the language of the heart. The faith of our people is not just in God, but also in those intermediaries that God has placed in our path. Therapists can be such intermediaries.
—ROSENDO URRABAZO

Those who work therapeutically with Latinos in the United States need a sensitivity to the history, language, and culture of the various Hispanic communities currently residing in this country. One of the most influential factors is the role played by religious beliefs in Latino cultures. I have chosen to speak very generally about Latinos in order to introduce therapists to some common elements present in most Latino subgroups. A more complete study would require extensive treatment of the various Latino groups and their particular ways of being religious. However, this chapter focuses primarily on the Catholic faith as it is the religious tradition of the majority of Latinos in the United States.

Throughout this chapter, I emphasize repeatedly that any talk of religious content should be at the initiative of the client or family.

Religious material should not be introduced by the therapist. The use of religious material is not to debate theology or to give an aura of "spiritual direction," but rather to explore how religious material affects our self-concept, our interpersonal relationships within the family, and our perception of reality. Clients with a sincere belief in God and a faith-oriented disposition may be able to draw strength from their religious tradition. On the other hand, delusional or misguided understandings about religion can result in harmful thinking and inappropriate behavior. Families who work with knowledgeable therapists may be able to expand their religious beliefs in ways that affirm a more wholesome approach to their own lives and relationships. Therapists may at times be able to provide Latinos an opportunity for personal growth and healthy family relationships by exploring fundamental religious beliefs.

FAITH AND RELIGION FOR SURVIVAL

The immigrant who comes to the United States from a rural village or small town in Mexico or Latin America is often completely overwhelmed by the contrasts found in modern U.S. cities. In many Latino communities, the cultural world view of the church, the society, and the school are all one and the same. The major institutions are in agreement about who you are and how you are to live your life. This is changing in the larger Latin American cities to the dismay of many Latinos.

In the United States, most Latino families live in urban centers (U.S. Bureau of the Census, 1990). The first challenge for them is one of survival. Although most enter legally, many stay past their legal time period in order to work and support their families. Those without proper documentation live in constant fear of discovery and are ready victims for exploitation (Morganthau & Brant, 1997; Smolowe, 1997).

The process of leaving their homeland, their family, and friends, where all is familiar, is often a traumatic experience occasioned by economic or political necessity and dreams of a better life. Crossing the border without documentation can be dangerous and expensive (Galan, 1994). Many have been robbed, raped, beaten, and left for dead in their effort to cross to *El Norte*, the United States. Many Central Americans come to the United States traumatized by war and suspicious of all government officials. Some estimate that one out of every three who cross the border illegally is caught and sent back. The process then begins again. Only hope and faith sustain people forced to undergo such inhuman experiences. Their hope is for a better life away from the poverty and starvation of their homeland; their faith is in a God who will watch out for them as they travel and care for those left behind. Latinos raised in religious families call on God, Jesus, Mary, and all the saints to help them along their path.

Immigrants often see the worse parts of our American society: the slums, the back alleys, the inhuman living conditions of farm workers, the backbreaking jobs that no one wants. The immigrant experience of America is often one that is without mercy, without justice, without compassion. With time, some may see a different picture of the United States. They can see that there is also a lot that is good in this country and that their experience of the shadow side of our society is just that one side. This is best expressed by immigrants who have been in the United States for many years and have been able to make a living and support a family. There is a sense of thankfulness for a chance to make a better life than was possible in their homeland.

Latinos raised in the United States are caught between two world views, two cosmologies, those of modern society as opposed to the mystery of their Latino soul. Values clash. In the pluralistic world of the United States, there exist many world views and ways of living life. Many Latinos see this as permissive and dangerous to the well-being of their souls. Given the certitudes of the Latino world, the certitude of God, the certitude of their role in the universe, and the purpose of life, the openness of our modern society seems chaotic and without clear direction.

One Latino perspective perceives economics as the North American religion. Those who have money are valued and those without are not. A Latino who works all day for a contractor and then does not get paid sees North Americans pay lip service to a Christian God on Sundays and rob the poor of their livelihood during the week. Given the conservative nature of Latino villages, where behavior is carefully determined by custom and tradition, North American cities may be likened to Sodom and Gomorrah (Gen. 13:13). Latinos tell stories of myths and abuse to other Latinos planning to work in the United States. There is a common expression among Latinos that highlights this situation: *"Pobre de Mexico tan lejos de Dios y tan cerca a los Estados Unidos"* ("Poor Mexico so far from God and so close to the United States").

When immigrants leave their home and come across the border, everything may be strange and unknown. Yet one place where there may be a lessening of that fear and anxiety is in church. The church, the priest, the Mass, are all familiar to them. Attending a welcoming church becomes an oasis away from the stresses of being in a foreign country. Although not all church communities are welcoming, there has been in the last twenty years a concerted effort by the Catholic church and other mainline churches to provide Spanish-language services for Latino immigrants. In addition, many small "store front" evangelical churches have sprung up, giving response to the cry of the Latino soul for religious expression attuned to its expressive needs.

The Hispanic American Soul: An Identity Caught between Two Worlds

Part of the survival of any culture is its ability to adapt and adjust to new situations and absorb new realties into its existing system of understanding. The permeability of Latino culture allows for many possibilities when it comes to identity. Although some members of the dominant society want us to choose between being Latino or being American, to do so is to reject one's cultural identity, one's parents and family, one's neighborhood; it is to do damage to one's soul. First-generation Latinos are not going to do that. But second- and third-generation Hispanic Americans, educated in our public schools and exposed to the Latino stereotypes, struggle with this question of identity. They are torn between the world of home and that of the non-Hispanic world of school and work. They may feel at once comfortable in either world and disquieted at not fitting into either. They may experience a certain embarrassment because of their brown complexion, their Hispanic name, their family of origin, their *barrio* (neighborhood), and even their religious upbringing. Some may experience shame at being Hispanic and coming from poor neighborhoods. Their souls are conflicted by the struggle with how they feel about themselves and their background. They know they are Latino, but they may not want to be identified with all that the United States says about Latinos. This confusion is a normal part of the process of cultural integration for second- and third-generation Latino children. It is normal to be a little confused. Sometimes just knowing that this inner conflict is normal and shared by others eases feelings of isolation.

Something new has been born. Some call it a mestizo personality, and I argue that it is also a mestizo spirituality. The mestizo is a blending of cultures and spiritualities and the integration of values, beliefs, and behaviors from many influences to meet the needs of a new generation of Americans. This is not the "melting pot" philosophies of the turn of the century, but rather a "symphony" of varied instruments, each maintaining its integrity by contributing to the common music of the whole. America is a symphony of cultures. Latinos participate in that symphony of ideas, traditions, and cultural values. To carry the analogy further, each of us is a participant in this symphony and it takes time and some guidance to bring the various sounds into harmony. It is the job of the therapist to help individuals and groups appreciate the different sounds and deal with any dissonance. This can be done by helping the individual or families accept the fact of biculturalism, or multiculturalism. It might be beneficial to explore with them the various cultural influences present in their families of origin and early childhood development. Bringing this to surface helps in assessing the degree of influence and the extent of conflict present. Second- and third-generation Latinos are often caught between the two worlds. Generally, this generation does not feel gratitude but anger—at the mistreatment of their people by industry, by the courts, by all the major institutions of the United States. Those who have studied the history of abuse and exploitation must come to terms with the rage inside them at how Latinos have been mistreated (Acuña, 1981; McWilliams, 1949/1990). Therapists need to listen to the stories of abuse and help Latinos manage their rage. Helping Latinos acknowledge how they have maintained their own self worth in an abusive and unjust situation can give Latinos a sense of control and dignity. However, helping Latinos recognize situations that are potentially unjust in addition to helping them gain the skills needed to fight for their rights is even better.

Many Latinos feel they just don't quite fit in the dominant culture. They feel different. They often look different. Their skin may be white as the lightest Anglo or black as the darkest African. They may be of any race and yet are bound together by a common language and religious tradition. On one hand, they have inherited something of the Latino indigenous spirit of their parents and grandparents: trust in God, faith in goodness of life, and a confidence in the rewards given to those who are respectful and obedient to their elders. On the other hand, there is also an American spirit within them, that "rugged individualism" that calls each one to make it on their own, to soar solo and establish their own career, family, and home, to live wherever the job takes you, and to expect and demand justice and fair play in all their dealings. The job, the career, the possibility of wealth and status take on a sacred character. Therapists can work carefully with Latinos to help them sort through the tensions of living in two worlds and help them choose what is best for them given their circumstances.

Latinos may speak English with a heavy, a slight, or no accent. They may like a variety of different music, different foods, and forms of dress. Latinos have a passion about life that is missing in the mainstream society. It is that passion that indicates the presence of a soul, a spirit that permeates feelings and actions. The Latino spiritual soul may be buried underneath years of poverty or education and living in the dominant culture. And yet it is only when one allows that soul to come forward that one can be at peace. Therein lies the mystery of who Latinos are and have become. It is not the soul of one's parents, yet their spirit is there. It is something new: a "*mestizaje*," a mixture. It is something truly American, the coming together of different world views, and the emergence of someone new without losing the elements of the mixture, but integrating them in a new way. A therapist can help Latinos appreciate their culture and affirm their values as strengths that will help them forge new realities for themselves and their families.

Through the process of conquest, exploitation, and domination, both economically and spiritually, the identity of the indigenous has become of little value apart from a curiosity for tourists. The impact of centuries of disparagement has reached to the very soul of Latino peoples in the Americas. Where there has been significant contact with Europeans, the indigenous populations have suffered both physically and psychologically. Although people maintain many of the foods, folklore, and ancient indigenous temples as a reminder of their countries' past, the popular view of the poor and lower working class is one of disapproval, as Nobel laureate Octavio Paz names "*pelado*" (worthless wretch) (Paz, 1961). According to Paz's controversial view, this negative image is passed on from one generation to the next and is a major source of stress and the foundation to many negative behaviors within the Latino community. Although not unique to Latinos, a common attitude among some is: "If I am worthless, then my actions don't matter and I might as well get from life as much as I can." A popular expression within the Latino community is "*La vida no vale nada*" (Life has no value). Aspects of this self-image has been passed along to the Hispanic Americans of North America. A therapist can help explore with Hispanics the awareness of self-worth for themselves and in their culture. Learning to learn from the past as a starting point for the future is the work of therapy.

Christianity teaches that there should be no distinction between Jew and Greek, male and female (Gal. 3:28). A similar struggle for cultural identity exists for second-generation Cubans, Puerto Ricans, and other Latinos. Although some Latinos will argue that this self-image does not apply to them, there can be no question that North American media portrayal of Latinos has historically affirmed this stereotype. As more positive images of Latinos emerge in our society, along with them are also new stereotypes related to welfare abuse, gang violence, and dysfunctional family life. In the struggle to move out of poverty and behaviors that are not healthy, Latinos sometimes lose heart and face despair and depression. Therapists can encourage Latinos to view their culture as a positive force for themselves, underlying their gifts and values as important and for which it is worth fighting.

With regard to any religious material that emerges, care should be taken not to disparage religious beliefs, but rather to acknowledge them as products of the human experience. Individuals and families who are able to acknowledge the influence of these practices may then feel more free to accept all or part of these practices into their own spirituality. Usually, some modified form of the religious practice will maintain the link with the cultural group without completely binding the person to the spirituality of the past. Total rejection of one's spiritual roots is certainly possible, but the therapist might want to explore any intense feeling behind such rejection. Their choice should obviously be respected especially in this area of religious beliefs and practices. Given the complexity of these religious issues, careful attention should also be given to providing a safe environment, wherein they can explore the options open to them within their social and cultural context.

Faith

Faith is common to all people. Even the absence of faith is a form of faith. Jerome Frank (1973) calls this the "assumptive world view," a set of assumptions or presuppositions for dealing with reality. Yet for many Latinos, faith means that belief in God and religion is a way of organizing religious beliefs, rituals, and laws for the purpose of worship and living. Faith involves a whole complex of beliefs and assumptions that arise from our experience and beliefs about the sacred. Most peoples of the world operate out of a set of religious assumptions about reality. It is not just about church attendance; it has to do with how we see the world. Thus, most Latinos have a religious world view and look to their faith and religious beliefs to interpret and make sense of the world around them.

Faith and religion are not necessarily equivalent terms. For Latinos, faith is about belief in the sacredness of the world and an experience of the divine presence and will. This is a source of strength for the person, the family, and the community. This faith comes from deep within the person and at once transcends the individual and connects him or her to others in the community. It is this faith that sustains them in times of insurmountable pain and loss; it is this faith that cries out for justice in the face of violence; it is this faith that celebrates new life at birth and mourns the loss of life at death. Faith is also a decision of the spirit. For many Latinos, faith is formed and nurtured in the family and community, through special prayers, rosaries, and devotions. Yet it is the church that can be the strongest support for the family. Church, family, community work together and nourish each other. The Latino faith community believes that all in the universe has meaning and purpose in God's plan. With this belief, one is able to survive the tragedies of life without despair, to celebrate and give thanks in good times, and to direct their complaints and anger in times of sorrow.

Religion

Religion, for Latinos, is also a mechanism for survival. It is the way to understand and put order to their universe. Religious beliefs and practices are for Latinos, like for many other cultural groups, a way of looking at the world that has been passed down from one generation to the next in order to give meaning and purpose to living. It touches the very core of who they are and helps them understand, survive, and thrive in the world around them. These religious beliefs have roots that go back to the indigenous past, and to the early Christian missionaries of the sixteenth century. It is important to note that the Roman Catholic Church has been reluctant to incorporate Latino practices until fairly recently. For some Latinos, their faith and culture also integrates elements of their African or Asian roots. It is a prescientific cosmology where humans are at the center of the universe and all that happens has a divine origin and part of a divine plan. People influence that plan by their prayers and petitions, sacrifices and pilgrimages. They are able to dialogue with God directly or through intermediaries who are able to intercede for them. They are able to negotiate with God and get him to change his mind as did the patriarchs of the bible (Gen. 18). Within the Latino community, there is an awareness of the divine presence and, like all people, they stand in awe, and struggle to understand the meaning of this presence (Otto, 1917/1959).

GOD: MEANING AND PURPOSE AMIDST CHAOS AND CONFUSION

As we have seen, a fundamental concept within the Latino world view is that of God. For Latinos, God is not so much a concept as an experience. The belief in the presence of God is an integral part of the religious heritage passed on from previous generations. Our Spanish language is full of expressions that underlie the collective belief in God and the acceptance of God's reality as a normal part of existence. Thus, people will greet each other in the morning with *Buenos dias de Dios* understood as "good morning," but literally "good day of God." Other common expressions like *Adios,* or *Vaya con Dios,* (Go with God), *Que sea la voluntad de Dios* (Let it be God's will), and *Si Dios quiero* (If God wanted it) are only a few of the many daily expressions that show the pervasiveness of religious beliefs. Just using these expressions doesn't mean that one is a believer, but their presence in the common speech of the people does bespeak to the religious sensibility within the culture and to the collective consciousness of the people. What does this mean? As stated earlier, most Latinos believe in

God and acknowledge so in religious surveys. How are we to understand the Latino concept of God and what implications are there for therapists? Therapists must be open to contemplate and deal with spiritual ideas that arise in session.

In many Latino cosmologies, the forces of good do battle with the forces of evil and the battleground is the human soul. Some Latinos, usually the uneducated and superstitious, are caught between two worlds and must constantly choose between one or the other. The chaos and confusion found in this world, and in the human heart, are put in order by belief in an all powerful God who calls the world into order and gives it purpose. Many Latinos seem themselves as pilgrims along a journey traveling between life and death and destined to be with God in heaven. They are kept from sharing in God's glory by temptation, sin, and abandonment of God's call. Without God, many Latinos believe that there can be no meaning nor purpose to life. Without faith in God one is *perdido* (lost). The purpose of the universe is to provide us with a temporary home until we reach the eternal peace of heaven. Life has meaning only in the context of divine love and that love shared among caring human beings. All other values are secondary to love of God and loving relationships.

Recent immigrants come from Mexico because they are poor; the drive to survive and forge a better life for themselves and their families is instinctive and real. Given this cosmology, it is understandable that some will make reference to their homeland as a land of faith and trust in God, and *"El Norte,"* the United States, as "faithless," a land in which there is little trust and little faith. The danger of coming north is not only physical, but also spiritual. One is in danger of losing one's soul, or one's purpose and meaning. This type of thinking can lead some to giving up their values, which they need to hold dear.

The Expression of Jesus Christ: Empathy and Compassion

Christ has a special place, although there is no one understanding of Jesus among Latinos just as there is no one understanding of God. There are many layers of belief that differ, depending on the depth of faith, life experience, educational background, and family history. Still, some common characteristics seem to emerge at least among the immigrants that come to the United States. Almost all Latinos (87%)

believe that Jesus is God (Gallup, 1985). Here we find a paradox. On the one hand, Jesus is all powerful and the maker of miracles.

On the other hand, there is a deep appreciation for the vulnerability of Jesus. He is the tortured, suffering Christ, falsely accused and condemned to death. His humanity is a reflection of the humanity of the Latino people. His suffering and persecution are venerated in paintings and artwork that depict a bloodied, beaten Jesus. Latinos believe that Christ understands their suffering and pain because he himself has undergone persecution and abuse. He can empathize with the people he saves because he has lived life poor like them, persecuted like them, ignominious like them. He is the savior of the poor, not from a position of strength, but from one of weakness. It is this empathy and compassion that characterizes the Latino Christ and the Latino hope for salvation. Jesus knows their suffering and is moved by it. They do not suffer in isolation. There is one who hears their cry.

Poor Latinos identify more with that Christ that most resembles their own existence. Many immigrants are poor, as Christ was poor, so their lives are perceived as honorable. Latinos pour out their heart in a cathartic release of concern, pain, and requests for divine intervention. This outpouring of one's soul is not just a pious act of petition for help, but more deeply is part of a healing process. A therapist must be ready to listen to the pain and suffering part of a Latino's story. The act of seeking help and expressing deep emotions within cultural sanctioned rituals opens up the individual to the possibility of insight (inspiration) into possible solutions to life's problems. These rituals are often outside the lexicon of official liturgies of the Church and thus carry the name of "popular religiosity" (Oktavec, 1995; Romero, 1991).

Therapists might want to encourage their clients to share with them their prayers to God. Therapy can become a place for ritual. This type of sharing cannot but help give deeper insight into the person and strengthen the therapeutic bond between client and therapist. Obviously, therapists should be careful not to impose this action where there has not been some religious content initiated by the client.

Mary: Unconditional Acceptance

Another faith-related element in the Latino soul is the role of the Virgin Mary, or Our Lady of Guadalupe. Catholics refer to the mother of Christ as their own mother. There is much encouragement on the part of the church teaching and preaching in this regard (McBrien, 1994). Although much can be said about this role in the unconsciousness of the Latino believer, I will mention only a few of the more basic concepts that I think are important for therapists to keep in mind. The Virgin Mary as an archetype in the Latino psyche can be an oppressive imposition of unrealistic expectations or an avenue for emotional healing (Garcia-Preto, 1996b; Rodriguez-Holguin, 1994; Urrabazo, 1986). Latinos see Mary as *"nuestra Madre"* (our mother) whether it be under the title of Our Lady of Guadalupe, *Nuestra Señora del Cobre*, or the Immaculate Conception; all relate to the same woman of the Bible Christians believe has been entrusted with the maternal concern and protection of God's people (John 19:25–7.n). She is revered as their mother and exemplifies the ideal mother who offers her children unconditional acceptance (Elizondo, 1997; Rodriguez-Holguin, 1994).

Many Latinos hold Mary as their ideal. Accordingly, a life of motherhood, devoting oneself to the children is an important role for Latinas. Very high expectations can lead to sacrificing all for the children. If these expectations are too high, a Latina can turn from the Church. Yet, paradoxically, she may keep Mary as esteemed above all others. An exploration might reveal something of the feminine nature and demands of one's soul. Some theologians see Mary as the feminine heart of God in Western Christianity (Boff, 1987; Gebara, & Bingemer, 1989).

For Latinos, Jesus and Mary represent love, compassion, and justice for the forgotten and lost. Psychologically, they also represent different aspects of the idealized Latino self and work contrary to social stereotype and internalized negative self concepts. Therapists must be aware for the gender roles that these may evoke in Latino women, when they deal with marital and family issues.

Saints: Models of Integrity and Character

In Latino cultures, people also turn to the saints and various forms of popular religiosity to seek divine assistance. Latino believers view saints and holy people (good people, living or dead, not officially declared saints) as helpers in life with the power to influence and bring about changes in persons and events. These heroes of Christianity are reminders that many who have come before have struggled to live the

Christian life and have been victorious over evil and the vicissitudes of human existence.

Latinos find encouragement in the lives of the saints. A therapist may access a client's hopes and dreams by sorting through the stories of others that they find inspiring. Part of the therapeutic process might include a realistic appraisal of "religious icons." Many of the problems within and between people are related to false conceptions of the self and of the world. A therapist needs to be careful to listen and accept a client's beliefs, searching for the metaphors and stories that promote growth and life.

Let me say again what should be obvious about religious content. This type of material should not originate with the therapist nor should the therapist use religious literature unless the individual or the family initiates the discussion. The fundamental rule of following the patient's lead is especially appropriate when dealing with such potentially cathartic material as religious beliefs and practices. Nor should therapists shy away from delving into such issues. Obviously, these discussions should not be theological debates, but, as William James (1902/1958) pointed out many years ago, should be an honest acknowledgment of real human experiences that can and do change peoples lives.

THE CHURCH: A SUPPORTIVE COMMUNITY

Many Latinos go to the church as a refuge from the temptations and struggles of living in modern city life. In the church, they find something familiar and true, the peace and security they often felt back home. Given the religious heritage that Latinos bring to this country, it is only natural that they will try to duplicate the sense of belonging they experienced in their country of origin. Therapists must give consideration to the meanings placed on immigration events, underscoring the pilgrim image, a search for God's will. The church community can be a strong resource in their present and future lives.

Forty-four percent of Latinos go to church at least once a week. Another 24% attend two or three times a month. Latinos want to belong to religious communities that are welcoming and that provide needed social and spiritual services. The church for Latinos can be a supportive community in the midst of strangers. The growing number of small store-front churches is testimony to the fact that when Latinos do not feel welcome in the mainline churches, they will leave and start their own. The point here is not the worthiness of one church over another, but the desire of Latinos to belong to a supportive and affirming group. In a new land with strangers all around, a different language, and different cultural ways, Latinos find comfort in their local church, where, for a brief time, they feel at home. For the vast majority of Latinos, this is the Catholic church. But as more mainline and evangelical churches reach out and offer services sensitive to the needs of Latinos, it is only natural for them to go where they feel most welcomed and most at home.

Church participation is an opportunity for therapists to explore the need for affiliation of Latinos. The choices made with regard to church membership will offer insight into authority issues, moral issues, social and cultural expectations, as well as issues about belonging, marginalization, isolation, and separation. For many Latinos, participation in church activities satisfies a need of the soul to search out kindred spirits. Many churches hire therapists to work with couples and families. It is also helpful to talk about the expectations of the church community on its members. The church community can be an important first step in the acculturation process and in feeling comfortable with being in this country.

Within this pluralistic society of competing moral and social values, Latinos can contribute something to the discussion as they bring with them their cultural and religious traditions. Perhaps by active community involvement, one does not necessarily have to lose one's soul in migrating north. Churches provide an opportunity for that not to happen.

Priests and Ministers

Within the Latino community, priests have historically been the chief interpreters of God's will. Latinos with little formal religious education live in a world dominated by the interpretations of priests or preachers. Their voices are seen as the voice of God. They are esteemed as sacred persons and their decisions are often viewed as unquestionable. The priest or minister may be the first person a Latino or Latina turns to for help or advice. Other members of the church, such as sisters, brothers, religious coordinators, can also be resources for Hispanic families in need of help. Ministers and priests are rich referral sources for therapists, as they often send their parishioners to counselors when pastoral counseling is not enough. A collaborative community that involves church, school, family, and mental health resources is ideal.

PARENTAL ROLES: DIVINE EXPECTATIONS, HUMAN REALITIES

The attitudes held about our parents influence our religious beliefs and teaching about God. Many uneducated and rural Latinos operate out of a pre-Newtonian view of the world and their theology reflects that cosmology. In a prescientific world, gods and demons play havoc on the lives of humans. People placate them by prayers, incantations, and rituals. As more Latinos get a better education, the old religious answers will be challenged. Although it is not the job of the therapist to engage in theological debate, some assistance might be given by encouraging clients to explore contemporary understandings that value the importance of symbols. Children will challenge their parents' ideas of the world they live in. Therapists will have to explore magical thinking without deconstructing a belief system based on another worldview. It is not an easy call to make, but often necessary when teenagers and parents view reality in drastically different ways.

Fathers

It is generally accepted by researchers in the field that one's idea of God is determined to a great extent by one's human experience of one's parental figure. If one's experience of his or her father is that of a loving and kind man who is also strong and protective, it is not difficult to believe in a God who is also loving, kind, strong, and protective. In one study, Hispanic children were asked to respond to a series of projective tests and they portrayed their fathers as authoritative rather than authoritarian, that is, as one who gives advice and as the one to go to with questions (Urrabazo, 1986).

Latino Fathers are more involved in the raising of children than has been previously portrayed in the literature (Gutmann, 1996). Too often, negative stereotypes about Latino fathers as distant and uncaring are just not true, at least not any more than any other cultural group in the United States. With the increase in divorce, more men are stepfathers to children of other marriages (U.S. Bureau of the Census, 1992, 1993). Others live in a committed relationship with the mother of their children. Within this group, there is every possible degree of commitment (or lack thereof). In fact, there are many types of fathers in the Latino community. Some men are single parents. The vast majority of fathers do live within a committed married relationship.

The cultural expectation of Latino fathers is not unlike that expected of God: to protect and provide for the family, to work hard and yet have time for the wife and kids; to be responsible in all dealings within and without the family; to be a good role model for the children, a tower of strength for his sons, and a compassionate heart for his daughters. In contrast, Hispanic men report feeling a common or general disparagement of their self-worth within the Anglo society. They are seen as *"braceros"* (arms) that work and not much more. Children and teenagers begin to deal with what the family culture says, what the church says, and what society says. The contrasts of these views will create a struggle for identity, especially for the young man wanting to be like his father.

There comes a point in the life of any child when he or she sees their parents as human beings and not as all powerful and omniscient. It is a moment of conscious awareness of the fallibility of human parents. It can be also one of deep appreciation for the efforts made to protect, provide, and care for the family. Still there may be a personal and perhaps a cultural desire to maintain the myth of the father in some way. The young men may feel great anger at the treatment of their fathers or become embarrassed and rebel from their cultural identity. If someone is in charge of ordering the events of the universe around us, there is then a sense of security and purpose to life's challenges and for the family. Realistic views of a father can help create maturity and responsibility.

In Spanish we say, *Que sea la voluntad de Dios* (That it might be God's will). This expression is used to address those events that cannot be controlled or do not make any sense. The belief is that God is in control and wills this event for reasons one cannot understand at this time. The expected response is one of passive acceptance of the divine will. Difficult moments such as the death of a young child, a painful illness, or a spouse being treated in a shameful manner by society must be struggled with. This attitude may give some strength to move on to life as they pray before the cross of Christ. At these times, some people may turn away from God as their feelings of hurt and alienation turn into anger and confusion. Therapists gently accept these varying views as a natural form of the grieving process. Anger and pain are a part of grieving. The importance is that someone does not get stuck in pain and indignity or become bitter in this anger and then turn on life.

Mothers

Hispanic children portrayed their mothers as authoritarian on projective tests. Mother was the one who makes you do things or made things happen (Urrabazo, 1986). Mary, God's mother, is the ideal that Latina women look to for guidance and help. Our Lady of Guadalupe is the protector of all. She is the powerful image for the entire culture. Our Lady is the first woman of the Americas. Our Lady of Guadalupe changed the course of history. The peasants of Mexico were generally ignored by the Catholic Church until her miraculous appearances. It is no wonder that Our Lady can make things happen. Mothers in the Latino family, as in most cultures, are the key "culture bearers" and often the most influential in the development of personal, social, and cultural identity. They are expected to be all giving of themselves for their children, wise, industrious, and the ultimate protector of their children. Pope John Paul II, in a papal letter, stresses virginity and motherhood for all Catholic women (McBrien, 1994, p. 776). Although this teaching has been fairly consistent within the Catholic Church, national statistics in the United States seem to indicate that women are viewing motherhood as important but are turning away from virginity. There is a growing increase in single-parent families headed by women. Others are opting not to marry and to have children. Many women want and demand for themselves opportunities and options to live their lives as they choose and not according to the dictates of any institution. Latina women living in the United States are gradually introduced to opportunities of lifestyle and work not encouraged by more traditional cultures or taught by the Catholic Church.

Many Latina women, like others from all socioeconomic levels in America, are exploring new ways of being a woman. They have long worked in the fields alongside their spouses but have not had an equal share in the fruits of their labor nor in the decision making of society. Today, more women are demanding to have a say in the spending of both the "house money" and the countries' money. While visiting a remote village in Oaxaca, Mexico, I asked an elderly woman what she thought about women's rights. She told me that she works just as hard as her husband and demands a say in the decisions that affect her life and that of her children. She said that young women today will not put up with abusive husbands.

Although education is an important factor in providing women with a variety of opportunities, another important influence is the American culture itself. Changes are helpful for women as they learn that living with an abusive husband is not necessary. Opinions are helpful, but at the same time, there is some cause for alarm. Many children are growing up without two parents. Our high divorce rate and increase in single-parent families puts added stress on women and places unrealistic expectations of being "super moms" for their children. In spite of the strong family values found in the Latino cultures, all indications are that the Latino community is moving in the same direction as the majority of American families.

With the many roles demanded of women (daughter, sister, wife, mother, career women, provider, etc.), women can become overwhelmed with little time for themselves. All theses roles reflect aspects of the female self and become an integral part of one's identity. But there is a deeper core that is at the center of all these activities. Women today are trying to speak to this often hidden dimension of the self. Many turn to religion to seek out direction. It is paradoxical that the same religion that can be oppressive of women can also be the source of their liberation. They find a spiritual prayer in church, which grounds them in their struggle. Many women find social network in church settings. Reading groups, retreats, divorce groups, and so on, all offer support for women. They also have opportunities to help each other and join programs that advance their skills in English or simple listening skills. Women join the parish church in all sorts of ways. They help as festival coordinators and volunteer in church offices and on parish councils.

The view of mothers as self-sacrificing women who have to give up their lives for the sake of the family is one of the key myths of the Latino culture. To say that this is a myth is not to deny that the reality has been idealized by the church and the Latino culture beyond the reach of many. Among Latinos, the cultural expectation may be so strong that many women live lives with constant feelings of inadequacy. Yet although many women are the main providers and the head of the family, it is often the mother who is running the household, paying the bills, and making the key decisions in the home. In relation to her children, mothers often have the last word (Unsworth, 1997).

The significance of this for therapists working with Latinos is to understand that the role of mother is charged with both emotional and religious significance. Women must learn to claim their strength and limitations. As women claim their identity as strong, they can use their devotion to Our Lady as real support. As Our Lady of Guadalupe made things happen, so can Hispanic women. Rather than reject this cultural icon as oppressive, a reading in contemporary theology may help to make Mary more human and more dynamic for Latina women. The Catholic Church is today seriously contemplating declaring Mary "co-mediatrix of salvation" for the year 2000. This is a title that has been part of the belief of the faithful for centuries. Mary, together with Jesus, has been instrumental in bringing about the salvation of the world (Unsworth, 1997). This is not to take away the specialness of the myth; rather, it is to deepen our understanding and show a different face of the traditional image. In doing so, we also show a different view of women (Boff, 1987).

Therapists: Intermediaries of God

In all of the preceding reflections, I have made reference to the role of the therapist as one who can explore aspects of religious thought in helping the troubled person or family. Understanding Latinos is more than being fluent in Spanish; it is also understanding the cultures of the Latino peoples. This has been clearly stated by McGoldrick in her interesting collection of essays on culture and family therapy (Bernal & Shapiro, 1996; Garcia-Preto, 1996a, 1996b; Hernandez, 1996; Korin,

1996; McGoldrick, Giorgano, & Pearce, 1996). The various essays in her work highlight the importance of religion in the various cultures studied and therefore the importance for the therapist to have some understanding of religious beliefs and practices. What I would like to add to this discussion is how the people view the therapist and how the therapist might view his or her self in working within the Latino community.

Latinos for the most part go to their local priest, minister, deacons, sisters, brothers, or religious coordinators when they seek help in resolving personal or family problems. Studies continue to show that most people will go to their religious leader first when seeking counseling (Clinebell, 1984). Most clergy persons do not have the training nor the time for long-term therapeutic relationships and often will refer people to a therapist whom they believe will be sensitive to the particular needs of the counselee. Nonetheless, it is important for the therapist to understand that good pastoral counseling dictates that even though people have been referred to a professional therapist, the clergy are expected to maintain some contact with their parishioner. There may be an opportunity to collaborate when the occasion warrants. Often, ministers welcome guidelines from therapists on who is appropriate to refer. Therapists can learn what help they can offer from ministers. Some Latinos may see the therapist as an extension of the services of the church and as such as an extension of the church ministry. In short, therapists may be seen as fulfilling similar functions as church leaders, with similar corresponding expectations.

It is common for Latino clients to ascribe a certain status and power to their therapist not unlike that of priests, *curanderas* (local spiritual leaders), magic, and miracle workers. These unrealistic expectations are best understood and cleared up from the beginning. Latinos expect therapists to have a special knowledge and insight into the problems of life that allow them to give sage advice. Although advice is rarely appropriate, some suggestions and guidance on how to think about their problems and how to explore unconscious motivations are helpful. This demands a careful response from the therapist so as to help individuals and families find their own way without feeling rejected.

Latinos also expect therapists to be what we call *"serviciales"* (of service). Therapists can be a positive force in the service of mental health and also a help toward spiritual wholeness. This service is both behavioral and attitudinal. Some therapists may not speak the language well nor understand all the nuances of the culture, but Latinos can pick up very easily when someone really is trying to help. At times, it this attitude of caring that is the most helpful for our people in establishing trust and confidence in the therapist. The language of Hispanic Americans is not just Spanish, it is the language of the heart. Latino faith is not just in God, but also in those intermediaries that God has placed in their path. Therapists may be seen as intermediaries with God by some Latinos.

CONCLUSION

This chapter has explored some basic concepts and issues related to Latinos, religion, and possible therapeutic opportunities and directions. When a Latino client or family enters into the therapeutic process, they should be able to freely discuss any aspect of their life that may have a bearing on their reason for seeking help. When religious material is presented, this may provide a valuable opportunity for therapists to explore some of the fundamental beliefs and attitudes that influence behavior within Latino communities. Therapists who are sensitive to the religious reality of Latinos will be better able to help their clients gain greater insight into themselves and into those aspects of their family and culture that may have a bearing on their current situation. Religious beliefs continue to be a major anchor of Latino identity and decision making. It behooves all of us in the helping professions to take Latino religious experience seriously.

REFERENCES

Acuña, R. (1981). *Occupied America* (2nd ed.). New York: Harper & Row.

Bernal, G., & Shapiro, E. (1996). Cuban families. In M. McGoldrick, J. Giorgano, & J. K. Pearce (Eds.), *Ethnicity and family therapy* (2nd ed., pp. 155–168). New York: Guilford Press.

Boff, L. (1987). *Maternal face of God.* New York: Harper & Row.

Boff, L. (1995). *Catechism of the Catholic church.* New York: Doubleday.

Clinebell, H. (1984). *Basic types of pastoral care and counseling: Resources for the ministry of healing and growth.* Nashville, TN: Abingdon Press.

DeVos, G. (1978). Selective permeability and reference group sanctioning: Psychocultural continuities in role degradation. In J. Milton Yinger & Stephen J. Cutler (Eds.), *Major social issues: A multidisciplinary view.* London: The Free Press.

Elizondo, V. (1997). *Guadalupe: Mother of the new creation.* New York: Orbis Books.

Falicov, C. J. (1996). Mexican families. In M. McGoldrick, J. Giorgano, & J. K. Pearce (Eds.), *Ethnicity and family therapy* (2nd ed., pp. 169–182). New York: Guilford Press.

Frank, J. (1973). *Persuasion and healing* (Rev. ed.). Baltimore: Johns Hopkins University Press.

Gallup, G., Jr. (1985). Religion in America—50 years: 1935–1985. *Report No. 236.* Princeton, NJ: The Gallup Poll.

Gallup, G., Jr. (1988). *The Unchurched American—10 Years Later.* Princeton, NJ: The Princeton Religion Research Center.

Galan, H. (1994). *Go back to Mexico.* [Documentary]. Austin, TX: Galan Productions.

Garcia-Preto, N. (1996a). Latino families: An overview. In M. McGoldrick., J. Giorgano, & J. K. Pearce (Eds.), *Ethnicity and family therapy* (2nd ed., pp. 141–154). New York: Guilford Press.

Garcia-Preto, N. (1996b). Puerto Rican families. In M. McGoldrick., J. Giorgano, & J. K. Pearce (Eds.), *Ethnicity and family therapy* (2nd ed., pp. 183–199). New York: Guilford Press.

Gebara, I., & Bingemer, M. (1989). *Mary: Mother of God, mother of the poor.* Maryknoll, NY: Orbis Books.

Gutmann, M. C. (1996). *The meanings of macho: Being a man in Mexico City.* Berkeley: University of California Press.

Hartshorne, C. (1948/1976). *The divine relativity: A social conception of God.* New Haven: Yale University Press.

Hernandez, M. (1996). Central American families. In M. McGoldrick., J. Giorgano, & J. K. Pearce (Eds.), *Ethnicity and family therapy* (2nd ed., pp. 214–224). New York: Guilford Press.

Holy Bible, King James Version. (1962). Grand Rapids, MI: Zondervan.

James, W. (1902/1958). *The varieties of religious experience.* New York: New American Library.

Korin, E. C. (1996). Brazilian families. In M. McGoldrick., J. Giorgano, & J. K. Pearce (Eds.), *Ethnicity and family therapy* (2nd ed., pp. 200–213). New York: Guilford Press.

Kuhn, T. S. (1962). *The structure of scientific revolutions.* Chicago: University of Chicago Press.

Kung, H. (1978). *Does God exist? An answer for today.* E. J. Quinn (Trans.). London: Abingdon Press.

McBrien, R. P. (1994). *Catholicism* (Rev. ed.). San Francisco: HarperCollins.

McGoldrick, M., Giorgano, J., & Pearce, J. K. (Eds.). (1996). *Ethnicity and family therapy* (2nd ed.). New York: Guilford Press.

McWilliams, C. (1949/1990). *North from Mexico: The Spanish speaking people of the United States* (Rev. ed.). M. S. Meier (Ed.). New York: Praeger.

Morganthau, T., & Brant, M. (August 4, 1997). Immigration: Cracking a slavery ring—How deaf Mexicans were smuggled into forced servitude. *Newsweek,* p. 39.

Oktavec, E. (1995). *Answered prayers: Miracles and milagros along the border.* Tucson: University of Arizona Press.

Otto, R. (1917/1959). *The idea of the holy.* J. W. Harvey (Trans.). Middlesex: Penguin Books.

Paz, O. (1961). *The labyrinth of solitude.* New York: Grove Press.

Rodriguez-Holguin, J. (1994). *Our Lady of Guadalupe: Faith and empowerment among Mexican American women.* Austin: University of Texas Press.

Romero, C. Gilbert. (1991). *Hispanic devotional piety: Tracing the biblical roots.* Maryknoll, NY: Orbis Books.

Smolowe, J. (August 4, 1997). Suffering in silence: Deaf slaves are set free, but are there more? *Time,* p. 33.

Unsworth, T. (July 18, 1997). Pope may declare Mary's coredemptrix. *National Catholic Reporter,* 11–12.

Urrabazo, R. (1986). Machismo: Mexican American male self-concept (Doctoral dissertation, Graduate Theological Union, Berkeley, California).

U.S. Bureau of the Census. (1990). Housing characteristics of selected races and Hispanic-origin households in the United States: 1987. *Series H121-87-1.* Washington, DC: U.S. Government Printing Office.

U.S. Bureau of the Census. (1992). Households, families, and children: A 30-year perspective. *Current Population Reports,* P23-181. Washington, DC: U.S. Government Printing Office.

U.S. Bureau of the Census. (1993). *Hispanic Americans today,* P23-183. Washington, DC: U.S. Government Printing Office.

10

HEALTHCARE TODAY: TREATING HISPANIC FAMILIES AND CHILDREN WITH CHRONIC ILLNESSES

HEATHER J. AMBROSE, MARIA T. FLORES,
AND GABRIELLE CAREY

My pledge as a physician is to ask God to be virtuous in my dealings.
I want to understand the cry of pain from those that are suffering.
I want to heal those that are injured and sick. In this way,
I can soothe the mourning mother, wipe away the tears of the innocent,
accept the noise and protests of the elderly, and be kind to the lost
and mentally tormented.

Saul S. Trevino, MD., Founder of the Diabetic Clinic,
Robert B. Green Hospital (1950), Cofounder of the Poly Clinic
with Ramiro Estrada, MD., Joaquin Gonzales, MD.,
Isikia Gonzalez, MD., and Eduardo Ximenez, MD.
—BENAVIDES, 1997

Culture provides a core perspective for viewing the healthcare of families of all ethnicities, but is especially important in understanding issues with Hispanic families who have chronically ill children in healthcare systems. Hispanic families approach health services for

229

their physical and mental health problems in ways that some professionals may find complex. Some families do not seek the care they need and others do not receive proper care for a variety of reasons. Hispanic families tend to be child-centered, placing the welfare of their children before their own needs. However, obtaining adequate healthcare is still a problem for many Hispanic children in the United States.

One goal of healthcare reform is to provide at least minimal care for all citizens. To a great extent, the advent of managed care has done much to set this goal in motion for Hispanic families who are struggling in the mid to lower economic levels. In the lower to middle economic class of American citizens, medical insurance was not affordable but they were ineligible for welfare or medicaid. Many more Hispanic families and families in general have basic medical health insurance through their employers. Still, working out ways to ensure proper medical and mental healthcare for Hispanic families remains a challenge for providers who wish to offer culturally competent healthcare services.

THE MEANING OF CHILDHOOD CHRONIC ILLNESS

While gathering my thoughts about what to write for this chapter, I (the first author) could not help but reflect on my own experience with having a chronically ill family member. When my niece was eleven years old, she was diagnosed with juvenile-onset diabetes. She is my sister's daughter and her father is a Native American. The diagnosis came as quite a shock to my family as we had never had a family member diagnosed with juvenile-onset diabetes. I knew at that time that my niece's diagnosis would have an incredibly large impact on the rest of her life. However, I was not prepared for the kind of impact her illness would have on the rest of the family.

Everyone in my family has had to learn some things about diabetes management and what to do in the case of a diabetes emergency. We have all had to make some adjustments in order to help my niece manage her diabetes to the best of her ability. Diabetes management has seemed to be a difficult task for my niece, as she is very angry about having the disease and at times behaves as if her diabetes is not a problem. Her attempts to deny the existence of the diabetes has, on a few occasions, resulted in some very serious reactions that could have ended in her death if my sister or brother-in-law had not been with her. Seeing the effects her diabetes has had on my family prompted me to investigate more about juvenile-onset diabetes, and how this illness affects other families.

At the time of my niece's diagnosis, I was finishing up my first year as a Master's student in marriage and family therapy. My first instinct was to find out as much as I could about juvenile-onset diabetes. Through reading countless journal articles and medical books, I quickly learned how serious the diagnosis of juvenile-onset diabetes was. I also discovered what lifestyle changes a person with juvenile-onset diabetes must make in order to live a healthy life. In addition to learning about lifestyle changes, I became amazed at the staggering statistics I found regarding juvenile-onset diabetes, particularly with regard to ethnicity. Juvenile-onset diabetes has reached epidemic proportions in Hispanic families, yet many do not receive the help they need to properly combat or deal with the stress of this chronic illness.

I spoke with Maria Flores and Gabrielle Carey about their clinical work and their supervision of Hispanic families with chronic illnesses. The result of my research on Hispanic families and juvenile-onset diabetes was my doctoral dissertation; the result of my own experiences in collaboration with Gabrielle and Maria's clinical experience was this chapter. Although I focused on diabetes, other chronic illnesses also have childhood onsets. Although each disease or chronic disorder presents unique challenges to professionals, the family dynamics can be relatively similar. This chapter will examine the importance of including family therapy with larger systems interventions, such as the extended Hispanic family, the healthcare system, the school system, and other social or governmental systems.

COLLABORATING FOR MEANING

Part of the role that mental health professionals treating families with chronically ill members can play is to help doctors understand the process of meaning construction in the family's adjustment to the illness. Rolland (1998) discusses the importance of exploring a family's benefits about and experiences with a health problem. Utilizing the services of mental health professionals can assist healthcare providers in discovering important aspects of a family's belief system. Some important aspects of a family's belief system include family beliefs about what is normal and abnormal; the importance a family places on conformity and excellence in relation to the average family; how the family views the relationship between the mind and body; ideas about what caused an illness and what can affect its course and outcome; and meanings attached by the family, ethnic group, religion, or the wider culture to symptoms or specific diseases (Rolland, 1998). Including the family in the treatment and care of a chronic illness is very important. As reported by Horowitz et al. (1998), it has been discovered that involving the family in the medical treatment process tends to shorten the length of hospital stays, reduces the chance of a relapse, and enhances the patient's level of comfort.

In order for collaboration among the healthcare workers, the mental health workers, and the family to exist and be beneficial, a good relationship must exist among all three parties. McDaniel and Campbell (1997) state that the relationship is the key component that determines how successful the collaboration will be. Rolland (1988) concurs by stating that the success or failure of collaboration between healthcare professionals and the family depends on the fit of beliefs among the family, the provider, and the healthcare system over time. Open communication and education also seem to be key factors involved in a successful collaboration process (Horowitz et al., 1998). Mental health professionals must be active in the community and must work to educate families with chronically ill members regarding what these families can expect to experience while going through the adjustment process. Education might also include practical aspects of disease management, which may not have been sufficiently explained by the medical professionals or adequately understood by the patients. Mental health professionals must not become easily discouraged when first attempts at community outreach fail. Through establishing a collaborative relationship with Mexican American families with a chronically ill member, medical and mental health professionals can better assist these families with their adjustment to a difficult and painful process.

COLLABORATION AND MANAGED CARE ISSUES

It appears as though more and more doctors are beginning to appreciate the benefits of taking a multidisciplinary approach to treating chronic illnesses. Strozier and Walsh (1988) discuss various models of collaborative practice, which include holistic practices, public health settings, and HMOs. Each of the three models will be discussed briefly.

Holistic practices involve multiple contributors from differing disciplines. Medical care is reframed as wellness care, with a shift toward healthier lifestyles. This model has typically been utilized only in affluent communities where the participants can pay for the services out of their own pockets. Public health settings typically have a structure that is compatible with the collaborative approach. However, these settings generally do not effectively implement collaboration. HMOs probably have the greatest potential for utilizing the collaborative process. However, according to Strozier and Walsh (1998), because of the HMO's heavy emphasis on cost containment and the separation of mental health benefits from general medical benefits, physicians in HMO settings may be discouraged from engaging in collaborative relationships. This is unfortunate because, according to McDaniel and Campbell (1997), collaborative healthcare tends to lead to better health outcomes for less money.

FAMILIES WITH CHILDREN IN MEDICAL CRISES

There is little doubt that the diagnosis of a severe or chronic illness in a family member has a tremendous impact on the family system. Once a family member is diagnosed with a sudden, long-term illness, the family system changes. Everyone in the family must learn how to adjust to the new illness, which creates stress for the family and interrupts normal patterns of family functioning. This may be especially true for severe and chronic illnesses with an acute onset. This chapter will be useful in the treatment of families whose children have been determined to have any number of chronic illnesses or disorders, such as juvenile-onset diabetes, rheumatoid arthritis, sickle-cell anemia, cystic fibrosis, birth defects, genetic syndromes, physical handicaps and disfigurements, HIV or AIDS, cancers, and asthma. It is estimated that 6 to 12% of all the children in the United States have a serious chronic illness (Hobbs, Perrin, & Ireys, 1985).

Family therapists are specially trained to help families adjust to the emotional and mental upheavals illness can bring. Therapists need to give proper attention to the particular educational, psychological, and emotional needs of the entire family, beginning as soon as the chronic illness is diagnosed. Facilitating the collaboration of families, medical care providers, and school personnel will ensure the continued well-being of children with chronic disorders (Younger et al., 1985). Families can seek help for alleviation of stress and pain, help with compliance to medical treatment regimes, and a general stabilization of family life. By working along with family physicians and other medical specialists, family therapists can serve as an anchor for the family amidst the ensuing maelstrom.

Stressors on the Family

The burden of caring for the disease can be even greater with time. For families with insurance, once the child with a chronic illness becomes an adult, he or she may not be able to obtain his or her own health insurance because chronic diseases are a preexisting condition. Without medical insurance, maintaining healthy management of the disease may become extremely difficult, and the person may begin to feel demoralized and rejected by the medical community. The costs of these chronic illnesses can be staggering. HIV and cancer treatments can be highly costly and experimental and often are not covered by HMOs, PPOs, or other affordable insurance. In addition to juvenile diabetes or the many forms of cancer, many young girls becoming women develop anorexia nervosa or bulimia and need ongoing attention. Women well into their postmenopausal years can still be found suffering from eating disorders that had an onset in early adolescence. These diseases are only a few of the areas in which health coverage needs to be extended.

Factors that contribute to aggravating any illness are stress, unresolved family conflict, and personal loss and depression (Bahnson, 1987, p. 31). Stress is defined as the response to a severe stressor. A person usually responds to a major stressor in three phases: (1) alarm and mobilization, (2) resistance, and (3) restructuring, and exhaustion of available resources, or death. The stressor itself may not kill, but the person's reaction to it can. According to Rolland (1987), acute onset illnesses require effective and instrumental changes compressed into a short period of time. In addition, if the illness follows a relapsing, episodic course, families must learn to be flexible to deal with the stress associated with the fluctuation between crisis and noncrisis stages (Rolland, 1987). Family conflict can be related to disease vulnerability and can be multigenerational.

Vulnerability or Resilience?

According to Figley and McCubbin (1983), the vulnerability of a family to crisis depends on the interaction of the stressor with existing resources and with family perception. Once a chronic illness has been diagnosed in a child, flexibility to change family roles, to take on new tasks and demands, mutual emotional support among family members, and the family's perception of the stressor event will determine how successfully the family will negotiate the inevitable changes that occur within the family's system.

An investigation of the characteristics, dimensions, and properties of resilient families that assisted these families in being resistant to disruption in the face of change and adaptive in the face of crisis situations was conducted by McCubbin and McCubbin (1989). Regenerative families were seen as the type of families that could handle change and crisis. According to McCubbin and McCubbin (1989), these families cope with difficulties through faith, acceptance, and working together to solve problems. Regenerative families are active, try new things, and encourage others to appropriately address their problems and concerns. These families are in control, active, and when faced with difficulties, they are more caring, loyal, and tolerant of hardships.

In a chapter on families with children coping with chronic illnesses, Judith Libow (1989) puts an emphasis on resilient families. So often in medical systems, the emphasis is placed on the pathology and the problems resulting from it such as family isolation, maternal depression, sibling and patient's emotional disturbances, and the overinvolvement of the primary caregiver with the patient. Libow argues for more studies on family coping skills, strengths, resources, and adaptive styles:

Interestingly, there is very little literature on strengths of families with chronically ill children, their adaptive styles, or the elements of medical care most facilitative of effective family coping. Yet many families with similar circumstances and hardships manage to successfully meet the challenges of the illness as well as the needs of their ill children and other family members, despite the ongoing problems of pain, disruption, uncertainty, family reorganization, and possibly life-threatening changes as the days go by. (p. 213)

Case Study 1: A Resilient Family Regenerates

Diana was a performer. She was selected by the art and drama team her freshman year to be a member of young performers of San Antonio. Diana loved to dance, sing, play piano, and act. Diana's parents were excited, as this provided their daughter with the opportunity to develop her talents and skills.

In her sophomore year, Diana began to lose her luster. She lost weight and her instructors noticed that her energy and performances lacked the focus to detail that had been one of Diana's best skills. In a routine meeting with the instructors, Diana admitted that she had been starving herself and whenever possible vomiting her food. The instructors gave Diana one week to inform her parents of her problem or they would call them with this information. They also suspended Diana for one year from the young performers of San Antonio.

Diana's parents took Diana to her medical doctor. He gave the family three referrals for psychotherapists from the approved list of providers. The new insistence by managed care companies for referrals from a family doctor has created a more consistent consultation with medical personnel from our office. These referrals are helpful when the physical and mental health issues are intertwined. Diana's parents chose from their PPO rather than their HMO list in order to pick their own provider, although it would cost them more money. They wanted a licensed family therapist who specialized in eating disorders.

They chose a Hispanic provider because they wanted a therapist who understood the special dynamics of Hispanic families. In this case, almost all treatment was done through family sessions. These parents acted as "cotherapists" in the therapeutic process. This Hispanic couple was very egalitarian in their interactions and parenting style. Diana made rapid progress. After Diana's admission, other girls in her performance group and school came forward with similar problems. Diana, although still in recovery, was hired to be the lead actress in a documentary on eating disorders.

Diana's family certainly was willing to work together for their daughter's improvement. The family's flexibility and effort for education and support were admirable. In Diana's case, education was a most important step in helping the family to understand what happened to her desire to perform. Diana explained to her family how she distorted her thinking process into fooling herself into vomiting after eating. She admitted that at first, this approach for losing weight worked, but over time, it sapped her energy and talents.

HISPANIC CULTURAL FACTORS AND FAMILY REACTIONS TO STRESS

Falicov (1982, pp. 137–139) described common aspects of Mexican American families. Falicov stated that Mexican American families tend to have traditional views about family life. Many conservative Mexican American couples tend to have a traditional division of labor in the household. The husband typically assumes the role of provider and protector of the family, and the mother typically assumes the expressive role of homemaker and caretaker. The relationship between parents and children is considered to be very important. Therefore, the Mexican American couple primarily focuses on parental functions during the child-rearing stages. Parents will sacrifice everything for their child. The extended family is extremely important, and there is typically a high level of interdependence and support between generations.

Chilman (1993) has conducted research on Mexican American families to determine if there are differences between Mexican American and Anglo American families. She discovered that there are many kinds of Mexican American families with differing cultural patterns. Diversity in Hispanic families is matched with diversity in Anglo American families. These patterns vary in accordance with how recently the family has immigrated to the United States, place of residence, socioeconomic status, degree of intermarriage with other ethnic groups, age, urbanization, and the employment of women outside the home. Recent studies have revealed egalitarian family patterns in urban and rural Mexican American families.

One Mexican American study found rigid differentiation of sex role tasks to be lacking, and that both men and women shared in homemaking and child-rearing needs (Chilman, 1993). However, fathers tended to have a stronger role outside the family, and mothers tended to have a stronger role in the day-to-day matters of child rearing and homemaking. Mothers were still viewed as being the center of the family and fathers were still seen as being the authority figure. Extended family was still viewed as being an important source of support, especially for the children in Hispanic families. Other authors (Flores & Sprenkle, 1988) found that among nonclinical families with comparable incomes, Mexican Americans (959) and Anglo Americans (1315) scored in *the balanced family* range on the FACES survey (Olson, Portner, & Lavee, 1985).

Juvenile-Onset Diabetes: An Epidemic among Hispanic Populations

Juvenile-onset *Diabetes mellitus* is the most common endocrine disorder of childhood and adolescence (Younger et al., 1985). In 1985, approximately 66 million children under the age of seventeen had been diagnosed with juvenile insulin-dependent diabetes, or Type I diabetes. In 1996, the Juvenile Diabetes Foundation estimated that within the year, another 650,000 people would be diagnosed with some form of diabetes. In the state of Texas, diabetes with its complications is the third leading cause of death. The high rate of deaths attributed to diabetes and related complications in Texas may be correlated with the large population of ethnic minorities that live in Texas. Recent research has indicated that Hispanic Americans, African Americans, and Native Americans are 1.5 to 2.5 times more likely to develop diabetes than other ethnic groups (Diabetes Fact Sheet, 1996).

However, as I found from doing my own research on Mexican Americans and juvenile-onset diabetes, Mexican Americans are less likely to seek appropriate medical care and tend to be more noncompliant with treatment regimens. The lack of appropriate medical care and noncompliance with treatment regimens may increase the likelihood of serious health complications occurring (Ambrose, 1997). It was because of the high incident rate of juvenile-onset diabetes among Mexican Americans, and their tendency to not adhere to treatment regimens, that I chose to take a more in-depth look at the impact juvenile-onset diabetes has on Mexican American families. According to the Juvenile Diabetes Foundation (1996), 9.6% of the Mexican American population has some type of diagnosed or undiagnosed diabetes. Mexican American families may deal with chronic illness differently than families of other ethnicities. There are many issues involved in managing a chronic illness like juvenile-onset diabetes. In these days of managed care, these issues become even more relevant.

A Serious Reflection on Research with Hispanic Populations

Through the process of conducting my research study, I ran into one very large obstacle. Although I was living in a geographical location with a large population of Mexican American families having children with juvenile-onset diabetes, I had a very difficult time gaining their permission to interview them about their experiences. Looking back, I may have gained some insight into why I experienced these difficulties.

One of the barriers to my interviews may have had something to do with my ethnicity, gender, and level of education. I am an Anglo female who, at the time of the interviews, was conducting research for my dissertation. Although I explained to the families that I wanted to talk with them about their experiences of having a child diagnosed with juvenile-onset diabetes and did not stress the research aspect, I believe that many of the families were uncomfortable with the idea of talking with me because of our cultural differences. Because I am an outsider, these families may not have trusted me enough to share their personal feelings and family struggles with me.

Keitel, Kopala, and Georgiades (1995) stated that Mexican Americans were more likely to receive substandard health medical care than Anglos, possibly because of deference to medical professionals and wanting to avoid embarrassment by not asking necessary questions. The deference and embarrassment factor may have played a role in the unwillingness of these families to speak with me. Deference and embarrassment may also play a role in the lack of support groups that exist for Mexican American families with diabetic children in the geographical location in which this study was conducted.

I was shocked and dismayed to find only one support group existed in this area of Texas to specifically help families with children diagnosed with juvenile-onset diabetes, and that there was only one outreach program aimed specifically at the Mexican American population at Santa Rosa Children's Hospital. When I asked about the lack of support groups and outreach programs, I was told that these services had not been utilized in the past and therefore no longer existed. It stands to reason then that the Mexican American population may be just as inhibited about seeking help from mental health professionals as they are from medical professionals. When Mexican Americans do present for mental health services, it would behoove the mental health professionals to take a systemic perspective in examining both health and mental factors that may be causing stress on the client.

I believe acculturation, class, and language were also factors that influenced which families consented to participate in the interviews. Of the four families interviewed for the study, one family was considered to be upper class ($120,000 gross annual income) and three were considered to be middle class ($50,000 gross annual income). Three of the families were second- or third-generation Americans, and all four families spoke fluent English. The four families willingly participated in the interview process and shared very personal family experiences. Three of the families spoke about the importance of seeking and gaining support from family and from the medical community, whereas one family was hesitant about participating in support groups because it did not want to focus on the diabetes. I am left wondering if more Hispanic therapists and researchers are needed, especially in areas heavily populated with Hispanics.

Because there is such a strong connection between mental health and physical health, I found it important to explore what factors might be involved in Mexican American families seeking out and obtaining mental health and medical services (Ambrose, 1997). Although I focused my research on juvenile-onset diabetes, similar reactions and dynamics may occur in Hispanic families with children diagnosed with other chronic illnesses. In the next few sections, we will be exploring more closely the family readjustment period, and we will explore some important issues discovered by the first author in her research with case studies about families dealing with other types of chronic illnesses in their children.

RESTRUCTURING THE FAMILY SYSTEM

While sifting through the literature on chronic illness and its affects on the family, I encountered several articles pertaining to family stress theory. Figley and McCubbin (1983), in their work with the creation of the Double ABCX Model of Family Stress, discussed the importance of family perception in handling crises. Patterson and Garwick (1994) expanded on the work of Figley and McCubbin by proposing three levels of family meaning in order to gain a better understanding of the family's definition of the crisis.

The first level of family meaning is the meaning the family gives to the situation. Patterson and Garwick (1994) state that in addition to interpretations about the cause behind the illness, the family will also develop ideas and expectations about who will be responsible for managing the illness. These expectations are important aspects of how well the ill child will adhere to treatment regimens, as well as how strong a relationship is formed between the family and the healthcare system.

The second level of meaning is how the family views itself, or family identity. Under this level of meaning, according to Patterson and Garwick (1994), family roles need to be reallocated and family rules need to be changed in order to form a new family structure that will more adequately meet the needs of the family. At this level, family resources become extremely important in helping the family adapt to the illness. The authors further state that under the family identity meaning level, families must be cautious not to direct a disproportionate amount of the family's resources toward the illness, which would result in the reduction of resources needed for normal family functioning. This unbalancing of resources can lead a family to identify itself as "a diabetic family" as opposed to a family with a diabetic member.

The third level of meaning deals with how the family views the world, and the family's relationship to the world. Restructuring the family during a crisis or a time of stress often requires changes in the family's relationships to others outside of the family and to life itself. According to Patterson and Garwick (1994), crisis often causes people to turn to significant others for emotional support and explanations of the crisis. During times of crisis, families often pull together to create a shared world view. Families who experience support from their community will adjust better to crisis than those families who experience stigmatization and isolation.

Hispanic Families Experiencing Restructuring: Research Findings

My research (Ambrose, 1997) on Hispanic families uncovered an overall theme surrounding the adjustment that occurs after a child is diagnosed with juvenile-onset diabetes. This family adjustment process entailed five steps: (1) reorganizing family resources; (2) finding ways to balance changes occurring within the families with a sense of stability or "normalcy"; (3) finding and utilizing support from the community; (4) giving and receiving support from immediate and extended family members; and (5) developing outlets to assist in coping with the stress associated with having a child family member diagnosed with juvenile-onset diabetes.

One dominant theme in the analysis of my study was the belief the families interviewed held regarding the children's ability to overcome serious illness. Properly managing the disease in order to live a long and healthy life with few or no complications was a primary goal for all of the families interviewed for this study.

In addition to proper disease management, triumphing over a serious illness may include the possibility of a cure being discovered for the disease in the near future. The possibility of a future cure seemed to be an exciting aspect for these families to contemplate. Every family interviewed for this study became more animated when talking about having a cure. Perhaps thinking in terms of a cure, for these families, places the illness into a more bearable or manageable context.

Preparing to Die and Fighting to Live: AIDS in the Family

Dr. X referred Tony (28) and Irene (22) for marital therapy. The couple's presenting problem was marital violence. Irene beat up Tony. The police were called and both were arrested although Irene admitted Tony did not fight with her. The family physician's referral was also based on Tony's medical history. Tony had AIDS and his condition was very serious and deteriorating. Irene had contracted HIV from Tony. When Irene learned of her HIV status, she took a broom and began yelling and beating Tony. The couple had a seven-year-old daughter with cerebral palsy who was confined to a wheelchair. The child, Marcella, was not at risk for contracting HIV because she was Tony's stepdaughter from one of Irene's former affairs.

Dr. X referred Tony and Irene to a bilingual marital therapist to help them deal with Tony's medical condition. Although both Tony and Irene were third- and fourth-generation Hispanics who spoke more English than Spanish, they both had parents who spoke more Spanish than English. The therapist's bilingual ability was an asset in assisting Tony, Irene, and their family with the healing and dying process.

The couple were Tejano fans who enjoyed dancing and partying on the weekends, especially if a new Tejano star was in town. Discussing Tejano music and artists was a major engagement point between the therapist and couple. This connection served to define and affirm their cultural lifestyle in an appropriate fashion for engagement (Holder, Turner-Musa, Kimmel, & Reiss, 1998). At first glance, this case does not seem to have any specific cultural overtones other than Tejano dancing. However, the importance of using cultural factors to connect with clients should not be underestimated. One does not have to be Hispanic to enjoy Tejano music or Mexican food, fiestas, or any other Hispanic traditions. There are a multitude of ways to embrace the Hispanic culture. The therapist's interest in and understanding of some part of Hispanic culture, such as Tejano music, served to strengthen the therapeutic bond, which was helpful in keeping this couple in therapy. Tony and Irene are good examples of how illness can overload a family system's ability to cope.

The work Tony and Irene accomplished in therapy was rewarding to them. Tony and Irene resolved the blaming involved in the pain of the illness; both had been reckless and had engaged in a number of affairs. Irene realized she could just as easily have given the virus to Tony. Both were willing to forgive each other for the infection and the violence. At year's end, Tony died of respiratory failure. Irene was able to support and love Tony by the time of his death. She had learned to manage her condition and cooperate with her doctors, which had been a problem when the couple first came to therapy.

We had invited Marcella into our sessions a few months before Tony's death. Irene made plans for the care of her daughter in case she became active with AIDS. Tony's family became Irene's greatest supporters. When Tony was hospitalized for the last time, his extended family held a vigil in the hospital. Each time he had been hospitalized, more of his family members came to wait for his recovery from the crisis. Some of the nurses would make snide remarks about the number of family members who were constantly present at the hospital. The family members would sleep on the benches, because they wanted to be there in case Tony needed them. The presence of Tony's family demonstrates the Mexican tendency toward togetherness and extended familial support.

Marcella and Irene's fears about Marcella's future welfare were greatly eased by the show of family support. Because of Marcella's need for special care with her cerebral palsy, finding a placement for her in the event that Irene should get sick or die would be difficult. Yet after the vigils in the hospital, they knew they could count on Tony's family. Tony died seven years ago and Irene has not yet been diagnosed with full-blown AIDS. She takes good care of herself and her daughter in hopes of surviving and beating the disease.

THE ASSOCIATION OF GRIEF WITH THE DIAGNOSIS OF CHRONIC DISEASES IN CHILDHOOD

The emotional reactions experienced by the families, immediately following the diagnosis of juvenile-onset diabetes in a child family member, formed one of the most prevalent themes found in my research. All of the families voiced experiencing emotional turmoil and grief on learning about the diagnosis. The families expressed their grief in different ways such as denial, having to adjust to physical pain, having a sense of being different, and varying emotional responses to the diagnosis. The families also reported being in varying stages of the grieving process. It appears as though grief reactions to having a child family member diagnosed with chronic illness have been a continual process for these families.

Case Study 2: Expect Anything and Facilitate the Support of the Extended Family

Claudia's family was from Mexico. Dr. Y called for a consultation because Claudia had juvenile diabetes. Claudia was not cooperating and her parents did not understand how important it was for Claudia to follow the treatment regimen in order for her to have a normal life.

My cotherapist and I thought we would be seeing Claudia and her mother and father. We were amazed when seventeen family members showed up to be educated and supportive. We quickly moved the session to a larger room and took advantage of the enormous support system. Discussing the importance of the role of parents and family in helping maintain the life of this child inspired the family to help Claudia. We explained to the parents that Claudia's illness was very serious and that it would be important to educate as many family members as possible in the care and management of her disease. We assured them that any explanation would be in both English and Spanish. We expected six to seven family members to attend; instead, thirty-two family members showed up for the educational meeting. Claudia's compliance improved dramatically. Using the parents' motivation of working together as a family and sacrificing for the child made a difference.

Sussman (1996, p. 473) states that in order to communicate about the treatment of diabetes (or other diseases) adequately with people of ethnically diverse groups, it is important to understand the nature of medical systems cross-culturally, the process by which individuals maintain health and seek health services, and sociocultural factors that influence healthcare decisions and behavior. Although some research has been conducted on the structure of Mexican American families, more research is needed in order to understand how these families adapt to crises. Through gaining a better understanding of the Mexican American perspective on chronic illness, a more collaborative relationship between these families and healthcare providers may be established.

On issues pertaining to health and medical care, Keitel and colleagues (1995, pp. 539–542) discovered that Mexican Americans are more likely to receive substandard medical care than Anglos. One hypothesis as to why Mexican Americans may not seek early professional medical care is belief in natural healing methods. Many Mexican Americans still believe in the spiritual aspects of healing and are often more willing to seek natural treatment as opposed to medical treatment. Poor communication between healthcare providers and patients may also compromise medical care for Mexican-Americans. Deference to medical professionals, lack of bilingual healthcare providers, and desire to avoid embarrassment may inhibit people from asking necessary questions.

Case Study 3: Spiritual Healing

While conducting research on resiliency in adolescent teens, I (the third author) visited a number of school- and clinic-based programs. During one of my visits, I was asked to sit in on a group support session. The group was made up of young mothers and expectant mothers. It was right after the Christmas holidays and the teens were catching up on each other's experiences. The facilitator asked Jessica, "How is your baby? Didn't she have a recurring fever before the holidays?" Jessica told the group about her part in getting her baby well.

Jessica was 15 and her baby daughter was 7 months old. The infant had respiratory problems and had been frequently ill since birth. They lived in a chaotic home environment with her parents who were on disability and sold marijuana and crack from their home. Although both parents smoked pot, Jessica felt that her baby was in safe hands with her mother during school hours. Child protective services was monitoring the home because Jessica had called them one night when her stepfather attacked her, but to date, no placement of Jessica and her baby had been made. In the meantime, she locked her bedroom door and had a safety plan. Her boyfriend, who was not the father of the baby, was 19, an artist, and living on his own. Jessica wanted to move in with him, but her parents were against the idea. Jessica had expressed her fears that if she moved in with her lover, her mother might refuse to take care of the baby, which would force her to drop out of school.

The baby was still sick, although Jessica had taken her to the doctor and was giving her antibiotics. Jessica wanted to take her to the emergency clinic, but her mother was sure it was not something a doctor could cure. They argued about what to do for the baby. In Jessica's mother's opinion, the baby had been given the *Ojo* (evil eye) by one of her elderly uncles. This uncle had a patch over one eye and the other had been staring at the baby during a family reunion that had taken place shortly after the baby's homecoming. Jessica agreed that there was probably a very good possibility that the baby had been cursed. I asked what *Ojo* was because it was a term I had heard before but did not understand; the group was glad to educate me.

Ojo is when you look at something and you want it; you're jealous of the other person for having it. If you don't touch the object of your desire, you leave a curse on the person. It is a superstition to some, but to many other Mexicans and Mexican Americans, it is the cause of many illnesses. *Curanderas* are spiritual healers who cure with natural herbs and mystical powers. These healers have an uncanny ability to heal those who believe and seek their help. There is a way to determine if someone has *Ojo.* An egg is broken over the head of the afflicted, then opened and left overnight. If bubbles appear, the person has been cursed and must seek the help of the *Curandera.*

Jessica's mother was insistent that they test the baby for *Ojo* that night. Jessica was equally insistent that the baby needed medical attention. They compromised by breaking the egg and then going to the clinic. The baby got the medical treatment she needed at the clinic and the *Curandera* came to visit the next day. According to Jessica, the baby was making an amazing recovery, so she wasn't sure whether it had been the doctors or the *Curandera.* She sparkled with pride when the facilitator and the other young women congratulated her on being assertive and taking the baby to the clinic. This case illustrates the powerful influence natural healers have on many Hispanic families. Jessica could have been more traditional and accepted her parent's decision to call the *Curandera* and not take the baby to the clinic. Many Hispanics do not seek medical attention because of these spiritual beliefs.

The Denial Factor: To Know or Not to Know?

Another influence in determining what families participated in the interviews is what I call the denial factor (Ambrose, 1997). Through the interview process, I found that all four of the families spoke of their belief that there will be a cure for juvenile-onset diabetes in the near future. This belief exists for these families in spite of medical research pointing to the contrary. I hypothesized that the belief in a future cure helped these families manage the disease because they believed management would only be a temporary endeavor. According to a survey conducted by Trulin (1995) at the University of Southern California, he found that 65% of Mexican Americans said they would want to be told of a terminal diagnosis as compared to 87% of European Americans. Trulin also found that 48% of Mexican Americans would want to be told of a terminal prognosis as compared to 69% of European Americans. It seems that ignorance is bliss when it comes to chronic illness and the Mexican-American population. That being the case, it stands to reason that they would not want to talk about experiences with a disease they do not wish to acknowledge exists.

Sometimes, the denial of illness is often harder to bear in terms of pain and human suffering than facing the inevitable reality. The wish to deny illness and death is found in many cultures and is expressed in many ways. McDaniel and Campbell (1997) state that patients and family members tend to accept a difficult diagnosis at different points in time. "It's almost as if someone in the family needs to deny the illness and advocate for life to go on, and someone else needs to help the family grapple with the hard realities" (p. 356).

CONCLUSION

Hispanic families need to learn how to access healthcare services for themselves and their children. When a child is sick, especially with a chronic illness, clear information needs to be given in both Spanish and English whenever possible if it is necessary. Healthcare providers must be trained in cultural engagement skills with Latinos and other minorities. They need to be aware that besides a cultural perspective, many Latinos may be intimidated by healthcare systems and are embarrassed to ask questions. Family inclusion of extended family members can be an asset to gaining compliance. Family therapists are uniquely trained and experienced in working with multiple family members simultaneously. Others may wish to seek training with multiple family members to learn how to listen and be attentive and to practice joining with family units. Some may have a natural ability to work with children and parents together; others may feel distracted. Training and experience can help alleviate anxiety in working with families and family units. Family therapy in collaboration with medical care will be an important facet of effective healthcare in the future.

REFERENCES

Ambrose, H. (1997). *Family meaning among Mexican-Americans following the diagnosis of juvenile diabetes.* Unpublished doctoral dissertation, St. Mary's University at San Antonio.

Bahnson, C. B. (1987). The impact of life-threatening illness on the family and the impact of the family on illness: An overview. In M. Leahey & L. M. Wright (Eds.), *Families and life-threatening illness.* New York: Associated Health Press.

Chilman, C. S. (1993). Hispanic families in the United States. In H. P. McAdoo (Ed.), *Family ethnicity: Strength in diversity.* Newbury Park, CA: Sage.

Falicov, C. J. (1982). Mexican families. In M. McGoldrick, J. K. Pearce, & J. Giordano (Eds.), *Ethnicity and family therapy.* New York: Guilford Press.

Figley, C. R., & McCubbin, H. I. (1983). *Stress and the family volume. II: Coping with catastrophe.* New York: Brunner/Mazel.

Flores, M. T., & Sprenkle, D. H. (1988). Can therapists use FACES III with Mexican Americans? A preliminary analysis. *Journal of Psychotherapy and the Family, 4*(1–2), 239–247.

Hobbs, N., Perrin, J. M., & Ireys, H. T. (1985). *Chronically ill children and their families.* San Francisco: Jossey-Bass.

Holder, B., Turner-Musa, J., Kimmel, M., & Reiss, D. (1998). Engagement of African American families in research on chronic illness: A multisystem recruitment approach. *Family Process, 37*(2), 127–152.

Horowitz, R. C., Horowitz, S. H., Orsini, J., Antoine, R. L., & Hill, D. M. (1998). Including families in collaborative care: Impact on recovery. *Families, Systems, and Health 16*(1,2), 71–84.

Juvenile Diabetes Foundation. (1996). Diabetes Fact Sheet. [On-Line]. Available: http://www.jdfcure.com/facts.htm.

Keitel, M. A., Kopala, M., & Georgiades, I. (1995). Multicultural health counseling. In J. G. Ponterotto, J. M. Casas, L. A. Suzuki, & C. M. Alexander (Eds.), *Handbook of multicultural counseling.* Thousand Oaks: CA: Sage.

Libow, J. A. (1989). Chronic illness and family coping. In L. Combrinck-Graham (Ed.), *Children in family contexts: Perspectives on treatment.* New York: Guilford Press.

McCubbin, M. A., & McCubbin, H. I. (1989). Theoretical orientations to family stress and coping. In C. R. Figley et al. (Eds.), *Treating stress in families* (pp. 3–43). New York: Brunner/Mazel.

McDaniel, S. H., & Campbell, T. L. (1997). Editorial: Training health professionals to collaborate. *Families, Systems, and Health 15*(4), 353–360.

Olson, D. H., Portner, J., & Lavee, Y. (1985). *FACES III.* St. Paul, MN: Family Social Service, University of Minnesota.

Patterson, J. M., & Garwick, A. W. (1994). Levels of meaning in family stress theory. *Family Process, 33,* 287–304.

Rolland, J. S. (1987). Chronic illness and the life cycle: A conceptual framework. *Family Process, 26,* 203–221.

Rolland, J. S. (1998). Beliefs and collaboration in illness. *Families, Systems, and Health 16*(1,2), 7–26.

Smith, W. (1988). *A profile of health and disease in America: Diabetes, liver, and digestive diseases.* New York: Facts on File.

Strozier, M., & Walsh, M. (1998). Developmental models for integrating medical and mental healthcare. *Families, Systems, and Health 16*(1,2), 27–40.

Sussman, L. (1996). Sociocultural concerns of diabetes care. In D. Haire-Joshu (Ed.), *Management of diabetes mellitus: Perspectives of care across the life span* (2nd ed.). St. Louis: Mosby.

Trulin, F. (1995). The Hispanic health link. [On-Line]. Available: http://www.aclin.org/other/society . . . spanic_latino/larasa/hhlnov95.html.

Younger, D., Brink, S. J., Barnett, D. M., Wentworth, S. M., Leibovich, J., & Madden, P. B. (1985). Diabetes in youth. In A. Marble, L. P. Krall, R. F. Bradley, A. R. Christlieb, & J. S. Soeldner (Eds.), *Joslin's diabetes mellitus*, (12th ed.). Philadelphia: Lea & Febiger.

11

INJUSTICE IN LATINO FAMILIES: CONSIDERATIONS FOR FAMILY THERAPISTS

YVETTE G. FLORES-ORTIZ

The first time I saw my mother get mercilessly beaten I was no older than five years. I had just been brought over from Mexico leaving behind my grandmother, who had raised me since Mom came to the states. It seems like I hadn't been here more than a day with my mother and stepfather when I witnessed my mother's torturer transform before my eyes. I had been out with my uncle and when I came home I found my mother on the floor shielding her face from the fury of kicks my stepfather inflicted on her. At that moment, I ran toward her but my uncle held me back and my stepfather told my uncle (his brother) to take me away. The calm room before transformed into violet lights, yellow streaks; green goblins seemed to dance on the walls of the apartment. My stepfather changed before my eyes. I wondered why did my mother want me to witness this? I stared at my stepfather and I knew then that something snapped inside of me and that I would never be the same again. It seemed as though my arms were cut off and I could never use them to harm anyone.
—JUAN, 23-YEAR-OLD COLLEGE STUDENT

Juan grew up in a family in which migration, dislocation, alcohol abuse, and violence created a context of injustice, pain, and distrust for all its members. Juan's experiences are not unique. In some of my earlier writings (Flores-Ortiz, 1993, 1997, 1998, in press; Flores-Ortiz, Esteban, & Carillo, 1994), I have addressed the problem of violence in the lives of Latinos. Specific figures of incidence and prevalence are limited and questionable given the methodological problems of large-scale studies (see Sorensen & Telles, 1991; Straus and Gelles, 1989) and the problems of generalizability of small-sample descriptive studies (Torres, 1991). Moreover, public health and emergency room studies (Bauer, Rodriguez, Flores-Ortiz, & Szkupinski-Quiroga, 1999) are beginning to document the extent of spousal and child abuse within Latino families.

Despite rising public concern about violence in families and evidence that Latino families experience rates comparable with European Americans, few studies have focused on Latina's experiences with violence (Flores-Ortiz, 1993). The few existing empirical studies find that U.S.-born Latinos have higher rates of domestic violence and sexual assault than immigrant Latinos. For example, Sorensen and Telles' (1991) survey of 1,243 Latino households found spousal abuse in 20% of households (compared to 21.6% of European American households); rates were highest for U.S.-born Mexican Americans (30.9%). In addition, their data indicated that if a Mexican-born woman was sexually assaulted in adulthood, one-third of the time the perpetrator was her husband or male partner. Variables that predicted sexual assault among Mexican and Mexican American women included gender (more women were sexually abused than men), history of psychological problems, and marital status (with married women reporting more sexual victimization than women never married). Clearly, such findings call attention to the need to examine both the social context and dynamics of Latino families who abuse.

Straus and Gelles' (1989) national survey of American households includes a large sample of "Hispanics." Although the sample was not identified in terms of national origin or generational level, and excluded monolingual Spanish-speaking Latinos, the study found extremely high rates of spousal and child abuse among Latinos. Almost one of every four of the Latino families surveyed had experienced one or more major assaults against a spouse or partner during the year of the survey. Although most of the violent acts consisted of pushing, slapping, shoving, or throwing things, about half of the assaults were acts that carried a high risk of producing injury: kicking, punching, biting, or choking. A smaller number of male partners used weapons (guns, knives, and other objects) against their spouses. In comparison with the "non-Hispanic white" sample, the Latino rate of spousal abuse was 54% greater.

Both Sorensen and Telles' (1991) and Straus and Gelles' (1989) surveys focused on married respondents. Little empirical information is available about the degree of violence experienced by Latinas in dating relationships, and although clinical evidence suggests a high degree of sexual violence toward Latino women and girls (Flores-Ortiz, 1997), definite rates have not been established.

THEORIZING INJUSTICE

Over the past ten years, I have researched, theorized about, and provided psychotherapy for Chicano/Latino families with problems of intrafamily abuse. Interweaving research, theory, and clinical practice, I have created a model of family violence that encompasses the multidetermined nature of family injustice. The model proposes that violent outcomes, including domestic violence, child abuse, sexual, emotional, verbal, and spiritual victimization of family members by those entrusted to care and provide for them, *la misma familia,* are propitiated by an interaction of specific forces within the context of the family and society. The forces that promote social injustice create imbalances of power within the family wherein strategies of disconnection and oppression replace the cultural ideals of familismo, *respeto y comprensión* (Flores-Ortiz, 1993, 1997, 1998a; Flores-Ortiz et al., 1994).

Flores-Ortiz et al. (1993) propose a Predictive Violence Model, which incorporates an analysis of structural factors (Yllo, 1984), psychosocial context (Flores-Ortiz, 1993), and familial context (Borzormenyi-Nagy & Spark, 1984). Our predictor variables are defined in three categories: (1) societal and family context, (2) mediating variables, and (3) power imbalances.

The social-context domain includes socioeconomic status variables such as educational level, occupation, access to resources, and family size. The social context of violence in the community is included as well. This construct is measured by an Exposure to Violence Index, which is based on census and criminal justice data that characterize the degree of aggravated assault and nonintimate violence in a given community. In addition, testimonies of community residents are collected to determine their subjective experience of and exposure to social violence. Finally, the social-context domain includes an analysis of race-, gender-, and sexuality-based crimes and the residents' perceptions of discrimination, racism, and other forms of oppression.

The family-context variables consist of family-of-origin characteristics, including household composition in childhood and adulthood, marital conflict (past and present), conflict resolution strategies, and the family's history of migration(s) within the United States and from the rest of the Americas to the United States. These two domains are central to the analysis of family dynamics in any Latino family and help determine whether family violence in any form predates or is subsequent to migration, whether family injustice is an intergenerational phenomenon, and to what degree social factors propitiate, maintain, or exacerbate dysfunctional family patterns of coping and relating.

The mediating variables as defined by our model include substance use and abuse and social supports. Alcohol use patterns of Latinos have been studied extensively (Alaniz, et al., 1998; Caetano, 1985, 1987, 1990; De La Rosa et al., 1990; Moore, 1990; Mora, 1997), and although the specific link between alcohol and other drug abuse and family violence has not been empirically demonstrated with Latinos, studies suggest a high correlation between substance abuse and violence for Latino males and substance misuse and victimization for Latinas (Flores-Ortiz, 1993; Miller, 1990; Mora, 1997).

Our model proposes that the use of alcohol and other drugs by perpetrators of violent acts or their victims and the extent of social support systems available to families have a mediating effect on family relationships and power imbalances in the family. Specifically, alcohol and other drugs can act as disinhibitors that may increase the risk of violence. Inadequate social supports isolate the family, which decreases the possibility of detection of the abuse or protection of family members. The absence of culturally relevant social supports may also isolate families, thus increasing the risk for violence.

Power Imbalances in Families

This construct is determined by the self-esteem of family members and their economic position in the household. Social inequities among Latinos often are manifested in undereducation and underemployment and contribute to gender imbalance within families, particularly where one spouse is economically dominant. Our model postulates that imbalances in the family are critically linked to the societal and family context. Spouses that experience disempowerment and oppression at work may have difficulty creating a fair division of labor within the home. Likewise, individuals who are disrespected at work may find it difficult to respect those whom they love. Thus, the family context is perceived as having a reciprocal relationship to power imbalances in families.

Self-esteem is operationally defined as the individual's perception of his or her worth, intelligence, attractiveness, and warmth relative to other family members. For immigrants and their children, self-esteem is connected to feelings of belonging or marginality, of acceptance by the dominant groups, and by the realities of subordination (Flores-Ortiz, 1998b; Hardy & Lazloffy, 1995).

The clinical usefulness of this model is described elsewhere (Flores-Ortiz, 1993; Flores-Ortiz et al., 1994). It is offered here to provide a template of areas of needed assessment and potential intervention. Moreover, our model suggests that to completely understand how and why those who love us victimize us, often in the name of love, we must include an analysis of the larger context within which social and familial injustice develop.

Sources of Injustice

Almeida and colleagues (1996) propose that the roots of interpersonal injustice within the family and society are located in the historical legacy of oppression and colonization and the stratified caste system based on race, ethnicity, religion, sexuality, and ability instituted when the First World collided with the American, African, and Asian continents. Injustice was historically institutionalized through education, employment, and access to power, resulting in a pyramid of oppression where belonging and dispossession are predicated on degree of acceptance by those in power.

Interpersonally, Almeida and colleagues (1996) argue, injustice results in a hierarchy of oppression in which those with more power use it over those perceived as having less. At an interpersonal and intrafamilial level, power over relationships lead to a culture of terror and disrespect where violence easily can occur.

At an individual psychological level, oppression, particularly exposure to injustices engendered by racism and racist policies, result in what Ken Hardy names "psychological homelessness" (Hardy & Laszloffy, 1995). Racism inflicts pain; discrimination in any form wounds the soul. The pain of disempowerment leads to a loss of community or sense of belonging and to profound feelings of outrage that may in turn lead to rage and explosive anger. Thus, the violence engendered by racism cannot be isolated from spousal abuse, child maltreatment, and acts of violence toward the self (Flores-Ortiz, 1998b).

THE EFFECTS OF INJUSTICE IN PEOPLE'S LIVES

As a consequence of the historical legacy of colonization and their subsequent colonial status, members of dominated groups often experience feelings of guilt and shame, anger, self-hate, and a sense of powerlessness. These feelings often are accompanied by fear and depression, particularly fear of genocide. These are sequelae of disempowerment and internalized oppression. Likewise, oppression often leads to isolation, breakup of families, loss of identity, and the destruction of the culture. Ultimately, oppression leads to inauthentic human relationships as individuals isolate, disconnect from feelings, and take a stance of stoicism and apparent (and sometimes real) disregard for the well-being of others (Aboriginal Health Council of South Australia, 1995; Flores-Ortiz, 1998b). The sequelae of oppression can become multigenerationally transmitted legacies of disempowerment, hopelessness, and despair. A reservoir of pain is then available to transform into explosive anger or rage (Flores-Ortiz, 1998b).

In conditions of social inequality, the oppressed often will experience a sense of loss of agency, but may internalize the repudiated images held of them by the more powerful and hold themselves accountable for their own victimization (Flores-Ortiz, 1997, 1998b; Hardy & Laszloffy, 1995). It is indeed this self-blame that can lead to self-loathing. Rage turned inward compromises the spirit and the individual's ability to fair and just treatment of others. This is part of the link that leads to family violence. An individual who experiences rage as a function of oppression has a limited capacity to protect, nurture, and treat fairly those whom she or he purports to love. An individual or family wounded by injustice cannot authentically connect to another human being. Instead, he or she may feel toxic, unworthy, and engage in strategies of disconnection to prevent the other from getting too close. Familial and romantic relationships often become the terrain where the pain and rage of oppression is avoided, engaged with, or contested since intimate relationships are safer than those with individuals located in hierarchically more powerful positions (Flores-Ortiz, 1998b).

CONSIDERATIONS FOR FAMILY THERAPISTS

The treatment of family injustice rests on several assumptions. Social injustice, or any form of oppression, leads to unfairness and injustice in relationships. If oppression occurs, it can lead to isolation, breakup of families, development of dysfunctional family patterns of relating, a loss of identity, and even a destruction of culture. Relationships may suffer, leading to inauthentic connections as individuals isolate, disconnect from feelings, and develop a veneer of stoicism and invulnerability. When unchecked, this sequelae of oppression can become multigenerationally transmitted legacies of disempowerment, hopelessness, and despair, thus creating a reservoir of pain on multiple levels. Not only is the individual and his or her family affected, neighborhoods, communities, and larger systems may suffer as well.

The pain of injustice is available to transform into explosive anger or rage. Intimate violence, social violence, self-abuse, and the maltreatment of children are some of the expressions of injustice and despair. However, in a more optimistic light, the pain of injustice is available to transform into creativity, *entereza* (wholeness), and resilience (Flores-Ortiz, 1998b). This is what the therapist must grasp onto in the face of clients experiencing injustice and despair.

Assessments of Hispanic Clients

Given these assumptions, treatment must be justice-based and multimodal (often including individual, group, marital, family, and social network therapies), interdisciplinary and culturally attuned. Treatment must be connected to the individual and family assessments conducted. Irrespective of the presenting problem, mental health professionals need to conduct thorough evaluations of Latino clients, including the following:

- Obtain a history of migration: stages, reasons, traumas, postmigration experiences, and stressors
- History of exposure to violence (including intimate violence) in the country of origin and the United States
- Degree of daily indignities and feelings of marginality and oppression experienced by each
- History of coping strategies, pre- and postmigration
- Safety assessment of all family members
- Socioeconomic and cultural resources (including material, spiritual, and familial supports)
- Level of biculturality, cultural connection and disconnection, and ethnic identity
- Level of bilingualism, comfort with use of each language, context of language use
- Cultural meaning of alcohol and drugs
- Intergenerational and cultural value conflicts

Case Study

Julie was 2 years old when her parents separated and later divorced. Juan, her father, was a sullen and depressed man. He was fired or changed jobs every year. He felt that his bosses were prejudiced because he had dark skin. He obsessed over most things. His skin color was another example of how he used one thing to blame for all his problems. He had to have things his way or he would arrogantly withdraw with a total lack of involvement as well as participation. Norma, Julie's mother, was sweet but flighty and disorganized in her household duties and ways according to Juan. Juan would sit in the evenings in his big chair drinking and smoking, usually getting drunk. He smoked marijuana on occasion and other drugs when available. Then out of this sullen state, he would begin verbally attacking Norma. He would interrogate her every move or activity in a nonstop monotone voice. Jealousy was a big issue. They would fight.

Norma would yell and Juan would push or throw something at her without speaking. He would walk off pushing furniture and slamming doors as he went. This episode continued until Norma took Julie and left. Norma had to financially support the family as well as take care of the household for several of these years. Norma maintained her job security and felt the family burden and that of carrying Juan was too great. Juan followed and harassed her for years until he found another partner. Norma had sole custody of Julie. Juan maintained distance and little involvement. Juan did not speak Spanish and his family of origin had been in the United States four or five generations. In fact, he claimed to be part Apache Indian and that his ancestors built the Alamo and some of the surrounding mission in the early 1600s, a plausible story given the area. He had a sense of pride about himself and his family that turned sour. For there was also a sense that he and his family had lost who they were and could not regain it. He admitted with bitterness that he was raised by relatives that tolerated him because his parents were into drugs and alcohol. He blamed the stealing of the Alamo and his history on his family destruction. Julie's mother was from Mexico and her father was born in the United States. She had grown up in a two-parent home. They were poor, but there were no drugs, alcohol, or physical abuse in her growing-up years.

Norma married Lalo when Julie was four. Lalo was from El Salvador. He had blond hair and blue eyes and spoke impeccable Spanish. They had two children immediately. Maybe Norma thought that if she married someone who looked different, things would be different. Unfortunately, Lalo, as Juan, also drank too much and within months of their marriage, they were fighting. Lalo and Norma would yell and scream at each other when Lalo drank too much. Lalo complained about the pain of war from his country and how he saw many good people die. The noise of their fighting would escalate and scare the children. When Julie was 9 years old, Norma and Lalo had a huge fight. Norma left Lalo and took Julie and her siblings with her for several days to her mother's and then returned. She filed a police report.

Julie was very frightened by her stepfather. She cried and cried as she saw Lalo slap her mother. She became fearful and told her Dad, Juan. Juan was now living with his common-law spouse and her son. He took immediate action and called his lawyer for custody of Julie.

He was concerned for her safety. Julie cried herself to sleep over her fears. As time progressed, Julie spent time between both families. With her father's constant watch and her mother's anxiety, Julie became depressed. She was caught between two worlds. The households were very different, yet violence in both places: at her father's, a violence that erupts from a sullen brooding, and at her mother's, a violence of yelling and screaming.

Julie wanted to go with her father for it was quieter there. Yet on all sorts of levels, it was her mother that cared about Julie. Her father wanted to win Julie in order to hurt her mother for leaving him as the old wounds awoke within him. His obsessive nature took over and groomed the child's words and behaviors for the court and he won. But Julie lost; she did not understand her father's hostility and brooding. Nor did she understand his depression and drug abuse and how it would affect her through the years. After living with her father for two years, Julie ran away. She ran to her mother's, grandmother's, and friend's houses. The parents went back to court and Julie was allowed to go back to her mother's house. Much damage, however, was done as Julie seemed confused and sad. Anger at her father was the issue that most predominated her therapy. She knew her Dad loved her, but his controlling and sullen ways of punishment were too much for a young girl growing up. She felt betrayed by her father for taking her away from her mother. After Julie had a run with alcohol, and drugs, she was able to return to a normal life without her father constantly watching her every move. Ultimately, she identified with her mother again.

Norma and Lalo were shocked at the time of the court trial. How could the judge take their child away over one violent incident. Julie was a well-behaved child with honor grades. Julie's grades declined while she was with her father. Norma regretted making a police report. Norma and Lalo continued in therapy with good results. Lalo stopped drinking heavily. They worked on conflict resolution skills between them. Lalo was shocked into reality by the courts, and a fear of losing the two children he and Norma shared motivated his treatment. Lalo began his journey of not living in the past in a Central American country torn by war. Norma, however, "cried" every night for her daughter's return. Her bout with depression was lengthy. She struggled with the fact that no one believed her, especially the judges, when she told them that her ex-husband, Juan, was violent. "No one believes Latinas, no one."

Violence combined with alcohol and drugs can have devastating effects on a family. Culture takes a back seat to the damage it causes family members. Culture is used as a preventative measure or as, in this case, more in recovery to gain a solid ground and a sense of self-worth. As Norma learned to value herself, so did her daughter.

CONCLUSIONS

Once a thorough assessment has been conducted, mental health professionals can plan culturally competent and congruent interventions to bring healing, balance, and health to the family as a system and to the individuals that constitute the family (see Flores-Ortiz, 1997, 1998, in press; Flores-Ortiz, 1994, for specific treatment models).

Ultimately, I see treatment as a process of healing the wounds of oppression, rebalancing damaged or unjust relationships with self and others, and fostering accountability. Interventions must be family-focused regardless of the modality used and designed for the specific culture of each family. As the wounds of injustice are healed, interventions must pay attention to the prevention of further injustice in the family, and building resilience in family members. In the treatment of substance misuse and family violence, the therapist must understand the social, cultural, and familial contributions to the problem. The therapist's role is often that of cultural broker, agent of prevention, and builder of resilience.

REFERENCES

Aboriginal Health Council of South Australia (1995). Reclaiming our stories: Reclaiming our lives. *Dulwich Centre Newsletter* (1).

Alaniz, M. L., Cartwell, R. S., & Park, R. N. (1998). Immigrants and violence: The influence of neighborhood context. *Hispanic Journal of the Behavioral Sciences, 20*(2), 155–174.

Almeida, R., Woods, R. M., Messineo, T., & Font, R. (1996). The cultural context model. In M. McGoldrick, J. Giordano, & J. K. Pearce (Eds.), *Ethnicity and family therapy* (2nd ed.). New York: Guilford Press.

Bauer, H. M., Rodriguez, M. A., Flores-Ortiz, Y., & Szkupinski-Quiroga, S. (1999). Social, cultural, and political barriers to help-seeking for abused Latina and Asian immigrant women. *Journal of Health Care for the Poor and the Underserved*, in press.

Boszormenyi-Nagy, I., & Spark, G. (1984). *Invisible loyalties*. New York: Brunner/Mazel.

Caetano, R. (1985). Drinking patterns and alcohol problems in a national sample of U.S. Hispanics. In D. Spiegler, D. Tate, S. Aiken, & C. Christian (Eds.), *Alcohol use among U.S. ethnic minorities*, pp. 147–162. Research Monograph No. 18, National Institute on Alcohol Abuse and Alcoholism, DHHS Publication No. (ADM) 89-143. Washington, DC: U.S. Government Printing Office.

Caetano, R. (1987). Acculturation and drinking patterns among U.S. Hispanics. *British Journal of Addiction, 82*, 789–799.

Caetano, R. (1990). Hispanic drinking in the U.S.: Thinking in new directions. *British Journal of Addiction, 85*, 1231–1236.

De La Rosa, M., Lambert, Y., Gropper, B. (1990). Exploring the substance abuse-violence connection. *Drugs and violence: Causes, correlates, and consequences.* Rockville, MD: US Department of Health and Human Services. National Institute of Drug Abuse, Research Monograph Series, 1-7.

Flores-Ortiz, Y. (1993). La mujer y la violencia: A culturally based model for the understanding and treatment of domestic violence in Chicana/Latina communities. In N. Alarcón et al. (Eds.), *Chicana critical issues*, pp. 169–182. Berkeley, CA: Third Woman Press.

Flores-Ortiz, Y. (1997). The broken covenant: Incest in Latino families. *Voces: A Journal of Chicana/Latina Studies, 1*(2), 48–70.

Flores-Ortiz, Y. (1998a). A reconstructive dialogue with a couple with a problem of violence. In T. Nelson & T. Trepper (Eds.), *101 more interventions in family therapy.* New York: Haworth Press.

Flores-Ortiz, Y. (1998b). *Theorizing justice in Latino families.* Paper presented at the "Innovations in Chicano psychology: Looking toward the 21st century" Conference. East Lansing, MI: Julian Zamora Research Center.

Flores-Ortiz, Y., Esteban, M., & Carrillo, R. (1994). La Violencia en la Familia: Un modelo contextual de terapia intergeneracional. *Revista Interamericana de Psicología, 28*(2), 235–250.

Hardy, K. V., & Laszloffy, T. A. (1995). Therapy with African Americans and the phenomenon of rage. *In Session: Psychotherapy in Practice, 1*(4), 57–70.

Miller, B. A. (1990). The interrelationships between alcohol and drugs and family violence. *Drugs and violence: Causes, correlates, and consequences.* Rockville, MD: US Department of Health and Human Services. National Institute of Drug Abuse, Research Monograph Series, 177–207.

Moore, J. (1990). Gangs, drugs, and violence. *Drugs and violence: Causes, correlates, and consequences.* Rockville, MD: US Department of Health and Human Services. National Institute of Drug Abuse, Research Monograph Series, 160–176.

Mora, J. (1997). Learning to drink: Early drinking experiences of Chicana and Mexicana women. *Voces: A Journal of Chicana/Latina Studies, 1*(1), 89–111.

Sorensen, S. B., & Telles, C. A. (1991). Self-Reports of spousal violence in a Mexican-American and non-Hispanic white population. *Violence and Victims, 6*(1), 7–15.

Straus, M. A., & Gelles, R. J. (1989). *Physical violence in American families: Risk factors and adaptations to violence in 8,145 families.* New Brunswick: Transaction Publishers.

Torres, S. (1991). A comparison of wife abuse between two cultures: Perceptions, attitudes, nature and extent. *Issues in Mental Health Nursing, 12,* 113–131.

Yllo, K. A. (1984). Patriarchy and violence against wives: The impact of structural and normative factors. *Journal of International and Comparative Social Welfare, 1,* 16–29.

12

A MULTISYSTEMIC LOOK AT MEXICAN AMERICAN GANGS: ADOLESCENTS AT RISK

LUCILLE MARMOLEJO ROMEO

> Mis carnales *fought with me against that* pendejo
> *and the "VNE" (Varrio Northeast) gang. He was trying*
> *to step in on my girl. We got them good. We hit them*
> *hard and some* vatos *got stabbed. My homies are* mi
> familia *now. They take care of me and protect me.*
> *I know I can count on them.*
>
> —*ANTONIO*

Antonio, a sixteen-year-old, handsome, tough-looking, Mexican American gang member was admitted to a local psychiatric hospital for alcohol and marijuana abuse. He had been involved in a gang-bang and was severely beaten. The fight was sparked by a member of a rival gang who attempted to date Antonio's girlfriend. With false bravado and pride, Antonio exclaimed, "I like to fight, and I don't care if I get hurt or I die. Anyway, I'm going to die later on."

GANGS AND GANG MEMBERS

Professionals who work with juvenile gang members will recognize Antonio's statements as typical. In fact, the belief that death is impending, combined with pride in gang violence and strict loyalty to the brotherhood are common phenomena among gang members (Harris, 1994; Moore, Vigil, & Garcia, 1983; Sanders, 1994). Rosier (1998) studied the phenomenon of getting in and getting out of gangs and found that even among those who successfully left their gang, the fear of death and violence was still very real in their lives. She quotes Kathy, a former female gang member, "when people say they are out of a gang, they're not really. . . . I can't go downtown because some girls are after me . . . the gang may not be there forever but your enemies will be. . . . I'm always worried about retaliation" (p. 117).

Gangs are present in all fifty of the United States (Sheldon, Tracy, & Brown, 1997). It is estimated that approximately 400,000 gang members exist today. Of the seventy-nine largest cities, 91% report gang problems. Most of the arrests for violent crimes are related to gangs and most of the serious gang violence is committed by youth (U.S. Department of Justice, 1994). Although gangs are not a new phenomenon in our country—the first gang activity was recorded in 1783 (*West Side Story*, 1996)—the brutality seems to be getting worse.

California has the most number of gangs, followed by Texas. It is estimated that San Antonio, Texas, has 797 gangs, El Paso, 471. The largest gang, the WSU Kings, centered in San Antonio, has a membership of over 1,000 (*Texas News*, 1998). The total number of gang members in Texas is estimated to be 10,000. According to Dan Morales, Attorney General of Texas (Morales & Durham, 1995), gang membership in Texas cities continues to increase. San Antonio and El Paso appear to be competing with Los Angeles for the title "gang capital of the world." El Paso presently has 5,073 gang members, 4,627 males and 446 females (El Paso Police Department, 1997).

The profile of the typical gang member evolved over time and tends to be geographically related (Yablonsky, 1997). However, Yablonsky notes four trends that seem to be evident in gang evolution: (1) gangs have more access to extremely lethal weapons; (2) historically, gangs fought those of different backgrounds, but now there is interracial violence between and among gangs; (3) drugs are commonly associated with gang activity; (4) gangs have multiple purposes and have become structurally more sophisticated.

Morales and Durham (1995) describe the typical gang member of Texas as Mexican American between the ages of 12 to 23 years, second or third generation born, and bilingual (Spanish dominant). Texas gangs are relatively new and not as organized as the gangs of Los Angeles, Chicago, or New York. Most of the Texas gangs have both male and female members; only 1% of the gangs are exclusively female, 34% exclusively male. Nearly one-half of the Texas gangs are racially mixed: approximately 34% of the gangs are Hispanic, 17% Black, 3% Vietnamese, and 2% White (*Texas News*, 1998). Gangs use identifying symbols such as clothing styles, colors, tattoos, and hand signs to distinguish themselves from other "turf-based gangs" who defend their perceived interests in a particular geographical territory against their rivals.

Cholos

Antonio lives in west Texas, in the El Paso neighborhood known as *secundo barrio.* The city borders Cuidad Juarez across the Rio Grande in Chihuahua, Mexico. He belongs to the "Fatherless gang," a turf-based gang that is one of the better known gangs of this region, notorious for a high incidence of crime and violence. Antonio, like his gang cohorts, is fatherless. His father died of a heroin overdose when Antonio was ten years old. Yet, not all fatherless youths join gangs. Antonio describes his twin brother as a "wannabe" gang member, explaining that he "is not tough enough to fight with knives or guns," but adopts their style and dress. Gang symbols and insignia are particularly dangerous to wannabe gang members. Senseless murders of innocent wannabes occur because in wearing gang insignia, they become walking targets.

Chicano gang youths are also known as *cholos.* These gang members dress in *"cholo* style," which distinguishes them from other adolescents. The *cholo* style often consists of baggy khaki pants, white T-shirts or long-sleeved flannel shirts, battered on the top, and black slipper-type shoes. In the past, gang youths would adopt the colors and clothing from a sports team. Then schools outlawed these "colors," and the police learned to recognize them. Schools are now battling the *cholo* style by adopting uniforms and dress codes. However, as soon as one symbol is identified and eliminated, another appears to take its place. By the time this chapter is published, symbols such as certain hairstyles, Mickey Mouse paraphernalia, and safety pins will be outdated. Therapists and other mental health workers who maintain connections and regular contact with schools and law enforcement can stay abreast of the changing gang underworld.

The members mark their gang turf with graffiti *placas* to identify their area. *Placas* may represent names of gang members or gangs, but most frequently, they are threats or warnings. Violence in the form of assaults, drive-by shootings, and homicide occur as a result of rivalries between one gang and another. Neighbors and relatives may be pitted against each other. During 1996, 165 drive-by shootings were reported in El Paso (El Paso Police Department, 1996). The good news is that the number of drive-bys has dropped precipitously. San Antonio had much success in this area. The answers seem to be found in working collaboratively with school, community, and law enforcement. However, some argue that trying teen perpetrators of violent crimes as adults has helped deter the violence.

Rosier (1998) notes that the drop in drive-bys could be due to the attitude of the gang members themselves, as former gang members felt disgusted by the increasing violence of modern gangs.

Miguel and Adam described the gang members of today as "cowards" because they no longer went up to someone and challenged them, but rather remained anonymous and shot them from a distance. Adam admits, "We never did the drive-by stuff . . . we fought hand to hand . . . now it's different . . . now they want to shoot you and your family . . . they take someone out for something ridiculous" (p. 140).

Although the media portrays the gang member as a criminal, rarely do we hear reports about the sociocultural, familial, and developmental factors that contribute to the formation of juvenile delinquency. Thus, the purpose of this chapter will be to address and discuss the systems and cultural issues that are specifically related to the Mexican American gang member residing in the U.S. cities close to or bordering Mexico. The case example of Antonio, an adolescent gang member, will demonstrate those systems issues that affect the gang individual. Therapeutic treatment and the importance of being culturally aware and sensitive to the gang youth and his or her family will also be highlighted and discussed.

Adolescent Identity Development

Developmentally, the adolescent is undergoing transition from childhood to adulthood and is in the process of forming a sense of identity. Erik Erikson (1963) defines adolescence as a stage of "identity crisis" in which the adolescent attempts to separate and differentiate from the world of his or her parents. Role confusion can occur through overidentification with "heroes," cliques, or bad crowds. If the adolescent is experiencing conflict and tension with his family, peers, and teachers, a sense of estrangement and aloneness can develop and lead to a strong identification with an outside group such as the barrio gang (Erlanger, 1979).

The process of affiliation with a negative peer group or gang can be very seductive, especially when acceptance, bonding, a sense of belonging, and protection are offered. The estranged youth may experience low self-esteem, powerlessness, and rage that may be manifested through aggression, violence, or risk-taking behavior. She or he may attempt to mask feelings of depression and turmoil through substance use and abuse. For example, Antonio stated that when he smoked "weed" and drank beer with his "homies" he felt "powerful and not afraid." He was also able to forget about problems with his family and at school. His affiliation and membership with his gang provided that sense of belonging and identification for which he yearned.

Considering Gender in Identity Development

Carol Gilligan (1982/1993) explored Erikson's life stages, developmental tasks, and conflicts for women. She illuminated the fact that women develop differently from men. In our society, we commonly assume healthy development means that adolescents need to separate, individuate, and become autonomous beings. Ironically, this alienates women and is aversive to their healthy development. Gilligan (1982/1993) describes the feminine self as a "connected self." Women develop in relationships, responding to others in caring, empathic, and nurturant ways (Miller, 1976, 1991). During adolescence, women face the tasks of developing intimacy and autonomy, simultaneously. The "loss of voice" (Brown & Gilligan, 1992) many adolescent females face leads to the same sense of estrangement and aloneness that can lead to gang membership or unhealthy behaviors.

Considering Ethnicity and Acculturation in Identity Development

It is important to consider the influence of ethnicity as well as the influence of gender on adolescent development, and gang involvement. Hispanic, African American, Native American, and Asian families usually develop in greater connection than families in our dominant Anglo culture. Overidentification with a counterculture can result in the loss of one's ethnic identity, or internalized cultural values, customs, beliefs, and styles (Bernal & Knight, 1997). When Chicano youths are confronted daily with negative, inferior images of Hispanic culture in comparison to the Anglo culture, they risk rejecting their own ethnicity. Yet the acceptance of one's ethnicity is crucial to the healthy development of self-concept, self-image, and for the identity of the Chicano community as a whole.

In *Outcry in the Barrio,* Garcia (1988) writes of the shame and embarrassment he felt when he was teased by peers for bringing a sack lunch of tacos to school. He later begged his parents to buy bologna and bread so that he could eat sandwiches instead of Mexican food. Similarly, Antonio disclosed feeling ashamed by his mother. She had migrated from Guanajuato, Mexico, to El Paso and was not literate in English. Embarrassed when he had to translate for his Spanish-speaking mother during a parent-teacher conference, Antonio swore to never attend another school conference with her.

These stories support Falicov's (1982) assertion that placing a child in the role of language mediator can create an imbalance in the parent-child relationship. The child can lose respect or even become ashamed of his or her parent(s). Respect is highly valued in Hispanic families. A Spanish-speaking teacher, counselor, or another person acting as translator can relieve some of the child's distress, and preserve the family pride of parents and guardians caught in these situations. This is just one example of why it is important to be sensitive to cultural beliefs, values, and the degree of acculturation when providing services to families of Mexican descent.

MEXICAN AMERICAN FAMILIES IN ACCULTURATION

Most Mexican people are *mestizos,* different from other Hispanic groups in their country of origin (Mexico), and mixture of racial roots (Spanish and Indian). Many lived in the Texas that was Mexico before it became part of the United States; others migrated here for a variety of reasons. Victor Villaseñor (1991) recounted his grandparents' stories about thousands of Mexican families who waited for weeks to catch a train that would transport them to the United States. These families crowded into boxcars, suffering malnutrition and risking disease from poor hygiene. They sought freedom from war and violence; and like today's immigrants, they desired employment, housing, education, and healthcare. Settling in *barrios,* they held on to their Mexican traditions, language, customs, and values. Although Mexican Americans are the majority of the population in border cities, they still hold minority status, both socioeconomically and politically. They continue to face the stress of acculturation into the dominant Anglo culture, and the pressure to assimilate and abandon their Mexican Heritage.

The Mexican nuclear family is organized in an extended family network, stressing family interdependence, cohesiveness, and cooperativeness. Close familial relationships are especially important in the immediate family, if they are separated from their extended kin or country of origin (Falicov, 1982). Individualism and autonomy such as in the Anglo culture are discouraged. *Familismo,* a tendency to rely on extended family for support and kinship, is emphasized as well as *personalismo,* building relationships (Levine & Padilla, 1980). The children are expected to pay *respeto* to their parents and elders, showing deference and obedience to their rules and decisions. Loyalty to the family of origin and generational interdependence are highly valued. The extended family members are invited to participate in family celebrations and rituals, which provides a sense of family unity and attachment.

Children are considered the center of the family; they are nurtured and protected by their parents. The father and mother provide an executive function in the parenting of their children. Parental roles are usually complementary, characterized as male *machismo* and female *marianismo.* The father assumes a dominant, authoritative role, protecting his wife and children in an honorable and viral manner (Falicov, 1982). The mother serves an expressive role with her children. She is expected to be self-sacrificing, devoted, and nurturing, as she places her family's needs above her own (Soto-Fulp, Del Campo, & Del Campo, 1993). The father disciplines the children, whereas the mother nurtures. Sibling ties are reinforced by encouraging cooperation and sharing. Competition and rivalry are not tolerated. Relational closeness and enmeshment help the family cope with stress, acculturation, and adaptation (Falicov & Karrer, 1980).

These processes of acculturation and assimilation can exacerbate and unbalance family functioning and stability, especially if the parent is worrying about basic survival needs; fulfilling needs for food, shelter, and employment. In addition to acculturational stress, other life difficulties or crises such as illness, death, separation, substance abuse, or unemployment, can contribute to family dysfunction and tension, thus creating further disharmony. The marginalized youth, caught between two cultures, may be more at risk for gang involvement when this imbalance occurs (Belitz & Valdez, 1997). Gang members look for kinship and alliance outside the family, rejecting family and cultural values such as cohesiveness, cooperativeness, interdependence, maternal nurturing and sacrifice, or paternal authority (Soto-Fulp et al., 1993). Why do some children and adolescents reject the values of their parents, whereas so many other Latinos embrace them?

Jefe de la Casa

Throughout the generations, Antonio's family followed Mexican traditions, culture, and values. Both sets of grandparents were born in Mexico. His father was born in El Paso and grew up in a bicultural, bilingual environment. In contrast, his mother was born in Guanajuato, and remains a Mexican citizen. Although she migrated to the El Paso/Cuidad Juarez area as a young woman, and is a legal resident of the United States, she never learned to speak English. Compared to her late, first-generation husband, and to her children, she is less acculturated to the American lifestyle. She remains in contact with her relatives from the interior of Mexico and from Juarez, and she retains a strong Mexican identity.

Antonio's mother described the early years of her marriage as stable and happy. Three children were born from this marriage: Antonio and his twin brother Alfredo, now 16, and Graciela, 12. However, the family atmosphere changed drastically after her husband's return from the Vietnam War. He suffered from depression and substance abuse. Although he was treated on numerous occasions for his addictions, he was not able to fully recover, and died of a heroin overdose.

After his father's death, Antonio became the *jefe de la casa* and was protective of his mother and siblings. On the loss of her husband, Antonio's mother suffered from depression and loss of energy. She became employed as a factory worker and consequently had less involvement with her children. Luckily, the family received some help and support from their extended family in Juarez and in El Paso.

Two years later, Antonio's mother met a Mexican man, ten years younger than she. Subsequently, he moved into their house, creating much conflict and tension, especially for Antonio, who had assumed the role of father and protector. Antonio felt jealous of his mother's relationship with her boyfriend. He felt replaced by him. Antonio reacted with rage and defied the boyfriend's attempts to discipline him. Several times they engaged in fistfights.

Antonio's rebelliousness extended to school, where he was expelled for truancy, fighting, and smoking marijuana. Typically, in the United States, the adolescent mind-set is to turn to one's peers. It was during this time that Antonio became involved with the "fatherless" who promised him friendship, alliance, protection, and power. They fulfilled the illusion of becoming his familia.

TREATMENT AND CULTURALLY RELEVANT ISSUES

When providing therapeutic services to Mexican American gang youth, it is necessary to address and assess all the variables that affect treatment outcome. It is imperative to view the adolescent within the contexts of his or her environment. The therapist would explore the youth's relationships in the family, at school, and with peers, while simultaneously assessing background factors such as ethnic and cultural customs, or traditions, and the dominant societal laws and beliefs (Bronfenbrenner, 1986). Due to the complexity of problems, the number of systems and contexts intertwined, and the severity of issues that Chicano gang youth and families face, treatment needs to be systemic and multimodal in order to be effective.

Treatment objectives for gang members on the individual level frequently include a focus on the individual's psychological state, reducing "acting out" behaviors, achieving sobriety, changing peer group involvement, and acquiring appropriate educational placement. Some of the newer postmodern approaches have shown success in reaching alienated youth (Anderson, 1997; Rosier, 1998). Listening, without judging or condemning, is just the first step in reaching out and instituting change. Trust has to be established, and this may be the most difficult step to accomplish as a therapist working with adolescents, especially gang youth. Each gang member must be listened to as an individual to hear what issues need to be addressed and what is needed in terms of treatment.

Preventative programs on a school or community level, such as Drug Abuse Resistance Education (D.A.R.E.) and Gang Resistance Education and Training (G.R.E.A.T.), are helpful, but they are not enough (Rosier, 1998). More intervention is needed for gang members who wish to leave the gang. Former gang members may be an excellent resource to help others leave gangs. One example from Albuquerque, New Mexico, is a school-based program called Respect Encourages Student Participation in Empowering Communication Techniques (RESPECT). The interventions are aimed at youths in gangs. Activities such as meditation, group meetings, and workshops offer alternative ways to solve conflicts. The goal is to keep students safe and in school (Tabish & Orell, 1996).

Rosier (1998) noted that gang membership, although frightening and destructive, also has many positive benefits for gang members. Gangs provide close relationships, financial gain, and a sense of protection from rivals.

> *Research has typically failed to describe how meaningful the gang is to the individual other than to indicate why individuals join a gang. . . . Being in a gang meant more than simple companionship but extended to developing deep and meaningful bonds with others in a context where one felt a sense of belonging. (p. 152)*

Once out of a gang, ex-members felt a profound sense of loss, a loss of close bonds with others, a lack of purpose in life, financial losses, and a loss of security. Perhaps the most profound losses were caused by the deaths of friends and family members. Many gang members and ex-gang members must live with daily reminders of the pain and destruction they have brought to others.

David and his brother were both involved in a gang when rivals shot his little sister in a drive-by, paralyzing her for life. David explained to Rosier (1998), "we [brother and subject] were hurting our family. . . . I feel it is such a personal thing because she has back spasms and disfiguration . . . tears come to my eyes . . . she still has her life to live . . . this is a constant reminder . . . it makes me break down" (p. 138). Although gang members are perceived as coming from dysfunctional or broken families, this is often not the case. In fact, the family may be the most powerful deterrent of gang membership. A close supportive family can rally together and provide a strong impetus for leaving the gang.

Systemic Therapy and Family Structure

Studies have shown that structural family therapy (Aponte, 1976; Haley, 1980; Minuchin, 1974; Minuchin and Fishman, 1981) is one of the most effective approaches in working with Hispanic families. As in collaborative approaches, joining and building trust is the first step. From a systems perspective, the gang member can be viewed and treated individually, relationally within the family, or more broadly as part of school and community systems. In approaching treatment from the family level, the therapist's primary emphasis is on reinstating family homeostasis and stability. This will be a difficult goal to achieve due to the adolescent's transfer of allegiance and loyalty to the gang.

Families may be affected in many ways. The gang member may bring the violent, dangerous lifestyle into the home. There may be danger and threats from rival gang members. Relationships will be strained, severed, or damaged. The client may be the gang member, some family members, or the whole family. Many therapists work with groups of current or ex-gang members in prisons or schools. The illegal activities, the secrecy, and the danger destroy trust. Emotions such as anger, grief, and fear will be at high levels.

Working with Antonio's Family

Through the process of family therapy, Antonio's negative behavior and rebelliousness was reframed as a manifestation of his grief due to his father's death. His mother and siblings were able to empathize as they had also experienced grief and depression. Unfortunately, the mother's boyfriend was not empathic or understanding, adding to the family's stress by dropping out of family therapy. The boyfriend's relationship with Antonio's mother grew problematic and strained. Temporarily, the paternal aunt and her husband assisted the family by taking Antonio and his brother and sister to live with them. This provided a chance to rest for the mother as she also needed to heal and gain emotional strength. The mother agreed to enter into individual therapy, sought a medical evaluation for clinical depression, and was prescribed medication. Antonio enrolled in the local Job Corp Program in which he was able to continue his education, acquire vocational training, and receive positive role modeling.

Throughout Antonio's therapy, the therapist maintained awareness and sensitivity to the family's cultural beliefs and values. Minuchin (1974) emphasized that it was necessary for the therapist to "join" the family in understanding and experiencing its reality as a way of helping to bring positive change in its functioning. This was accomplished by having a bicultural, bilingual therapist who integrated a systems and cultural approach in therapy. The therapist worked on not stereotyping Antonio as being a hardened criminal nor his family as being uneducated or lacking in strengths or resources. The therapist was able to understand how Antonio became the adult in the house during his father's absences and after his death. Culturally, the oldest son is often given more responsibility and authority in these situations. Helping Antonio to undergo the adolescent developmental phase of separation and individuation was complicated by his parentified role. It was important for the therapist to proceed slowly with the family's input rather than pushing for his separation and reinforcing his individuation too quickly.

Morales (1992) related that in the provision of therapeutic services to minority clients and families it is not sufficient to be "culturally sensitive"; one must be "culturally responsive." The culturally responsive therapist actively integrates cultural beliefs with therapeutic interventions. Two examples of culturally responsive therapeutic interventions with Antonio's family were used. The first was reinforcing the mother's religious beliefs and joining in prayer with her *curandero* (barrio healer) for Antonio's recovery.

In the second intervention, Antonio was encouraged to get involved and follow his maternal grandfather's love of horsemanship. His grandfather had worked as a *vaquero* (cowboy) on a ranch in Juana. For Antonio's seventeenth birthday, his aunts and uncle gave him a gift, three horseback riding lessons. Finding new interests, hobbies, and occupations helps fill some of the void left after leaving a gang.

Antonio's progress in recovery from drugs and gang involvement was not a smooth nor easy one. He had a drug relapse three weeks after his release from the treatment program and was rehospitalized for another two weeks. His relapse was due to smoking marijuana. Like many Mexican American youths, Antonio had insurance coverage because his father had been a war veteran, so he was able to receive hospitalization. His family, although frustrated, continued to work with him and Antonio was able to gradually withdraw from his gang. The mother ended her relationship with her boyfriend and continued her individual treatment. While this case had a successful outcome, many do not. It is often easier for ex-gang members to drift back to the gang and illegal activities than to remain out, struggling financially, and grieving lost relationships. Unfortunately, most gang members end up incarcerated in a penitentiary or at their own funeral. Family therapy provides a hopeful and necessary component in this country's war against gangs.

REFERENCES

Anderson, H. (1997). *Conversation, language, and possibilities: A postmodern approach to therapy.* New York: Basic Books.

Aponte, H. J. (1976). Underorganization and the poor family. In P. Guerin (Ed.), *Family therapy: Theory and practice.* New York: Gardner Press.

Belitz, J., & Valdez, D. M. (1997). A sociocultural context for understanding gang involvement among Mexican-American male youth. In J. G. Garcia & M. C. Zea (Eds.), *Psychological interventions and research with Latino populations* (pp. 56–72). Boston: Allyn & Bacon.

Bernal, M. E., & Knight, G. P. (1997). Ethnic identity of Latino children. In J. G. Garcia & M. C. Zea (Eds.), *Psychological interventions and research with Latino populations* (pp. 15–38). Boston: Allyn & Bacon.

Bronfenbrenner, U. (1986). Ecology of the family as a context for human development: Research perspectives. *Developmental Psychology, 22*(6), 723–742.

Brown, L. M., & Gilligan, C. (1992). *Meeting at the crossroads.* New York: Ballantine Books.

El Paso Police Department. (1996). *Gang unit statistical information.* El Paso, TX: Author.

El Paso Police Department. (1997). *Gang unit statistical information.* El Paso, TX: Author.

Erikson, E. H. (1963). *Childhood and society.* New York: Norton.

Erlanger, H. S. (1979). Estrangement, machismo and gang violence. *Social Science Quarterly, 60*(2), 235–247.

Falicov, C. J. (1982). In M. McGoldrick, J. K. Pearce, & J. Giordano (Eds.), *Ethnicity & family therapy.* New York: Guilford Press.

Falicov, C. J., & Karrer, B. (1980). Cultural variations in the family life cycle: The Mexican American family. In E. Carter & M. McGoldrick (Eds.), *The family life cycle and family therapy.* New York: Gardner Press.

Garcia, G. G. (1988). *Outcry in the barrio.* San Antonio, TX: Fredie Garcia Ministries.

Gilligan, C. (1982/93). *In a different voice: Psychological theory and women's development.* Cambridge, MA: Harvard University Press.

Haley, J. (1980). *Leaving home.* New York: McGraw-Hill.

Harris, M. G. (1994). Cholas, Mexican-American girls, and gangs. *Sex Roles, 30*(3/4), 289–301.

Levine, E. S., & Padilla, A. M. (1980). *Crossing cultures in therapy.* Belmont, CA: Wadsworth.

Miller, J. B. (1976). *Toward a new psychology of women.* Boston: Beacon Press.

Miller, J. B. (1991). The development of women's sense of self. In J. V. Jordan, A. G. Kaplan, J. B. Miller, I. P. Stiver, & J. L. Surrey (Eds.), *Women's growth in connection: Writings from the Stone Center* (pp. 11–26). New York: Guilford Press.

Moore, J., Vigil, D., & Garcia, R. (1983). Residence and territoriality in Chicano gangs. *Social Problems, 31*(2), 182–194.

Morales, A. J. (1992). Therapy with Latino gang members. In J. D. Koss-Chioino & L. A. Vargas (Eds.), *Working with culture.* San Francisco: Jossey-Bass.

Morales, D., & Durham, D. J. (1995). Gangs in Texas. *Results of the 1995 Attorney General gang survey.* Austin, TX: Office of the Attorney General.

Minuchin, S. (1974). *Families and family therapy.* Cambridge, MA: Harvard University Press.

Minuchin, S., & Fishman, H. C. (1981). *Family therapy techniques.* Cambridge, MA: Harvard University Press.

Rosier, C. (1998). *Former gang member's experiences of getting in and out of the gang: A phenomenological study.* Unpublished doctoral dissertation. St. Mary's University, San Antonio, Texas.

Sanders, W. B. (1994). *Gangbangs & drive-bys.* New York: Aldine de Gruyter.

Sheldon, R., Tracy, S., & Brown, W. (1997). *Youth gangs in American society* (pp. 2–13). New York: Wadsworth.

Soto-Fulp, S., Del Campo, R. L., & Del Campo, D. S. (1993). *Mexican-American families and acculturation implications for family therapy.* Paper presented at the Texas Association for Marriage and Family Therapy Conference, Houston, Texas.

Tabish, K., & Orell, L. (1996). RESPECT: Gang mediation at Albuquerque, New Mexico's Washington Middle School. *School Counselor, 44*(1), 65–70.

Texas News. (1998). [WWW document]. http://texnews.com/1998/texas/index.html.

U.S. Department of Justice. (1994). *The gang problem in America: Formulating an effective federal response.* Washington, DC: U.S. Government Printing Office.

Villasenor, V. (1991). *Rain of gold.* New York: Dell.

West Side Story. (1996). [WWW document]. http://alphabase.com/westside/gangs.htm.

Yablonsky, L. (1997). *Gangsters.* New York: New York University Press.

Zatz, M. S. (1985). Los cholos: Legal processing of gang members. *Social Problems 33*(1), 13–30.

PART IV

HISPANIC FAMILIES IN ACCULTURATION

13

ACCULTURATION AND FAMILY THERAPY WITH HISPANICS

CYNTHIA DIEZ DE LEON

*Physical uprooting entails living without the familiarity
of people's faces and the sound of their voices, without the
feel of the streets and the comfort of the houses, without
the odors of the foods, the myriad smells, sounds, and
sights, the cold and the heat of the air, without the color of
the sun, or the configuration of stars in the night sky. The
landscape that had been internal as well as external—a
very part of the immigrant's soul—is gone. All is changed
now. Imagine the move from a sleepy little rural village in
Latin America to a bustling American metropolis. Even if
you could reinvent yourself, how do you reinvent a whole
physical, social, and cultural landscape?*
—FALICOV, 1998, p. 52

I am a native of San Antonio and a fourth-generation Mexican American. Both of my parents speak Spanish fluently and have used this ability in their respective areas of work, though we did not speak Spanish at home as I was growing up. I learned Spanish as a child speaking with greatgrandparents and other extended family members and later went on to major in Spanish in college. Although I do not believe knowledge of Spanish is a prerequisite for cultural identity as a Mexican American, for me it has provided an insight that would have been difficult to grasp otherwise. The proximity of Mexico to San Antonio has also given me the opportunity to examine my own sense of cultural identity and the process of acculturation that I, as well as the rest of my family, have experienced and continue to experience. Additionally, my family and I are Presbyterians, which has prompted me to examine the intersection of culture and religion within the Hispanic community. I currently work primarily with children and families, both Hispanic and non-Hispanic.

ACCULTURATION DEFINED

Acculturation is the process by which ethnic groups accept the cultural patterns and traits of other groups with whom they are in contact. Frequently, in the United States, acculturation refers to the changes that members of a minority group undergo as they move toward adoption of the majority group's culture (Mena, Padilla, & Maldonado, 1987).

Acculturation is manifested at the behavioral, affective, and cognitive levels of functioning. Behavioral components include language, customs, music, and food choice, whereas the cultural symbols one loves or hates and the meaning one attaches to life are included in the affective domain. Within the cognitive domain fall beliefs and attitudes about gender roles, health and illness, and values in general (Cuellar, 1995).

MEASURING ACCULTURATION

Acculturation has been measured in a variety of ways over the years. One of the most widely used acculturation measures is the Acculturation Rating Scale for Mexican Americans (ARSMA) (Cuellar, Harris, & Jasso, 1980), which reflects a unidimensional measurement of acculturation. That is, an individual's level of acculturation can be rated on a continuum from "Mexican" to "American." Factors included in the determination of an individual's level of acculturation in this model include language usage, generational status, and ethnicity of peers. Other authors have posited multidimensional models of acculturation and its measurement (Mendoza & Martinez, 1981; Padilla, 1980). Such measures focus on factors such as cultural awareness and ethnic loyalty in determining the level of a person's acculturation. Yet other authors suggest that the acculturation process may be bidirectional and reflect incorporation of values and beliefs from both cultures (Szapocznik & Kurtines, 1980).

Similar to the latter understanding of acculturation is the orthogonal model of cultural identification (Oetting, & Beauvais, 1991). This model suggests that an individual's level of identification with every culture is separate, or orthogonal to identification with every other culture. For example, a person's identification with the Mexican culture can be rated from high to low, as can identification with the Anglo culture. Thus, an individual could have a high level of identification with the Mexican culture, while also identifying highly with the Anglo culture.

ACCULTURATION AND THERAPEUTIC ISSUES

Knowledge of the acculturation process is an important issue for the therapist working with Hispanic families. Level of acculturation has been examined with regard to a number of therapeutic issues. For example, increased levels of acculturation have been found to correspond with an increased willingness to seek mental health treatment and follow through with treatment recommendations (Mena, Padilla, & Maldonado, 1987). In addition, acculturation has been identified as a variable in the content and extent of self-disclosure and overall success of therapy (Barón & Constantine, 1997). Level of acculturation has been found to correspond with preference of counselor ethnicity and type of treatment preferred as well. Namely, ethnically similar therapists are the choice of unacculturated or low-acculturated individuals, whereas bicultural persons have no strong preference with regard to the ethnicity of their therapist, and acculturated individuals tend to prefer therapists of the dominant culture (Atkinson, Casas, & Abreu, 1992). Further, there is a difference in the style of therapy preferred by a client. Low acculturated persons seemed to prefer a shorter course of treatment with a directive therapist who helped focus on concrete goals, whereas more acculturated individuals seemed to expect a longer course of treatment that was more focused on personal development issues (Atkinson et al., 1992; Ponce & Atkinson, 1989).

Emotional Stress in Immigrants

Although acculturation has been found to be a critical factor in issues related to psychotherapy, it has also been found to impact the nature of problems presented by individuals and families. First, it is important to understand that the process of immigration and the subsequent process of acculturation can result in a high level of emotional stress and, at times, distress. Espin (1987) describes a three-step process that newly arrived immigrants undergo as they adjust to life in a new country. These steps include happiness and relief, followed by disappointment with the new country, and, finally, in the successful adaptation, the incorporation of good and bad aspects of the host country.

The emotional reaction to the process of adjustment has been labeled acculturative stress. Certain factors, such as whether the person participated in the decision to immigrate and age at the time of immigration, have been identified that may exacerbate this feeling of stress. For example, women who had little to no voice in the decision to relocate have been found to have increased difficulty in adjustment (Espin, 1987).

The stress of acculturation seems to be more intensely experienced by individuals who immigrate after the age of fourteen (Padilla, Lindholm, Alvarez, & Wagatsuma, 1985; Szapocznick et al., 1987). A subsequent study suggests that immigration for persons twelve and over is found to be the most stressful and disruptive (Szapocznick et al., 1987). Regardless of the exact age, authors seem to agree that the developmental issues of adolescence are exacerbated by the stress of adjusting to a new cultural context. These youngsters find themselves outside the "in" group, which leads to a sense of not belonging and feelings of inadequacy. In addition to the difficulties noted in adolescents, increased depressive and somatic symptomatology have been found in female immigrants (Salgado de Snyder, 1987).

Emotional Stress in Successive Generations

Although the acculturation process is stressful for recently arrived immigrants, the stress associated with acculturation appears to cause increased psychological distress in successive-generation individuals as well. More acculturated individuals may come to incorporate the views and negative stereotypes of their own culture, while having little emotional access to cultural resources that may help them deal with the feelings. Thus, it has been speculated that individuals who adhere to their cultural values and beliefs use these beliefs to buffer them from the stressors associated with adaptation to American life. For example, feelings of loneliness and alienation in college students have been found to be inversely related to biculturalism (Suarez, Flowers, Garwood, & Szapocznik, 1997). Those students who possessed a bicultural identity appeared the most well adjusted and it was speculated that they were able to use the strengths of both cultures to adjust to their new situation. Likewise, individuals who maintain a strong cultural orientation were found to have a healthier overall adjustment (Buriel, 1975).

UNEVEN RATES OF ACCULTURATION

Not only is it important for the therapist to recognize the stress of immigration and the acculturation process that affects new immigrants, as well as subsequent generations, but also it is important to understand that the acculturation process will not be uniformly experienced by each family member, nor will changes in values and beliefs necessarily be constant across issues. Studies of Cuban families suggest that male children acculturate to American culture most rapidly, whereas the acculturation rate of adult women appears to be the slowest (Szapocznik, Scopetta, Kurtines, & Aranalde, 1978). Conversely, Hernandez (1996) suggests that in Central American families, women may more easily find employment outside of the home, thereby accelerating their rate of acculturation.

Generational Rates

Both of these uneven acculturation patterns can have a significant impact on the family structure. In the case of a more rapid acculturation rate for children, it is not uncommon for the children to serve as translators for their parents as they interface with societal structures involving school, work, and financial issues. Such a move may violate the cultural norm that children should be silent in the presence of adults or strangers (Garcia-Preto, 1996). More importantly, allowing the children to intervene between their parents and the structures outside the home can upset the hierarchical structure of the family (Hernandez, 1996), thereby lessening the perceived power that the parents hold in the family (Belitz & Valdez, 1997).

During adolescence, youngsters who have become accustomed to serving as "cultural brokers" for their parents outside of the family may begin to challenge the authority of the parents, particularly around issues of traditional values and beliefs (Hernandez, 1996). Parents may either respond by increasing their protectiveness and becoming increasingly strict and rigid (Hernandez, 1996), or they may begin to doubt their own abilities as parents and acquiesce power, becoming quite permissive and lenient (Garcia-Preto, 1996). A particular source of conflict for families of adolescent females comes from issues of overprotectiveness, which is more consistent with a traditional cultural view, and the youngster's desire for more independence as perceived in mainstream American culture (Szapocznik et al., 1997).

The role reversal between parents and children in families in which the children acculturate at a markedly more rapid rate than the parents can have upsetting consequences for the youngster as well. These youngsters may experience feelings of anxiety at the parents' perceived inability to offer support and intervention on their behalf as they interface with agencies outside of the family, and is one possible explanation for the youngster's decision to turn to gangs as a means of finding a support group that appears powerful (Belitz & Valdez, 1997).

Traditional Values at Stake

In families where the wife may acculturate at a more rapid rate than the husband, issues over power in the relationship between the partners may result. Husbands may frequently become resentful of the more independent stance adopted by their wives and upset by the real, or perceived, challenge to their patriarchal authority (Espin, 1987). Issues of anger and domestic violence in such families may result.

In addition to an uneven rate of acculturation for family members, particular values and beliefs also appear subject to change at an uneven rate as individuals acculturate. For example, in a study of the concept of *familismo*, which reflects the centrality and importance of the family in Hispanic culture, Sabogal et al. (1987) found that some aspects change, whereas others remain regardless of an individual's level of acculturation. Familism has been found to be comprised of three factors: "Familial Obligations," "Perceived Support from the Family," and "Family as Referents." Hispanic individuals were found to maintain a high level of "Perceived Support from the Family" regardless of their level of acculturation. Whereas levels of "Familial Obligations" and "Family as Referents" declined as acculturation levels increased, these levels still remained higher for Hispanics than for Anglos across levels of acculturation to Anglo culture (Sabogal et al., 1987). These findings were similar for Hispanic individuals of Mexican, Cuban, and Latin American ancestry.

Although other family values have been found to change at an uneven rate with increased levels of acculturation, Reuschenburg and Buriel (1995) found that, despite increased levels of acculturation, Hispanic families maintained an internal family structure that was similar to that of unacculturated families.

CLINICAL IMPLICATIONS

These findings have significant implications for the therapist working with Hispanic families. Incorporation of an acculturation measure as part of the intake process may be a helpful means of better understanding the client and may be helpful in the assignment of a therapist in facilities where this is an option (Barón & Constantine, 1997). In addition, awareness of the stress related to immigration and acculturation can help the therapist normalize some of the feelings for families and offer some information about the process, such as in the following case.

Case Study 1: Becoming Bicultural
Patricia and Miguel sought therapy after thirty-five years of marriage when Patricia threatened to leave the marriage because she believed Miguel to be having an affair. Four years prior, the couple had moved from a small, rural Mexican town to a large urban city in the southwest

United States. In Mexico, the couple worked together as street vendors, and Patricia was involved in a group of women involved in community affairs. Their move was prompted by a desire to improve their economic situation, as well as more educational opportunities for their youngest daughter.

At the time of the initial session, Miguel was working as a maintenance worker for an apartment complex. Not only was he paid a good salary, but he and his family were allowed to live in one of the apartments. The family had purchased one vehicle and had clearly experienced financial improvement in a short period of time. However, the apartment complex was located in a predominantly Anglo part of town, far from the "*barrio.*" Patricia did not speak English and was unable to find full-time employment. She spent most of her day alone waiting for Miguel to come home. The only other employee of the complex who spoke Spanish was a female co-worker with whom Miguel developed a friendship. Over time, Patricia's suspicions about Miguel being unfaithful increased and the marital difficulties escalated.

On their first appointment, the couple arrived with a litany of complaints about each other. As the therapist obtained background information, she began to point out the number of changes that the family had experienced in recent years and the stress related to the changes. Patricia's lack of *comadres* and connection to extended family was addressed, as well as the sense of isolation both experienced due to the language difficulties. Both Patricia and Miguel became tearful as they spoke longingly of the times filled with family and friends that they left behind in Mexico and the sense of sacrifice that accompanied their recent financial gains.

Therapeutic Outcome and Reflections on Process

Although this insight did not resolve their marital woes, it did allow them a forum to grieve together at the loss of the lifestyle that they left behind. They were also able to begin to see the emotional difficulties that the relocation had brought for each. The couple was able to move from there to address longstanding marital conflicts that appeared to have been exacerbated by the move.

Intergenerational, gender role, and intrafamilial conflicts may also be exacerbated by the acculturation process (Espin, 1987; Szapocznik et al., 1997). That is, difficulties often experienced by families, such as the tension over an adolescent's desire for increased independence, are exacerbated in Hispanic families when there is a significant difference in the level of acculturation of parents and children. In such a case, it is not uncommon for the parents to move to an extreme position of control in an effort to maintain family cohesion, whereas the youngsters may become "overly American" in an effort to pull away. The therapist can serve as a cultural mediator for the family, helping families recognize positive and negative aspects of both cultures, which can, in turn, help the family develop a more integrated cultural model.

A model of therapeutic intervention called Bicultural Effectiveness Training (Szapocznik et al., 1997) has been developed specifically to assist therapists in teaching families to "feel enriched rather than stressed by the unique opportunities provided them in their daily cross-cultural existence" (p. 171). Such a model can help the family and individual family members understand that rigid adherence to either end of the cultural spectrum for an individual who is confronted with both cultures is likely to lead to dysfunction and difficulties in adjustment.

Finally, it is important to recognize the process of acculturation as ongoing as individuals seek to consolidate their cultural identity. That is, years in the United States as well as successive-generation status is not necessarily an indicator that an individual has resolved all issues related to incorporation of two cultural views. This is illustrated in the following vignette.

Case Study 2: Maintaining Traditional Family Roles

Marta is a Mexican woman in her mid-fifties who was referred for treatment of her depression subsequent to a job-related injury that she sustained working on an assembly line. After surgery to correct the situation and months of physical therapy, Marta complained of chronic pain and limited use of her arm. Results of physical examinations indicated that Marta had an exaggerated pain response and her own self-limiting behavior was exacerbating the tension she felt in her arm, shoulder, and neck.

Marta has lived in the United States for twenty-five years and became a legalized resident after marrying her husband, Enrique, a U.S.

citizen of Mexican parents. Enrique worked in the field of construction until a fall at work left him with a disability for which he currently receives Social Security benefits. After his injury, Marta left her job to stay home to care for Enrique for several months. She had worked successfully outside the home for approximately ten years prior to her husband's injury and had attained a considerable level of responsibility in her job. She described feeling somewhat independent in her ability to drive across the city and to use her money to buy gifts for her family. Three months after Marta returned to work at a new job, she was injured. She and Enrique have remained at home for the past six years, both complaining of depression and chronic pain. Their depression has limited their involvement with persons outside the home, including extended family with whom they had often visited prior to the injuries. Marta reported that she has not attended church since she had her accident, but explained that she had been quite involved in church life prior to this time. She is no longer willing to drive, something she did daily prior to her accident, and has begun to experience paniclike attacks when she is in public places for a prolonged period of time. Over the course of treatment, Marta reported that her current behavior is in marked contrast to her behavior prior to her accident and, more specifically, prior to her husband's injury.

After Enrique was disabled and Marta returned to work, he became responsible for the home and particularly enjoyed cooking in the kitchen. Marta described her annoyance one evening when she returned home and the kitchen had been rearranged to his liking, explaining that she felt he had violated her domain. She was injured at work one month later. Over the years, as Enrique has experienced functional and social limitations, Marta's own difficulties have become more profound. They support themselves with Enrique's disability check and he is the only one who can drive at present.

Therapeutic Outcome and Reflections on Process

Marta's increased disability can be understood as a means of maintaining the existing family structure in which Enrique is the provider and strong one. In addition, her presence at home helps to reestablish Marta as the one in charge of the household domain. Her depression appears to result, in part, from a gender-role conflict that is exacerbated by her level of acculturation. That is, while she was working, Marta seemed to increase her confidence to function adequately outside the home. However, now that Enrique is disabled and stays at home daily, Marta does not feel free to function independently outside the home. She essentially seems unable to incorporate her ability and desire to function more independently into the traditional gender roles with which she was reared, stating, "we weren't brought up that way."

Marta's therapeutic goals must take into account a way to help her return to premorbid functioning without threatening the gender roles with which she and her husband are comfortable. As such, increased contact with family members, a return to her previous hobby of gardening, and beginning to do volunteer work at church, or a community center, or possibly a part-time job may be the most realistic for Marta at present.

CONCLUSIONS

As has been discussed, the process of acculturation can have significant effects on individuals whether they be recently arrived immigrants or successive-generation offspring. Familiarity with the factors involved in the process, as well as particular areas of stress and conflict, can help the therapist working with Hispanic families as they deal with these issues. Providing validation and empathy for the stressors involved in managing the process, as well as acting as a mediator to help families discover or create options for themselves that draw from the cultural realities with which they live are among the valuable contributions that can be made by the well-informed therapist.

REFERENCES

Anzaldúa, G. (1987). To live in the borderlands means to. In *Borderlands—La frontera: The new Mestiza* (pp. 194–195). San Francisco: Aunt Lute Books.

Atkinson, D. R., Casas, J. M., & Abreu, J. (1992). Mexican American acculturation, counselor ethnicity and cultural sensitivity, and perceived counselor competence. *Journal of Counseling Psychology, 39,* 515–520.

Barón, A., & Constantine, M. G. (1997). A conceptual framework for conducting psychotherapy with Mexican-American college students. In J. G. García & M. C. Zea (Eds.), *Psychological interventions and research with Latino populations* (pp. 108–125). Boston: Allyn & Bacon.

Belitz, J., & Valdez, D. M. (1997). A sociocultural context for understanding gang involvement among Mexican-American male youth. In J. G. García & M. C. Zea (Eds.), *Psychological interventions and research with Latino populations* (pp. 56–72). Boston: Allyn & Bacon.

Buriel, R. (1975). Cognitive styles among three groups of Mexican children. *Journal of Cross-cultural Psychology, 6*(4), 417–429.

Cuellar, I. (1995). Acculturation rating scale for Mexican Americans. II: A revision of the original ARSMA. *Hispanic Journal of Behavioral Sciences, 17*(3), 275–304.

Cuellar, I., Harris, L. C., & Jasso, R. (1980). An acculturation scale for Mexican American normal and clinical populations. *Hispanic Journal of Behavioral Sciences, 2*(3), 199–217.

Espin, O. M. (1987). Psychological impact of migration on Latinas: Implications for psychotherapeutic practice. *Psychology of Women Quarterly, 11,* 489–504.

Falicov, C. J. (1998). *Latino families in therapy: A guide to multicultural practice.* New York: Guilford Press.

Garcia-Preto, N. (1996). Puerto Rican families. In M. McGoldrick, J. Giordano, & J. K. Pearce (Eds.), *Ethnicity and family therapy* (pp. 183–199). New York: Norton.

Hernandez, C. (1996). Central American families. In M. McGoldrick, J. Giordano, & J. K. Pearce (Eds.), *Ethnicity and family therapy* (pp. 214–226). New York: Norton.

Mena, F. J., Padilla, A. M., & Maldonado, M. (1987). Acculturative stress and specific coping strategies among immigrant and later generation college students. *Hispanic Journal of Behavioral Sciences, 9,* 207–225.

Mendoza, R. M., & Martinez J. L. (1981). The measurement of acculturation. In A. Baron, Jr. (Ed.), *Explorations in Chicano psychology.* New York: Praeger.

Oetting, E. R., & Beauvais, F. (1991). Orthogonal cultural identification theory: The cultural identification of minority adolescents. *The International Journal of the Addictions, 24*(5A & 6A), 655–685.

Padilla, A. M. (1980). The role of cultural awareness and ethnic loyalty in acculturation. In A. M. Padilla (Ed.), *Acculturation: Theory models and some new findings* (pp. 47–84). Boulder, CO: Westview Press.

Ponce, F. Q., & Atkinson, D. R. (1989). Mexican American acculturation, counselor ethnicity, counseling style, and perceived counselor credibility. *Journal of Counseling Psychology, 36,* 203–208.

Rueschenberg, E. J., & Buriel, R. (1995). Mexican American family functioning and acculturation: A family systems perspective. In A. M. Padilla (Ed.), *Hispanic psychology: Critical issues in theory and research.* Thousand Oaks, CA: Sage.

Sabogal, F., Marín, G., Otero-Sabogal, R., Van Oss Marín, B., & Perez-Stable, J. (1987). Familism and acculturation. *Hispanic Journal of Behavioral Sciences, 9*(4), 397–412.

Salgado de Snyder, V. N. (1987). Factors associated with acculturative stress and depressive symptomatology among married Mexican immigrant women. *Psychology of Women Quarterly, 11,* 475–488.

Suarez, S. A., Flowers. B. J., Garwood, C. S., & Szapocznik, J. (1997). Biculturalism, differentness, loneliness and alienation in Hispanic college students. *Hispanic Journal of Behavioral Sciences, 19*(4), 489–505.

Szapocznik, J., & Kurtines, W. (1980). Acculturation, biculturalism and adjustment among Cuban Americas. In A. M. Padilla (Ed.), *Acculturation: Theory models and some new findings* (pp. 139–160). Boulder, CO: Westview Press.

Szapocznik, J., Kurtines, W., Santiesteban, D. A., Pantín, J., Scopetta, M., Mancilla, Y., Aisenberg, S., McIntosh, S., Pérez-Vidal, A., & Coatsworth, J. D. (1997). The evolution of structural ecosystemic theory for working with Latino families. In J. G. García & M. C. Zea (Eds.), *Psychological interventions and research with Latino populations* (pp. 166–190). Boston: Allyn & Bacon.

Szapocznik, J., Scopetta, M. A., Kurtines, W., & Aranalde, M. A. (1978). Theory and measurement of acculturation. *Interamerican Journal of Psychology, 12,* 113–130.

14

DEMOGRAPHICS: HISPANIC POPULATIONS IN THE UNITED STATES

MARIA T. FLORES

The most amazing statistical trend projected by the U.S. Census Bureau predicts that by 2050, the Hispanic population will reach 81 million, approximately one-fourth of the U.S. total population (U.S. Bureau of the Census, 1995, 1996, 1997). Most social analysts contend that 20% representation within any given group creates a *critical mass* that provides the opportunity for a minority group to influence social and political forces in that society (Barker, 1992; Holland & Henriot, 1980). Hispanics will be the new voices, and Hispanic culture will have a great impact on our society.

DEMOGRAPHICS

The official count of Hispanics in the United States to date is 22.8 million, or 9% of the total population. This represents a 100% jump from 1970 to 1980 and a continued 50% increase during 1980 to 1990. One of every four Americans will be Hispanic by the year 2050. This growth rate is three to five times faster than the general population. Hispanics also maintain the youngest median age of 18 years compared to the general population of 28 years. Seventy-five percent of Latinos are under the age of 39 versus 60% of the general population. Also, among those over the age of 65, Latinos represent just less than half of the entire senior citizen population of the United States (U.S. Bureau of the Census, 1995, 1996, 1997).

These increases do not take into account the illegal immigrants residing in many U.S. cities. Nor do they reflect the Hispanics that marry Anglo Americans and who choose to assimilate or those who say they are Americans and refuse any other label. Or people, who given a choice between race or nationality, choose the label Caucasian in answering census reports. Another group not accounted for are those from Mexico and South America who are full-blooded Indians and choose the census label American Indian. All of these labels are correct and apply, yet the result is an underestimate of the number of Hispanics in the United States.

Who Is This Population Labeled Hispanic or Latino?

One way of understanding the Latino population is to trace the country of origin. However, when I speak about Hispanics, I do so in recognition of a past, a present, and a future. Therefore, any history is necessarily linked to the present living situation. Thus, place of origin is a beginning and present location is a helpful addition. Hispanic is a term often interchanged with Latino or Latina. I use these terms interchangeably, which perhaps reflects a bicultural identity and respect for the diversity of the Hispanic population as a whole.

Clearly, Hispanics are a diverse population that represents twenty-one Spanish-speaking countries and two with the native language of the Portuguese. In North America, Hispanics come from Mexico; in Central America: Belize, Guatemala, El Salvador, Honduras, Nicaragua, Costa Rica, and Panama; in South America: Columbia, Venezuela, Ecuador, Peru, Bolivia, Chile, Argentina, Uruguay, Paraguay, and Brazil. Hispanics come from the Caribbean islands, Puerto Rico, and Cuba, and from the European countries, Spain and Portugal.

Maps can be distorted, depicting the United States as larger than it really is in comparison to other nations. When we consider that Texas, Arizona, Utah, and Nevada can all fit in the country of Peru (Rand McNally International World Atlas, 1996), we feel a sense of awe that such distinct people and countries are grouped under one category, Hispanic. As you can imagine, even within the country of Peru itself, the southern and northern regions have quite distinct populations. Each of the aforementioned countries has its own unique history, culture and traditions, foods and people. All the countries, with the exception of Portugal and Brazil, share a common official language, Spanish. The Spanish language is a common thread, yet it varies from place to place and it is often integrated with Native Indian dialects or other European or African languages.

Despite the similarities that exist due to a similar linguistic heritage, it is an overwhelming endeavor and somewhat ludicrous to assume that a single generalization within or between Hispanic groups can be made and projected onto all. A stereotypical view characterized therapeutic attempts in the past, but they met with failure and assessment errors (Facundo, 1991; Padilla & Lindholm, 1983). The new multicultural view, which takes into account culture, country of origin, social class, religion, acculturation, family history, gender, personal choice, idiosyncratic individuals, distinct geographical settings, immigration, and discrimination, has helped to shatter the myth of sameness.

I will briefly describe the ethnic composition of three of the twenty-one countries, Mexico, Puerto Rico, and Cuba, because they represent the most prevalent populations. Mexican Americans make up 67% or two-thirds of the Hispanic population in the United States. At 13.5 million, Mexican Americans are also the fastest growing Latinos. This is due to both birth and immigration increases. Puerto Ricans number 2.7 million and maintain a stable population rate. Cubans have slightly more than one million inhabitants in the United States. The other Hispanic groups from Central and South America represent another 5.1 million (U.S. Bureau of the Census, 1997).

It is important for a therapist to be willing to read about a client's country or region of origin if additional background information is desired. Clients can provide a wealth of information and most are quite willing to educate their therapist about their country of origin.

This knowledge is most important because of the clear connection most Latinos have to their country of origin. It is also essential to understand the context of the environment in which Latinos find themselves. Some strong recommendations for those involved in seeing Hispanics that can be adapted to any identifiable cultural group are to study the political climate of Hispanics in your city and to find out about the economic or perceived social class of your clients. However, a necessary stance for a therapist is to realize that the appreciation or understanding of individuals in any group, or of the group itself, is distinct and unique, and cannot be completely captured by any single generalization or description.

I will portray a snapshot view of where Latinos have settled in the United States and how they are doing economically. The family's location within the United States allows culture to develop in unique and distinct ways. Therapists need to be aware of the areas in the United States where the Hispanic family may have dwelled previously. Children raised in Los Angeles will have a very different experience than children who grew up in the "Valley of South Texas." This knowledge combined with a history of their country of origin can be a great help in understanding the client or family that seeks help.

Mexican Americans

Mexican Americans are people who can trace their immediate ancestry to Mexico, but within this category are a great number of variations. Some Mexican Americans born in the United States have never visited Mexico, and other Mexican immigrants consider themselves Mexicans living in the United States. Mexico borders the southwestern states: Texas, New Mexico, Arizona, and California. Mexican Americans are concentrated in these states and in Colorado, which is understandable considering they were once part of Mexico. As one "park bench historian" commented to me, "they have returned from Mexico and are reclaiming their native lands." California and Texas are the largest Hispanic states. California's population is 30% Hispanic and is projected to outnumber non-Hispanic Whites by 2020 (U.S. Bureau of the Census, 1995). Many Mexicans were living in California when it became part of the United States, but more than 80% of the Hispanics have immigrated to California since 1970. Newcomers from Central America and Mexico are constant. Half of all the Salvadorans and Guatemalans in the United States live in Los Angeles.

Most Mexican Americans, like their Mexican counterparts, are *Mestizos*, a mix of Caucasian, from their European ancestry (predominantly Spanish), and Native American Indian (Novas, 1994; Padilla and Ruiz, 1974). Hispanic presence in America predates the founding of the United States; the first Spanish settlers arrived more than 400 years ago (Clinton, 1998). Aztec, Mayan, and Tarahumara Indian tribes are the best known groups in Mexico. Yet, there exist more than one hundred distinct Indian tribes in Mexico. Some Indians can trace their original tribal locations to Arizona, Michigan, or other areas in the United States. Some Mexicans maintain only American Indian ancestry and others only European. There are other European mixes besides Spanish that are not claimed or simply ignored by Mexican or Mexican Americans. Like most cultural groups, Mexicans attempt to maintain their original ancestry, yet location, settlements, and life circumstances often disrupt this ideal.

Mexican Americans, as well as other Latinos, are people that have balanced two or more cultures, integrating them into a whole way of life. The skill of balancing at least two cultures is a basic tradition to all Hispanic groups. That ability can be a great resource for balancing the new with the traditional, a skill that is necessary for adjusting to their new country. This is especially true as we enter the era of the multicultural perspective.

In addition to the stress of immigrating to a new country, many Latinos have other obstacles to overcome in the United States. Poverty is rampant in some neighborhoods, which spawns gangs and crime. There are second- and third-generation Hispanics caught in the vicious cycle of poverty with inadequate housing and education or job opportunities. Despite this desperate situation, many new arrivals hold two jobs and two-thirds of these families somehow manage to stay above the poverty line (Morganthau, 1993). As one person told me, "I worked just as hard in Mexico, but the wages were not enough to provide for my family. This is a miracle."

Some second- and third-generation Hispanics are now, for the first time, seeing their children go to college, choose a career, and become professionals. Six percent of Hispanics are professionals and this rate is incremental in growth. Family is a source of inspiration and motivation for Hispanics to succeed (Castro, 1993). Half of the Hispanics from southern California are middle-class (U.S. Bureau of the Census, 1995), yet most of their jobs involve unskilled or skilled labor. They will be a strong political power in the future (Meyer, 1992). Education will continue to be a critical issue for Latinos.

Texas has one of the older populations of Mexican Americans, many of whom have been in the United States for generations, dating as far back as the 1700s, and perhaps earlier, although Texas always has new arrivals as well. Many second- and third-generation citizens of Mexican descent are middle-class and are active participants in their local communities as indicated, for example, by the city council representatives in modern times and in old San Antonio. In the Rio Grande Valley, one of the nation's poorest areas, 90% are Mexican Americans, yet most are laborers and working class (Bower, 1997). There have been bitter fights over economic, job, and school discrimination in Texas, but the hostility is less volatile than in California. In Texas, many Anglos speak Spanish and intermarriage is common (Robinson, 1998).

Other Hispanics in Texas who blend in with the dominant Mexican group are Cubans, Puerto Ricans, and Salvadorans. There is also a noticeable group of Mayan Indians from Guatemala who fled from political upheaval during their country's civil war. They settled in Houston, Texas, and joined the working class. They are full-blooded American Indians (Robinson, 1998) and have their unique style and customs. Most of the Mayans wanted to escape their war-ridden country and have found "peace" in a new land.

Even an older Hispanic community than in Texas exists in New Mexico. When one visits Santa Fe, one can capture the sense of a distinct Spanish ancestry. Some Hispanics are the original descendants from the Spanish conquistadors. Others came from Mexico or are Native Americans that intermarried with Mexicans, Spaniards, or other Europeans. Some Native Americans denounce any Spanish, Hispanic, or Latino heritage with much fervor, claiming to be the First Nation of this land. Foreigners who came to take land in Canada, the United States, and Mexico are seen as the oppressors. The settlers usurped the Native American's countryside. A therapist could lose a client or a family very quickly if any assumptions of heritage are made in this community.

Puerto Rican Americans

Puerto Rican Americans are natural U.S. citizens. In Puerto Rico, the island's indigenous population was virtually eradicated by the

Spaniards, who replaced them with African slaves (Fitzpatrick, 1971). Today's Puerto Rican culture reflects the blend of African, European, Spanish, and native Tainos influences (Garcia-Preto, 1996). Modern Puerto Rican ancestry is not as easily traced because of travel and new settlements from the United States. Most Puerto Ricans have settled in the northeast, particularly in New York City.

Chicago is an ethnic city and Hispanics are an important addition. An HBO comic said, "Chicanos founded Chicago, I bet, where else did they get that name?" In Chicago, there is a high comfort zone for ethnic groups. There are Puerto Ricans, Ecuadorans, Guatemalans, Mexicans, and Cubans in record numbers. Though Puerto Ricans are American citizens by birth, they have the highest rates of poverty (38%), unemployment (11.2%), and households headed by single women than any other Latino group (Roy, 1998).

In New York and New Jersey, Puerto Ricans represent half of the Latino population but still do not fare any better than their Chicagoan compatriots. Other established communities include immigrants from the Dominican Republic, Colombia, and Cuba. Together, they make up four million of the city's population. Dominicans have not fared well either, as they maintain a 53% unemployment rate, are often on welfare, and have experienced some difficulty adjusting and learning the English language.

Critical steps need to be taken to reach these Latinos who are struggling to make a living for themselves. School and job opportunities must be expanded. Therapists from these communities need to be supported in helping Latinos in the struggle to gain opportunities in educational systems and the career possibilities that seem to elude them.

Cuban Americans

Cuban Americans are people who can trace their immediate ancestry to Cuba, the largest Caribbean Island. The Cuban culture historically has been a blend of Spanish and African cultures (Bustamante & Santa Cruz, 1975; Ortiz, 1995). However, most Cubans who immigrated from Cuba during the early phases of Castro's take-over were of White European backgrounds (Bernal, 1982). Many of these political immigrants had professional training and quickly adapted their skills to the United States culture. The first forced migration of Cubans indicates a class divide in Cuba along racial lines that have strong and dominant roots. Political refugees from Cuba came in waves. Many came to escape the economic hardships that the new Cuban government imposed. The second wave was poor and of Black or mixed cultures and races. Black Hispanics have very unique difficulties with identity and with whom they belong. They represent a tricultural perspective of three vastly distinct cultures. This is also true of some Latinos from Panama, Brazil, and Puerto Rico.

Cuba has had a unique geographical position, and has played a critical political, economic, and military role in its relation to the United States. Cuba has also been highly influential due to its position with Russia. The United States census reports 60% of Cuban Americans reside in the state of Florida with New York and New Jersey coming in a strong second.

In Miami, Cubans dominate the city as they represent 60% of the population. They dominate the city both politically and economically. They believe firmly in democracy and free enterprise and are against communism or any socialistic form of government. Many wealthy and professional Cubans on their arrival to the United States immediately established a marketplace and commerce. They built subdivisions, and started restaurants, coffee shops, and small malls. They established businesses such as clothing and furniture, thus creating jobs and opportunities. When the poorer Cubans came, they found jobs and a welcome sign from wealthier Cubans who are very sympathetic to the peoples oppressed under Castro's regime. This may have bridged the racial divide for some Cubans. Cubans now mirror the general Anglo population economically.

South American Hispanics

Colombians, like Cubans, have gained economic success. Two-thirds of Colombians' median income is comparable to that of non-Hispanic Whites, and one-fifth of the Colombian families earn at least $50,000 annually (Robinson, 1998). Colombians, like many Cubans who have come to the United States, are often educated professionals and entrepreneurs. They are fluently bilingual and bicultural, which allows them to move easily between cultures without losing their own identity. This type of industry is also true of about 100,000 wealthy South Americans and Peruvians who had the money to flee their countries during economic crises. They have settled in Miami suburbs such as Kendell and often own the best of the waterfront property (Robinson, 1998).

Central American Hispanics

Central Americans, with the exception of Panama with its strong African roots and Venezuela with some African settlements, are a blend of Indian and European cultures. South Americans as Brazilians, though Portuguese, are also indigenous or a blend of Indian and European. Brazil also has strong African settlements. As we move down south, the European mixes with the indigenous Indian populations change with diverse immigration patterns through wars and resettlements. Guatemala is probably the one Central American country that has "strong" indigenous groups (Menchu, 1998). Wars in El Salvador and Guatemala have created some dangerous situations for these immigrants. Many Central American immigrants have fled torture and persecution and are often in need of therapeutic assistance in addition to financial and social services.

When we talk about cultural backgrounds and cultural mixes in the various Latin American countries, we are talking about cultures in continual change. Much like the United States, there has been constant immigration and therefore the possibility of all sort of mixes and groupings. Though most African Americans fled north during and after the Civil War, some fled from the southern United States to Texas and Mexico. Panama was an American possession and therefore had African slaves. The French had strong claims in Mexico until one of the civil wars. The Jews fled to Latin America during World Wars I and II, and the Germans fled to Latin America to avoid persecution after the wars. The Irish came to Latin America during the potato famine or to evangelize the natives. This is just to mention a few of the many foreign settlers. Historically, we can trace much of the migration of the various countries that came to the "New World." Why the South American immigrants mixed with the indigenous natives whereas the U.S. and Canadian immigrants did not mix is a question for historians.

The trend of immigration through the Americas has been constant. Hispanics have immigrated to the United States and are now in all fifty states. I have mentioned some regions with strong concentrations of Latinos, but there are growing numbers in Arizona, Kansas, Maine, Massachusetts, and North Carolina, to mention a few. It is therefore important to become prepared to deal with these new immigrants and their healthcare needs. Training programs for mental health professionals that include specialized training in family therapy will be an important step for the future (Padilla, Ruiz, & Alvarez, 1976).

WHAT'S IN A NAME?

Language is considered the strongest force uniting Hispanic groups. Regardless of the dramatic difference between Latino groups indicated by geographical origin and historical influences, these groups are categorized by the U.S. Census Bureau as Hispanic because they speak a common language, Spanish. Similarly, Anglo American is often used to categorize the diverse population of Whites in the United States, whose predominant language is English, not only those of British heritage. However, the term Hispanic is not particularly accepted by many Spanish-speaking immigrants (Roy, 1998). One of the most obvious and annoying reasons for most Latinos is that the letter "h" is silent in Spanish. So almost every time the word Hispanic is used, it seems like a mispronounciation of "Hispana." There continues to be much disagreement among Latinos about what to call themselves. There are national, regional, and generational preferences. How a Salvadoran, Guatemalan, Puerto Rican, Cuban, or Mexican is categorized makes a difference to each group.

What a group calls itself is important. Naming is a fundamental human act. With Latinos, there are many names for a variety of reasons. Another obvious reason is that Hispanics represent a variety of cultures from distinct countries, and by owning a name that encompasses everyone one's identity is lost. Another reason is that names develop around movements and political agendas. The closeness to particular social agendas might sway choices in naming oneself. Other reasons might range from regional preference, traditional names verses new names, simply no desire to be categorized, to the confusing idea of being combined with a group of people from a hostile or warring nation in the old country. Rosendo Urrabazo (personal communication, 1997) writes:

> *Immigrants tend to retain their country of origin as their main self-identifier. Thus, those from Mexico call themselves* Mexicanos. *Within Mexico and among Mexicans there are numerous regional and class distinctions, for example,* Nortenos, Oaxaquenos, Veracruzanos, Indios, *etc. Latinos from Puerto Rico call themselves* Puerto Ricans *or* Puerto Riquennos. *Those born or raised in New York may call themselves* New Yorquenos. *Latinos from Cuba call themselves* Cubans, Cubanos, *or* Cuban Americans. *Those from*

the Caribbean Islands, Central or South America use their country of origin, such as Salvadorenos, Nicagaruenos, Columbianos, Dominicanos. *Within the United States among those of Mexican descent, a variety of names are used. In Texas there are* Tejanos; *in California,* Californianos. *In addition, you have names like* Chicano, Raza, *Mexican American, Americans of Mexican ancestry, Latin American,* Latino, Hispanic, *and some who refuse to be known as anything other than American.*

Daniel Roy (1998) has an excellent survey on the Internet that gives a helpful understanding of the major preference chosen regionally by middle-class Hispanics. The term *Chicano* is used in many western states and is most popular in California. In Texas, the terms Mexican, Mexicano, or Mexican American are preferred by 71% over any other names (Roy, 1998). This is probably due to the connection with the many border crossings to Latin America, as NAFTA (North American Free Trade Agreement) has made the Pan American Highway a natural corridor between countries.

The word Latino has two basic connotations: (1) Latino marks the connection with all the Romantic languages and cultures, which include Spanish, Italian, Portuguese, French, and Romanian; and (2) Latino symbolizes the Spanish language, which is the strongest connection with North, Central, and South America of all the other names. As a general category, Californians use Latino more than Hispanic. The *LA Times* officially adopted Latino instead of Hispanic. Texans interchange Latino and Hispanic regularly. Roy (1998) found that those who identify themselves as Mexican Americans most readily use multilevel descriptions of themselves depending on sociopolitical context more than any other Latino groups. Northeastern and mid-Atlantic regions prefer Latino, although Hispanic is still in common use.

The word Hispanic is based on a connection to Spain and the use of the Spanish language, thus it is thought to be less inclusive by some. Hispañola was the term for "New Spain," or areas in the "New World" settled by Spaniards. Hispanics argue about the appropriate name for their group. It is clear that there is much emotional and symbolic meaning in naming oneself. Latino and Hispanic are popular in the media, yet many people interviewed prefer to be identified with the name of their "Country of origin–American" as Roy's survey indicate (1998). Some subgroups prefer to identify with names like

Mestizo (Elizondo, 1995), which describes a mix of the Spanish and Indian cultures. A new group calls itself *Mexica,* which they announce is not Hispanic and not Latino, but pure and indigenous to the Americas. And one of the oldest names for Latinos, yet still popular because it can denote anyone living in the United States or on the North or South American continents, is *Americano* (Sosa, 1998).

Latina feminists do not like using Latino unless Latina is also used consistently when both males and females are being discussed. The basic rule for a therapist is not to presume to know clients' preferences about how they identify themselves. This is an excellent place, while in therapy with Hispanic clients, to apply the "non-knowing" stance of collaborative language systems (Anderson & Goolishian, 1992). Latinos are not monolithic; the diversity of their names demonstrates this fact.

Therapists need to let go of labels. Let clients describe for themselves what their ethnic background should be called. Ancestry is something that a client might appreciate the opportunity to share. The clients' trust level with therapists will determine how much information will be shared. Many Hispanics will label all ancestral mixes as Spanish and/or Indian unless trust is established with the therapists. This is probably because Spanish is the language spoken in their country of origin. Mixes of Spanish and Native American, German, French, Jewish, and African are some possible combinations (Meyer, 1992; Robinson, 1998). As one client told me, "We say we are Spanish but actually also one of my grandfathers was Irish. He was an alcoholic and I think that is why we do not talk about it." However a common response is, "Well, with these green eyes, I assumed we were Spanish. We say we are Spanish; after all this is the language we speak, but I don't really know."

CONCLUSIONS

Social scientists have found that the longer a person can trace his or her ancestry in the United States, the less they argue over the use of general categories such as Hispanic or Latino and Latina. The more educated and middle-class the Hispanic, the less important they say ethnicity is to success, though they often claim it personally very important. This, of course, follows the historical patterns of immigrants. The longer a group is in the United States, the less important it claims specific ethnicity is to achievement. As one of my graduate students responded, "I have been checking Hispanic on school forms and job applications for 27 years, so I am used to the name." In this way, the country of origin may be lost in the ancestral pool.

Yet I find, because of Latinos' geographical closeness to their country of origin, the Spanish language is reinforced as the means of communication, with 77% of Hispanics speaking Spanish in their homes (Garcia and Marotta, 1997). This continental connection reinforces the unity that is not as readily available to other ethnic groups. The proximity prevents a complete break with the motherland and the loss of cultural roots normally predicted by social scientists. The language loss that other immigrants have experienced is dramatically reduced for Latinos. This reality creates a tension over a general name or category versus the country-of-origin designation.

Some clients might want to do a family-of-origin search by asking their grandparents about the origins. Others might take these leads and research historical records on births, marriages, and deaths. As clients look back, it is also important to remember that culture is created and maintained in families and communities. Families create or develop a new part of their ethnic or racial identity that is meaningful to them. What is stated as a cultural piece today will probably take a different form with different families. Therapists must be open to the diversity of Latino families.

It is less difficult to speak about cultural distinctions if one feels comfortable and trusts the therapist. It is also difficult for clients who feel distrust and are defensive about their culture and how they identify themselves to share this reality with others. For this reason, taking the time to listen and join to make a trusting, genuine relationship is of the utmost importance to work with Hispanic people.

It is important to look at the changing demographics of the United States and look particularly at the Hispanic populations since they are the fastest growing part of the population. Understanding Latinos and where they come from, where they settle, and how they label themselves is a backdrop to who they are. This, of course, is simply like setting up the stage props and footlights. Then we wait for the players to enter for real understanding.

REFERENCES

Anderson, H., & Goolishian, H. (1992). The client is the expert: A not-knowing approach to therapy. In S. McNamee & K. J. Gergen (Eds.), *Therapy as social construction*. Thousand Oaks, CA: Sage.

Barker, J. (1992). *Paradigms: The business of discovering the future* [Video]. New York: HarperCollins.

Bernal, G. (1982). Cuban families. In M. McGoldrick, J. K. Pearce, & J. Giordano (Eds.), *Ethnicity in family therapy*. New York: Guilford Press.

Bower, P. (1997, March 25). *San Antonio Express News*, B4–B5.

Bustamante, J. A., & Santa Cruz, A. (1975). *Psiquiatria transcultual*. Havana: Editorial Cientifico-Tecnica.

Castro, M. (September 6, 1993). The Hispanic family: Its strength and values are challenged in a changing U.S. society. *Express News: Vista*.

Clinton, W. J. (1998, September 15). Presidential Proclamation of National Hispanic Heritage Month [online document]. Retrieved January 4, 1999, from the World Wide Web: http://www.aoa.gov/pr/WH=HHM.html.

Elizondo, V. (1995). *The Future is Mestizo*. San Antonio, TX: Mexican American Cultural Center.

Facundo, A. (1991). Sensitive mental health services for low-income Puerto Rican families. In M. Sotomayor (Ed.), *Empowering Hispanic families: A critical issue for the '90s*. Milwaukee: Wisconsin Family Services of America.

Fitzpatrick, J. P. (1971). *Puerto Rican Americans: The meaning of migration to the mainland*. Englewood Cliffs, NJ: Prentice Hall.

Garcia, J. G., & Marotta, S. (1997). Characteristics of the Latino population. In J. Garcia & M. C. Zea (Eds.), *Psychological interventions and research with Latino populations*. Boston: Allyn & Bacon.

Garcia-Preto, N. (1996). Latino families: An overview. In M. McGoldrick, J. Giordano, & J. K. Pearce (Eds.), *Ethnicity and family therapy*. New York: Guilford Press.

Holland J., & Henriot, P. (1980). Social analysis: Linking faith and justice. Washington, DC: Center of Concern.

McNamee, S., & Gergen, K. J. (Eds.). *Therapy as social construction*. Thousand Oaks, CA: Sage.

Meyer, M. (November 9, 1992). Los Angeles 2010: A Latino subcontinent. *Newsweek*, 32–33.

Morganthau, T. (August 9, 1993). America: Still a melting pot. *Newsweek National Affairs*, 16–25.

The new international atlas. (1996). Chicago: Rand McNally.

Novas, H. (1994). *Everything you need to know about Latino history*. New York: Plume/Penguin Books.

Ortiz, F. (1973/1995). *Contrapunteo Cubano de tabaco y el azucar.* Barcelona: Editorial Ariel.

Padilla, A. M., & Lindholm, K. J. (1983). Hispanic Americans: Future behavioral science research directions. *Occasional Paper No. 17.* Los Angeles: University of California, Spanish Speaking Mental Health Research Center.

Padilla, A. M., & Ruiz, R. A. (1974). Latino mental health: A review of literature. DHEW Publication No. 73-9143. Washington, DC: U.S. Government Printing Office.

Padilla, A. M., Ruiz, R. A., & Alvarez, R. (1976). Community mental health services for Spanish-speaking populations. *America Psychologist, 30,* 103–109.

Robinson, L. (1998, May 11). Hispanics don't exist. *U.S. News & World Report,* 27–32.

Roy, D. (1998). Strangers in a native land: A labyrinthine maze of Latino identity. *Latino attitude survey.* [On-Line document]. Available Azteca: University of Kansas.

Sosa, L. (1998). *The American dream: How Latinos can achieve success in business and life.* New York: Dutton.

U.S. Bureau of the Census. (1995, 1996, 1997). *Hispanic Today.* Washington, DC: U.S. Government Printing Office.

INDEX